BRUMBACK LIBRARY

3 3045 03152 4867

  W9-BGW-465

$24.95
379.73 RHO
Rhodes, Jesse H.
An education in politics

8/12

BRUMBACK LIBRARY
215 WEST MAIN STREET
VAN WERT, OHIO 45891

AN EDUCATION IN POLITICS

A volume in the series
American Institutions and Society
Edited by Brian Balogh and Jonathan Zimmerman

A list of titles in this series is available at
www.cornellpress.cornell.edu.

AN EDUCATION IN POLITICS

The Origins and Evolution
of No Child Left Behind

Jesse H. Rhodes

CORNELL UNIVERSITY PRESS ITHACA AND LONDON

Published in association with the University of Virginia's Miller Center of Public Affairs

379.73
RHO

Copyright © 2012 by Cornell University

All rights reserved. Except for brief quotations in a review, this book, or parts thereof, must not be reproduced in any form without permission in writing from the publisher. For information, address Cornell University Press, Sage House, 512 East State Street, Ithaca, New York 14850.

First published 2012 by Cornell University Press
Printed in the United States of America

Library of Congress Cataloging-in-Publication Data

Rhodes, Jesse H. (Jesse Hessler), 1980–
   An education in politics : the origins and evolution of No Child Left Behind / Jesse H. Rhodes.
        p. cm. — (American institutions and society)
   "Published in association with the University of Virginia's Miller Center of Public Affairs."
   Includes bibliographical references and index.
   ISBN 978-0-8014-4971-0 (cloth : alk. paper)
   1. Education and state—United States—History—20th century.   2. Education and state—United States—History—21st century.   3. United States. No Child Left Behind Act of 2001.   I. White Burkett Miller Center.   II. Title. III. Series: American institutions and society.
   LC89.R47   2012
        379.73—dc23   2011044129

Cornell University Press strives to use environmentally responsible suppliers and materials to the fullest extent possible in the publishing of its books. Such materials include vegetable-based, low-VOC inks and acid-free papers that are recycled, totally chlorine-free, or partly composed of nonwood fibers. For further information, visit our website at www.cornellpress.cornell.edu.

Cloth printing   10 9 8 7 6 5 4 3 2 1

Contents

Acknowledgments

Though a single author (or a few authors) usually claims the credit, the truth is that a book is almost always a collaborative enterprise. One of the great satisfactions of completing a book is acknowledging the contributions of colleagues, friends, and family. In the course of writing this one I have been fortunate to have received assistance, in all its myriad forms, from many people. It is my pleasure to thank them here.

Sidney Milkis, Eric Patashnik, and Paul Freedman at the University of Virginia were a great help to me as I conducted the research for this book, providing encouragement when I needed it and tough love when I deserved it. Sid has played the central role in helping me become a scholar of politics and history. Much of what I know about the craft of research and writing comes from Sid, and I have always been struck by his thoughtfulness and generosity. For all of his contributions to my intellectual development I am profoundly grateful. The Department of Politics at the University of Virginia provided an excellent intellectual environment in which to do historically informed political science and granted fellowship funding during my time there. Thanks go to the Miller Center of Public Affairs, which also gave me generous fellowship assistance. Cathie Jo Martin, who agreed to serve as my "dream mentor" during my Miller Center fellowship, deserves many thanks for providing insightful criticism and pushing me to link the study of education to broader debates about education, training, and social policy.

Since arriving at the University of Massachusetts, Amherst, I have been fortunate to have been surrounded by generous colleagues, who made pivotal contributions to this book. Ray LaRaja and Jerry Mileur each read and commented on several chapters, and provided excellent advice on how to better frame my arguments. Amel Ahmed and Tatishe Nteta went through several chapters line by line and asked questions that led me to clarify and strengthen key points. Angelica Bernal provided extensive comments on a paper, which helped me hone claims that appeared in the book, and Maryann Barakso and Jillian Schwedler graciously invited me to present work in progress at their Ambiguities of Democracy workshop. I also benefited from conversations and critiques offered by Charli Carpenter, John Hird, M.J. Peterson, Dean Robinson, Fred Schaffer, Brian Schaffner, and Stuart Schulman. Michael Hearn and Caroline Koch provided able research assistance.

Colleagues from other universities also deserve thanks. Perhaps against his better judgment, Rick Valelly agreed to serve as a mentor and provided invaluable advice about the book and life in the discipline. Vesla Weaver read an early version of the book from cover to cover and offered extensive recommendations on how to improve the writing and analysis. At several points during the writing, Dan Galvin gave much needed advice and encouragement. I also thank the anonymous reviewers who reviewed the manuscript for Cornell University Press, whose cogent and constructive criticism greatly improved my arguments and use of evidence.

Brian Balogh and Jonathan Zimmerman, the editors of the American Institutions and Society series at Cornell University Press, were outstanding series editors. I am particularly indebted to Brian, who went above and beyond the call of duty by reading and commenting on early drafts of each of the chapters contained in this book. Brian's advice—particularly his recommendations on how to improve the structure and flow of the narrative—have made this book infinitely more enjoyable to read. At Cornell University Press, many people deserve thanks. Michael McGandy took an early interest in the project and provided encouragement as it evolved into a book. Michael deserves special credit for pushing me to make the book more accessible and attentive to contemporary political concerns. Susan Specter guided the book through production with patience and skill, while Sarah Grossman and Kitty Liu answered my many questions about the publication process.

My research took me to archives around the United States, where archivists and librarians answered my questions and helped me find useful documents. I am especially grateful to the archivists at the William J. Clinton Presidential Library, the George H. W. Bush Presidential Library, the Library of Congress, the National Archives and Records Administration, the New York State Archives, the Special Collections Division at the University of Rhode Island, the Walter P. Reuther Library at Wayne State University, the Hoover Institution on War, Revolution, and Peace at Stanford University, and the Carl Albert Center of the University of Oklahoma.

Some parts of chapters 4, 5, and 6 appeared, in somewhat altered form, in "Progressive Policymaking in a Conservative Age? Civil Rights and the Politics of Federal Education Standards, Testing, and Accountability," *Perspectives on Politics* 9 (3): 519–44. Thanks go to *Perspectives on Politics* and editor Jeff Isaac for excellent advice on strengthening that article.

Seeing this project through to completion would have been impossible without the support of my family. My parents, Sam and Fran, helped lift my spirits during periods—some of them prolonged—when I doubted whether the book would ever be finished. By helping me put the project in perspective, they made the long hours of research and writing much more bearable. My brother Eliot was always up for a jam session on the guitar. My father-in-law, Tom McElroy, showed me that trips to the beach can help take my mind off work, while my mother-in-law, Susan McElroy, helped with the book's bibliography. My wife, Megan, deserves the greatest thanks. She put up with the long hours at the office, frequent stays away from home, and weekend research and writing that were a necessary part of completing this book, and always reminded me that there are more important things than academic writing. For her love and constant support I am eternally grateful. As the book neared completion, my son Jake was born. My life has been infinitely enriched by his laughter, even though his crying often keeps me up at night. Because they make me realize what really matters, I dedicate the book to my wife and son.

AN EDUCATION
IN POLITICS

EXPLAINING THE DEVELOPMENT OF AMERICAN EDUCATION POLICYMAKING

When President Barack Obama took office in January 2009, he called for sweeping federal efforts to improve the nation's elementary and secondary schools. "Our schools fail too many," the president declared in his inaugural address. "Everywhere we look, there is work to be done....We will transform our schools and colleges and universities to meet the demands of a new age."[1] Building on policy proposals that had been championed by a counterintuitive alliance of business leaders and civil rights activists, Obama instituted a "Race to the Top" initiative that would induce states to embrace sweeping new education reforms, such as "college and career ready" graduation standards, data systems capable of tracking students' performance over time, and policies that linked teachers' evaluations to their students' test scores. Obama and his allies in the business and civil rights communities also proposed to reauthorize the No Child Left Behind Act of 2002, the controversial law that required states to institute comprehensive standards, testing, and accountability reforms, so that it reinforced the priorities of Race to the Top.

Between March 2009 and November 2010, Race to the Top pushed dozens of states to commit to implementing far-reaching education reforms, leading education commentators to declare that the administration was "carving a deep mark" on education policy.[2] But less than two years after its initial announcement, the education agenda promoted by the administration and its business and civil rights allies was in trouble. States chafed against the centralizing elements of the administration's proposal, with some governors going so far as to

1

forgo federal funds in order to avoid federal requirements. Of equal importance, questions lingered about whether states would remain faithful to their pledges to institute changes to their curricula, teacher recruitment strategies, and account-ability regimes, especially given the (sometimes severe) education budget cuts brought on by the recession and slow economic recovery.[3] To make matters worse, Obama's ambitious proposal to reform No Child Left Behind made little headway in Congress, delaying reauthorization of the law until after the 2010 midterm elections, a full three years behind schedule. As the economy remained sluggish and criticism of the administration's handling of health care, financial regulation, and the wars in Iraq and Afghanistan intensified, the Democrats' authority to manage the nation's affairs—not to mention education policy—declined precipitously. The Republicans' seizure of the House of Representatives, and their significant gains in the Senate, in the 2010 midterm elections seemed to further threaten the ability of the Obama administration, business leaders, and civil rights activists to accomplish their objectives in federal education poli-cymaking. Indeed, the new Republican Speaker of the House, John Boehner of Ohio, promised voters that he would "take a new approach [to education policy-making] that hasn't been tried before in Washington—by either party.... It starts with cutting spending instead of increasing it. Reducing the size of government instead of expanding it."[4] Under pressure from conservative Republicans—and facing looming deadlines for academic progress under NCLB—in mid-2011 the Obama administration began to issue waivers exempting states and localities from some of the core requirements of the law.[5]

The sudden turn of events in federal education policymaking experienced by Obama and his allies in the business and civil rights communities echoed similar reversals during the George W. Bush and Bill Clinton administrations. Like Obama, both of these presidents had begun their administrations by joining hands with business leaders and civil rights activists to extend federal involve-ment in education standards, testing, and accountability. As was the case in the Obama administration, these crusades had wrought major changes in the orga-nization of federal authority in education, strengthening federal influence in the day-to-day workings of the nation's elementary and secondary schools. Yet each of these campaigns met with significant resistance, setting back efforts to wholly recast governing relationships in education. Moreover, while each had its virtues, neither effort produced a dramatic improvement in student achievement. Even the No Child Left Behind Act, which was widely viewed in 2002 as a culminating moment of federal leadership of education, is now usually acknowledged to have "produced uneven results."[6]

In this book, I shed new light on this puzzling, and ongoing, political dynamic. At its core, my argument emphasizes the enduring tension between Americans' yearning for national leadership and their celebration of political pluralism and local control, illustrating the consequences of this conflict for social policymaking in the United States. On one hand, I show how a counterintuitive coalition of business leaders and civil rights activists worked as political entrepreneurs, combining disparate ideas, exploiting institutional opportunities, and building diverse coalitions to drive a program of federally led education reform to the top of the national political agenda. On the other hand, however, my work suggests how even the most politically successful projects can be "institutionally bounded" in practice by durable institutional commitments, hostile interests, and public ambivalence about excessive federal involvement in schools. New federal initiatives were layered atop—rather than displaced—a diverse, highly decentralized education system. This approach, animated in significant part by a genuine interest in strengthening the academic achievement of students, especially students historically disadvantaged by race and poverty, has had the effect of dramatizing educational inequities and generating ongoing pressure for reform. Additionally, there is some evidence that standards, testing, and accountability reforms can produce modest-to-moderate gains in student achievement, particularly in mathematics. However, this approach has also proven politically and administratively unwieldy, simultaneously limiting the impact of federal reforms and imposing serious burdens, from the state level and down, on governments, schools, and teachers. Further complicating matters, standards, testing, and accountability reforms may also narrow the curriculum, encourage rote, teacher-directed education, and induce schools to undertake other undesirable behaviors to try to artificially boost student achievement. Over time, the tension between the demands for greater national unity of purpose and the desire for local control has contributed to a churning, haphazard style of development in education.

The Place of Education Policy in American Political Development

Schooling occupies a central place in American life. All told, Americans spend enormous sums on education—about $596 billion on public elementary and secondary education in 2007–8—more than the federal government spends on Medicare each year and slightly more than the base budget of the Department of Defense.[7] The United States' investment in education is not merely impressive in terms of raw numbers; it is notable in comparative perspective, as well. In fact, average education spending per student in the United States ($10,768 in 2007–8) is 45 percent higher than the average spent by other members of the Organization for Economic Cooperation and Development (OECD), while the proportion of GDP devoted to elementary and secondary education (4%) is above the OECD average of 3.6 percent.[8] Notably, over the past decade the federal share of education spending also increased significantly: between 2002 and 2008, the federal share routinely topped 8 percent of all education revenues, reaching its highest levels since the 1980–81 school year.[9] This investment finances a truly massive social enterprise: the nation is dotted with almost one hundred thousand elementary and secondary schools, which are attended by approximately 55 million students and staffed by more than 5.5 million teachers, administrators, aides, and other staff.[10]

Schooling is not only a major component of the contemporary American economy, however; it also has a profound influence on a broad range of economic outcomes. Countless studies have pointed out that individuals with more education often enjoy higher incomes, more-stable employment, and even better health.[11] More recently, evidence has begun to accumulate that nations with better-educated populations experience faster economic growth, making schooling an essential element of global economic competition.[12] It is also likely that the economic effects of education and training extend beyond individual welfare and national economic growth. Indeed, students of comparative political economy suggest that different skill formation regimes may have consequences for broader outcomes such as income inequality. In this work, the United States emerges as a nation that provides a broad, generalist education to the vast majority of its citizens, as well as higher learning to a significant fraction. Those who do well in primary and secondary education, and are able to attend college, receive training that prepares them for relatively high-skill, high-wage employment. However, because vocational training and school-to-work assistance for lower-performing students are weak in comparison with that offered by some other nations, many of those who do not go to college enter the workforce without marketable skills. As a result, the American education system is consistent with a comparatively high level of inequality of earnings, in which the highly educated earn much more than those with less education.[13]

Schools are also charged with major social and cultural responsibilities. The institution of the public school is grounded in the notion that a "common education" for every American child would help individualistic citizens form lasting community ties and identify a common understanding of the public good.[14] As Jennifer Hochschild and Nathan Scovronick argue, "[public schools] are the *only institution* in which, in principle, American children are taught to become good citizens through learning a common core of knowledge, acquiring a common set of democratic values and practices, and developing a common commitment to their nation and its people."[15]

It is clear that Americans expect a great deal—indeed, perhaps too much—from their schools. Concerns that American schools are inadequate to the task of promoting economic growth, reducing economic inequality, or preparing young citizens for democracy are perennially voiced in contemporary debate, providing much of the impetus for efforts to restructure schools and educational governance. Perhaps unsurprisingly, education now enjoys a spot at or near the top of the nation's list of policy priorities. In June 2011, 67 percent of Americans complained that lawmakers in Washington were paying too little attention to education, despite the fact that the nation was still feeling the effects of the most serious economic crisis since the Great Depression.[16] Writing in the midst of the downturn, New York Times columnist Nicholas Kristof tapped Americans' faith in education as a key to broader economic and social reform when he declared that "education reform could be the most potent antipoverty program in the country.... Unless we succeed in [this] effort and get more students through high school and into college, no bank bailout or stimulus package will be enough to preserve America's global leadership in the long run."[17] Scholars such as Jacob Hacker, Christopher Howard, Torben Iversen, Jill Quadagno, and John Stephens concur with Kristoff's view that public education is an integral facet of the United States' system of social protection. Iversen and Stephens make a particularly strong case for including education policy as a core component of the welfare state: "Skills and education are at the core of the welfare state. Incentives to acquire particular types of skills are closely related to both social protection and economic performance, and educational spending is not only a partisan issue but also one with profound implications for the distribution of income. Education and training systems can fruitfully be reintegrated into comparative welfare state analysis."[18]

This brief discussion indicates that the political and institutional developments embodied in initiatives such as Race to the Top and No Child Left Behind, which have important (if not always intended) consequences for American schooling, deserve close historical scrutiny from scholars of social policy. Yet students of the historical development of U.S. social policy have not paid much attention to schooling and education policy. Leading analysts of the American welfare state usually focus on the origins and development of social welfare and antipoverty programs such as Social Security, Medicare and Medicaid, unemployment compensation, and Temporary Assistance to Needy Families, as well as tax expenditures for home mortgage interest, employer pensions, and earned income.[19] The most important exception to this trend, Suzanne Mettler's magisterial work on the GI Bill, gives a central role to federal policies related to collegiate and postsecondary vocational training.[20]

However, in failing to examine the trajectory of American education policy, especially at the federal level, students of American social policy fail to appreciate dynamics that coexist uneasily with commonplace assumptions in current scholarship on the welfare state. The dominant view, propagated by scholars such as Mettler, Paul Pierson, Jacob Hacker, Diane Pinderhughes, and Theda Skocpol, is that the welfare state has experienced a period of retrenchment and drift since conservatives ascended to power with the election of Ronald Reagan in 1980 (though Obama's recent achievement in health care may be an important exception to this trend).[21] In the context of intensifying social risks, exacerbated by the severe economic downturn, these developments have imposed formidable burdens on many Americans, especially the most vulnerable. Yet the expansion of federal authority (and investment) in American schooling marks an important departure from this general trend in social policymaking—indeed, federal involvement is greater than at any previous point in American history. Even more puzzling, the law contributing most profoundly to the extension of federal involvement and investment—No Child Left Behind—was enacted during a period of Republican control of the presidency and House of Representatives and strong Senate representation. Growing federal involvement and investment in education suggests that there might be more to the story of the welfare state than a simple narrative of retrenchment and drift.

As a possible rejoinder to my view, some scholars would argue that the American welfare regime has been reconstituted rather than retrenched, transformed from an "enabling" system that provided citizens with resources and protected them from the vagaries of the market into a "paternalistic" or "punitive" system that employs monitoring, testing, and sanctioning to control citizens' behavior.[22] In these accounts, conservative entrepreneurs take center stage, championing new federal initiatives in areas such as welfare and criminal justice in order to bolster market capitalism, discipline unruly minority and poor citizens, and attract electoral support from anxious middle-class whites.[23] In the field of education policy, some analysts, such as Michael Apple, David Hursh, and Pauline Lipman, have pursued an analogous line of argument, charging that the growth of federal control over education standards, tests, accountability, and teacher quality represents a conservative effort to discipline teachers and students, promote competitive values, and bolster corporate capitalism.[24] According to Lipman,

> With George W. Bush's federal education legislation (endorsed by Congress), the *No Child Left Behind Act of 2001* (NCLB), school accountability, high stakes tests, standards, and systems of punishment and reward have been made official policy and the dominant education agenda in the U.S.... These policies are just one aspect of the larger neoliberal project to privatize public institutions and commodify public and private life while increasing state regulation of individuals and institutions through new forms of accountability, testing, standards, and surveillance.[25]

But this viewpoint does not adequately characterize federal standards and accountability reforms. First, it ignores the fact that many civil rights organizations, including the Leadership Conference on Civil Rights, the Citizens' Commission on Civil Rights, the Education Trust, and the National Council of La Raza, have been among the chief advocates of federal involvement in standards, testing, accountability, and teacher-quality reform in education since the early 1990s. Second, it obscures the fact that most conservative Republicans, as well as major conservative think tanks such as the Heritage Foundation and the American Enterprise Institute, have generally opposed the expansion of prescriptive federal authority in education, preferring block grants and measures promoting private school choice (such as so-called school vouchers), as well as voluntary state and local reforms, as panaceas for problems facing schools. Third, the role of business in federal education reform is considerably more nuanced than often presented in mainstream studies of retrenchment in social policymaking since the 1970s. In the case of federal education policy, major corporate organizations such as the Business Roundtable, the U.S. Chamber of Commerce, and the National Alliance of Business were among the primary advocates of expanding federal influence over education standards, testing, accountability, and teacher quality. Notably, they repeatedly banded together with the civil rights activists described above, rather than with ideological conservatives, to enact legislation embodying these reforms—along with significant new spending—into law.

Finally, and as a result of the dynamics discussed above, Lipman's perspective on the neoliberalism of NCLB misses how the role of partisanship and party competition in the development of federal education policy over the past generation has not conformed to patterns evident in other areas of social policy. Federal education policy has not followed the path described by the conventional narrative in which conservative Republicans waged an all-out political and organizational attack on the ideological underpinnings of New Deal–Great Society social policymaking, exploiting the economic and racial upheavals of the 1960s and 1970s to cast aspersions on liberalism and generate broad support for conservatism and Republican leadership.[26] Ideological conservative attacks on the federal role in education have in fact been repeatedly rejected by voters. The real story is much more complicated. Democrats and Republicans have converged on a policy agenda that borrowed themes from both partisan camps without simply splitting the difference between liberalism and conservatism. Furthermore, and against claims that partisan polarization obstructs federal involvement in social policy, increasing polarization has not forestalled expanding federal involvement and investment in schooling.[27] Indeed, federal intervention has grown alongside partisan polarization.

While federal involvement in education has expanded significantly since the 1980s, however, it has operated through traditional, indirect channels. Even today, there is no truly national system of education standards, tests, or accountability. Instead, the federal government has sought to shape education reform through what sociologist Elisabeth Clemens calls a "Rube Goldberg-esque" array of incentives and conditions-of-aid to state and local governments.[28] Race to the Top is a competitive granting program to state and local governments, while No Child Left Behind operates through categorical conditions on a venerable education grant-in-aid program to the states, the Elementary and Secondary Education Act (ESEA) of 1965. In spite of these convoluted means, federal education policy has had a major impact on the organization of elementary and secondary education, and may make beneficial contributions to students' academic achievement, at least in mathematics.[29] In important ways, the federal government's involvement in education reform has attempted to compensate for the weaknesses of state and local education policies, pushing them to strengthen their education standards and pay much closer attention to the educational advancement of historically disadvantaged students.

However, this indirect method of exercising power has also had important consequences for the operation of federal programs, sometimes undermining federal intentions, sometimes overburdening state and local governments (as well as teachers and schools), and sometimes doing both at the same time. School officials have also complained that standards, tests, and accountability have encouraged teacher-directed education, narrowed schools' educational offerings, and encouraged excessive preparation for standardized examinations. Consequently, reforms like those featured in No Child Left Behind have faced harsh criticism both from those who believe that the law fails to do enough to accomplish its laudable intentions, and from those who charge that it does too much, undermining the capacity of local schools to provide quality education.[30] Moreover, the "layering" of new federal initiatives atop old programs and traditional patterns of authority—and the resulting tensions produced—has been a principal spur to the ongoing development of federal involvement in education.

Two Schools of Thought

How should we explain these important, complex developments in federal education policymaking? The study of institutional development is divided between theories that emphasize the agency of political entrepreneurs in leveraging institutional change, and approaches that stress the constraints on entrepreneurship imposed by existing institutions and political commitments. Despite their considerable virtues as ways of explaining institutional development, these approaches have complementary flaws that limit their ability to explain the puzzling outcomes of federal education policy. So far, most social scientists have favored one or the other approach in their research; few have managed to blend entrepreneurship and institutional constraints into a unified explanation of institutional change.[31]

Scholars of American political development are increasingly turning to political entrepreneurs to explain important instances of institutional change.[32] Political entrepreneurs are "individuals whose creative acts [may] have transformative effects on politics, policies, or institutions."[33] Seeking to upset existing arrangements and install new institutions that further their ideological and material interests, entrepreneurs engage in an array of creative behaviors to foster institutional change. First off, entrepreneurs exploit moments of uncertainty or instability—common in complex political and institutional settings such as the United States—to reshape political discourse. Such moments of ambiguity provide entrepreneurs with opportunities to draw attention to a new issue or alter the way a salient issue is discussed.[34] Drawing together normative, causal, and political arguments, entrepreneurs craft a powerful narrative that transforms the brute facts of the uncertain situation into a "problem" or "crisis" demanding attention in the political arena.[35] Having identified a "problem" in need of remediation, entrepreneurs develop a causal story that identifies the origins of the problem in some existing set of institutions, discrediting the status quo and setting the stage for a new departure. This causal story carries an obvious "moral"— if existing commitments were changed, the problem would be resolved.[36] Entrepreneurs complete the rhetorical circle by proposing a "solution" or "blueprint" that explains how to change existing institutions in order to resolve the problem at hand.[37] Weaving together facts, norms, and rhetoric, then, entrepreneurs provide cause for abandoning existing institutional commitments and establishing new ones.[38]

A central part of entrepreneurs' rhetorical project is the creative recombination of existing problem and solution ideas. Indeed, the multiple—and sometimes contending—ideas that constitute the American political system are, in the hands of political entrepreneurs, resources with which to forge new political criticisms and agendas. Political actors appropriate claims of authority from diverse sources, combining various ideas to make their purposes resonate with a variety of audiences.[39] As political scientist Adam Sheingate suggests, "The capacity to present single innovations consistently from multiple perspectives and points of view allows entrepreneurs to consolidate their innovations by building robust coalitions in support of institutional change."[40] In truth, the ability to appeal to multiple ideologies and interests—to develop ideas that serve as "common carriers," to use Eric Schickler's term—is a crucial feature that distinguishes entrepreneurs from more orthodox advocates, whose proposals generally partake of more ideologically homogeneous themes and thus appeal to narrower audiences.[41]

Entrepreneurial activity is not limited to ideational innovation. Effective ideational innovation is tied to entrepreneurial mobilization, organization building, and coalition formation. Such efforts take time and resources, and political entrepreneurs distinguish themselves by paying these costs. It is well known that even when individuals and groups identify shared interests or objectives, they may fail to coordinate their actions to achieve them. Moving from the realm of ideas to the field of action, therefore, entrepreneurs undertake the hard work of organizing potentially sympathetic groups and brokering political compromises among contending interests.[42] Political entrepreneurs also pay the costs of disseminating ideas, developing means for presenting their proposals in an accessible format and conveying them to a broad audience. Finally, identifying potential opportunities with which to pursue an agenda—for example, a sympathetic foundation willing to fund a think tank or policy network, an enthusiastic legislator willing to submit legislation, an effective venue in which to plead one's case—is itself a costly activity that political entrepreneurs may undertake. In short, political scientist Justin Crowe suggests, entrepreneurs are "engaged in a constant search for political advantage, a constant search for 'speculative opportunities'—overlays, cleavages, and fissures, for example—that are pregnant with possibilities for change but require an act of leadership in order for any to materialize."[43]

If the set of ideas is powerful and the coalition building is successful, political entrepreneurs may drive shifts in the positioning of other actors in the political system. Recognizing the rising popularity of the causal stories and programmatic proposals pitched by entrepreneurs, even opponents of a proposed institutional change may be forced to mimic, at least publicly, these ideas, in a process that has been dubbed "strategic pursuit." Public validation of entrepreneurs' ideas by others (however grudging) reinforces their impact, pushing the discussion further from the status quo and toward entrepreneurs' framing.[44]

As Robert Kagan has noted, the contemporary policy process in the United States is characterized by a dense maze of laws, regulatory agencies, courts, and litigants, and thus presumes that new lawmaking will be highly technical and inclusive of multiple institutions. It goes without saying that this system puts a premium on knowledge and expertise.[45] Unlike elected officials, who have to juggle multiple responsibilities and placate diverse interests, unelected political entrepreneurs are intimately familiar with policy details in a given area and can commit the preponderance of their time and resources to developing and marketing favored reforms.[46] While it is possible that these figures may be career bureaucrats, as Daniel Carpenter has argued, it is even more likely (especially in the United States, with its comparatively weak tradition of careerism at the highest levels of administration) that they will be career policy advocates who circulate among various positions in government, as well as in think tanks, universities, foundations, and interest groups.[47] In the end, what distinguishes these figures and makes them successful is their extensive knowledge—not just of the intimate details of policy, but of the important ideas, people, and institutions that compose the policy community—and their longevity, which allows them to learn from past experiences, apply lessons to new contexts, foster long-term relationships with individual policymakers, and serve as a form of institutional memory for less-experienced participants.

An important limitation in analyses based on the efficacy of political entrepreneurs is that such works may present an overly voluntaristic view of political action that fails to appreciate the real constraints on entrepreneurial activity.[48] An alternative perspective, prominent in contemporary research on American political development, emphasizes the ways in which features of the political environment limit efforts to affect major changes.[49] As work in this field makes clear, entrepreneurs' efforts are likely to be challenged by organized interests and the "veto points" they control; the budgetary context and the limited availability of slack resources; and the broader environment of public opinion. These constraining factors shape the prospects of entrepreneurs' success both during the process of designing and establishing a new institution, and after the innovation is up and running.

Existing institutions and interests assert themselves directly in the process of formulation, debate, and enactment. In the American national political system, characterized by a separated presidency, Congress, and judiciary, as well as by multiple power sites *within* each of these institutions, there are many places in which opponents of a given entrepreneurial innovation can exert their influence. During most moments of institutional creation, opponents of proposed reforms remain in positions of power from which they can shape institutional outcomes.[50] Furthermore, opponents of proposed reforms are often the beneficiaries of the institutions entrepreneurs seek to change, and have acquired resources and organizational strength from their access to government largesse which they can use to resist entrepreneurs' proposals.[51] Thus, even if entrepreneurs have the political support to enact some version of the measure they propose, they will almost always have to offer concessions as the price of opponents' acquiescence.[52] And if opponents are in possession of important institutional veto points—for example, the filibuster pivot in the Senate, one (or more) house of Congress, or the presidency—they will likely be able to extract considerable concessions from entrepreneurs, limiting the new institution's reach and perhaps seriously eroding its impact.[53] In truth, organized interests may be so well entrenched that entrepreneurs may engage in a form of "self-censorship," in which they do not even bother to pursue certain kinds of proposals because they know in advance that such efforts will fail.

Existing institutions and interests also inevitably shape an entrepreneurial initiative after it begins to operate in the political environment. The ordinary day-to-day operation of the new initiative is likely to throw it into conflict with existing institutions.[54] As James Mahoney and Kathleen Thelen note, opponents of a new reform, particularly those who stand the most to lose from its operation, may use their power to undermine it when and where they can.[55] The problem of compliance is especially fraught in federal systems, in which implementation is frequently delegated to subnational, and partially autonomous, governments. In fact, the U.S. federal system provides particularly fecund terrain for political opposition, or at least ambivalence, to flourish.[56]

The scope of any entrepreneurial agenda will also be delimited by the attendant budgetary situation, which partially reflects existing institutional commitments and interest group pressures. In good fiscal times, entrepreneurs' efforts to establish new institutional and financial commitments will be eased by the availability of fiscal resources. However, difficult fiscal times limit the budgetary slack needed to finance major departures.[57] Not only are new resources less available but defenders of existing programs are on high alert to protect their pet programs from "raiding" in order to finance new initiatives. Since the mid-1970s, the combination of uneven economic growth, large tax cuts, and mature spending commitments has placed the United States on unsure fiscal footing. This has tended to lower the sights of entrepreneurs seeking expanded federal involvement in areas of social policy, channeling them away from the most expansive— and potentially costly—measures and toward more fiscally and politically tractable ones.[58] Even after a reform sought by entrepreneurs is in place, it can still suffer attacks on its budget from hostile interests or fall victim to cuts demanded by lean fiscal times.

During both the process of institutional formulation and the process of implementation, public sentiments may impose important—albeit complex and ambiguous—limitations on entrepreneurs' innovations. When an issue is highly salient and citizens have clear views about it, public opinion may have a powerful impact on the outcome.[59] Although the entrepreneurs' hand may be strengthened when citizens favor the innovations they propose, they face limited prospects of success when public opinion is steadfastly opposed. Even in situations where opinion is more ambiguous, political entrepreneurs have to tread carefully. If such situations offer opportunities for entrepreneurs to influence public opinion, they also entail considerable risks: opponents may attempt to counter-mobilize public opinion, reducing the effectiveness of the entrepreneurs' efforts.[60] Finally, attempts to cultivate public opinion are easily overtaken by events: as conditions change, or the nation experiences a crisis, entrepreneurs may find that citizens have suddenly stopped listening.

Studies emphasizing institutional constraints make a valuable contribution to our understanding of institutional change; however, these too provide an incomplete picture. Too often, researchers have focused on developing hypotheses about how different kinds of institutional configurations determine which kinds of institutional changes occur, without clearly explaining *how* the changes happen.[61] Alternatively, scholars sometimes argue that "friction" among institutions induces change; but reliance on this ambiguous metaphor tends to obscure the precise mechanisms of change.[62] If studies featuring political entrepreneurs are inattentive to the ways institutions channel the scope of change, then, as Daniel Beland, Lawrence Jacobs, and other scholars have noted, research studies highlighting institutional constraints often do not adequately theorize the mechanisms by which political actors change institutions. This observation highlights a second, related problem: approaches emphasizing institutional constraints are limited in their ability to account for the substance and direction of institutional change. Precisely because these approaches tend to take important actors' beliefs, preferences, knowledge, and expectations as given, they are often ill-equipped to explain which particular menu of substantive choices receives serious consideration from policymakers and the public.[63]

Institutionally Bounded Entrepreneurship

Institutionally bounded entrepreneurship illustrates how entrepreneurs and institutions interact to produce bounded, ongoing institutional change. This approach is sensitive to issues of timing and sequencing as well. Indeed, entrepreneurs and institutions interact in complex ways over extended periods of time, producing varied, unexpected, and sometimes ironic consequences. My approach is grounded in five core claims, which I illustrate by discussing some of the central empirical themes of this book.

First, political entrepreneurs foster institutional change with creative rhetorical and organizational maneuvers. In my analysis of the development of federal education policy, unelected political entrepreneurs—rather than the elected officials featured in studies by Maris Vinovskis, John Jennings, and Elizabeth DeBray Pelot—take center stage.[64] Indeed, major business organizations, especially large employer organizations such as the Business Roundtable, the National Alliance of Business, and the Business Coalition for Education Reform, and civil rights organizations such as the Education Trust, the Citizens' Commission on Civil Rights, and the National Council of La Raza, were the most consistently influential political entrepreneurs in the realm of education policy. These groups endorsed education standards, testing, and accountability—and federal leadership to promote these policies—for very different reasons. Business leaders understood this agenda as the ticket to renewed worker productivity and economic growth; civil rights entrepreneurs viewed it as a path to more equal opportunity for historically disadvantaged students harmed by low expectations and unchallenging curricula. Despite these different (though not incompatible) emphases, these groups have engaged in parallel—and at times coordinated—entrepreneurial efforts to establish new educational institutions that would achieve their objectives. These groups developed a powerful political narrative that threw existing educational commitments into question and established grounds for a new agenda featuring high standards for all students, testing to gauge student progress, and school accountability for results. To advance their agendas, they invested heavily in efforts to build supporting organizations and coalitions and established close working relationships with presidents, influential members of Congress, and Department of Education staff. They also generated new research and data of their own, which they used to attempt to persuade policymakers. At the same time, these entrepreneurs committed consistent attention to education policymaking over the course of several decades.

Second, creative recombination of ideas and interests is central to entrepreneurs' success. The fact that both business leaders and civil rights activists embraced expanded federal involvement in improving schools was essential to the relative success of this agenda. Not only did federal leadership of standards, testing, accountability, and teacher quality attract a major Republican bloc (large business) and a prominent Democratic constituency (civil rights lobbies); it was also carefully framed to appeal to ideological themes cherished within each party. Business leaders extolled the economic benefits when justifying standards, testing, and accountability reforms to Republican audiences, claiming that these policies were needed to prepare America's youth for the rigors of economic competition in a globalizing economy. At the same time, civil rights activists appealed to Democrats' identification with historically disadvantaged groups by contending that federal standards, testing, accountability, and teacher-quality reforms were civil rights measures designed to ensure that disadvantaged students had equal access to a rigorous education. Sometimes the proposals of business entrepreneurs and civil rights entrepreneurs were not the first choice of either mainstream Democrats or Republicans; however, *and unlike either liberal-led or conservative-backed reforms,* they were always within the "zone of acceptable outcomes" of both.[65]

Third, the existing institutional context bounds the scope of entrepreneurial change during moments of institutional creation. The education reform agenda promoted in significant part by business and civil rights entrepreneurs has held the rhetorical high ground since the early 1980s but has faced considerable obstacles to realization in public policy. Navigating these obstacles required business entrepreneurs and civil rights entrepreneurs to build on, rather than replace, existing institutions. Previous initiatives established a durable and widely accepted mode of federal involvement in education—categorical grants to state and local governments—and acquired a diverse and powerful set of supporting constituencies, creating formidable institutional and political constraints on what business and civil rights entrepreneurs could safely propose. Rather than challenge existing arrangements head-on, entrepreneurs have made the strategic choice to layer their reforms atop them, resulting in more-modest institutional changes. The tight budgetary context has also routinely discouraged business and civil rights entrepreneurs from advocating proposals that would require dramatic enhancements to federal administrative capacity. Lacking fiscal slack with which to finance more sweeping initiatives and seeking to consolidate support from other education interests, business and civil rights entrepreneurs have gravitated to more-modest proposals that effectively piggybacked on already-existing (and already-funded) federal commitments in education. Finally, whereas scholars such as Patrick McGuinn have generally viewed public opinion as a strong source of support for federal education standards, testing, and accountability,[66] I argue that it often served as a constraint on what entrepreneurs were able to accomplish. Indeed, public ambivalence about federal involvement in education reinforced the drift toward an incremental strategy that built on previous federal investments in education.

Fourth, the existing institutional context bounds the scope of entrepreneurial change during the process of implementation. The federal structure of the American polity—especially in education—effectively ensured that implementation of standards, testing, and accountability reforms would fall to states and localities. Uneven political enthusiasm and administrative capacity at the state level have contributed to considerable variation among states in the scope of implementation of standards, testing, and accountability reforms, undermining entrepreneurs' hope for higher standards and accountability for results for all students and schools. Also, state and local leaders have lobbied vociferously—and often successfully—for greater freedom from federal regulations throughout the period analyzed in this book. Thus, contrary to Paul Manna, who suggests that federal education reforms "borrowed strength" from state and local policies, I argue that business entrepreneurs and civil rights entrepreneurs more often experienced federalism as a stumbling block to the realization of their programmatic objectives.[67]

The fact that business and civil rights entrepreneurs ultimately layered their proposals atop existing categorical education programs has also tended to limit the realization of these entrepreneurs' goals over time. The result has been a recurrent disconnect between what reformers have proposed to accomplish through categorical grants—those federal funding streams that provide state and local governments with federal dollars in exchange for promises to implement federal priorities—and what governments have been positioned to achieve.

Fifth, entrepreneurs respond to constraints on their agendas by rejuvenating their entrepreneurial projects, promoting a churning process of development over time. Entrepreneurs tend to respond to the constraints imposed on their initiatives by the political and institutional context in a characteristic, and predictable, fashion. Rather than rethink their underlying assumptions or question the validity of earlier efforts in light of their experience, entrepreneurs are far more likely to blame the "system" for undermining their proposals. Viewing existing institutional constraints as problems to be overcome, entrepreneurs thus tend to propose new initiatives to regulate, remove, or circumvent those constraints.[68] In practice, this usually means more elaborate, and specific, rules and regulations governing policy in a given area. Each new bout of entrepreneurship is likely to intensify inter-institutional tensions, leading to more complicated policymaking and heightened polarization between entrepreneurs and their critics.

On one hand, business and civil rights entrepreneurs have advocated more-stringent versions of a "standards-based reform" paradigm that would rationalize standards, testing, accountability, and teacher-training policies; on the other, they have urged that the federal government take increasingly vigorous steps to pressure state and local governments to adopt standards-based reform elements. But these victories have not resolved the problem of institutionally bounded entrepreneurship. To the contrary, each political success has only increased the gulf between what business and civil rights entrepreneurs have sought and what the education policy system has been able to deliver, frustrating both entrepreneurs and their critics. Furthermore, these reforms have produced undesirable side effects, such as teacher-directed education, excessive test preparation, and even perverse efforts to artificially inflate test scores. Contemporary controversies over Obama's education initiatives indicate that this is likely to be an endemic challenge to federal leadership of school reform in the United States.

Institutionally bounded entrepreneurship incorporates both entrepreneurial creativity and institutional constraints into a dynamic model of institutional development that can account for the complex patterns of change that we frequently observe in American politics. This approach sheds new light on the politics of federal education reform and provides scholars with useful tools for examining institutional change in other areas of public policy.

The Major Players in the Drama

Uncovering the institutionally bounded entrepreneurship of business leaders and civil rights activists requires placing these actors in the context of some of the most important issues and interests that are involved in the contemporary debate over elementary and secondary education reform. This will illuminate the relationships between the political entrepreneurs at the heart of my analysis and other major actors who influence education policy, providing a sense of the major alternatives to the proposals offered by business and civil rights entrepreneurs, as well as a visual representation of various possible reform coalitions. To be sure, any effort to map the terrain of education policy requires simplifications; but it also fosters analytical clarity, winnowing the complexity of education policymaking to its most essential elements. Building on the insights of scholars such as Patrick McGuinn, Elizabeth DeBray-Pelot, and Maris Vinovskis, as well as my own reading of thousands of primary and secondary sources, I believe we can fruitfully analyze these politics by considering how five over-arching groups (business entrepreneurs, civil rights entrepreneurs, educational liberals, educational conservatives, and organizations representing state elected officials) approach five major educational issues (federal involvement in education; standards, tests, and accountability; federal education spending; school choice; and block grants and other means of decentralizing policy decisions).[69] The table below summarizes the positions taken by these groups on each of these major educational issues and provides examples of the leadership and political allies of each.[70]

Business entrepreneurs, often hailing from organizations such as the Business Roundtable, the National Alliance of Business, and the Business Coalition for Education Reform, emerge as strong proponents of federal involvement in education to promote rigorous standards, testing, and accountability policies in education. Business leaders have generally viewed standards, testing, and accountability policies as economic development measures, broadly understood. From their perspective, such reforms would enhance schools' capacity to produce students with stronger reasoning and analytical skills; as employees, these individuals would in turn help power the nation's economy. Fearing that decentralized approaches produce educational inefficiencies, business entrepreneurs have also favored federal leadership because they believed it would promote

TABLE 1. The positions of major players on salient education reform issues

	EXPANDED FEDERAL INVOLVEMENT IN EDUCATION	STANDARDS, TESTS, ACCOUNTABILITY, AND TEACHER-QUALITY REFORM	EXPANDED EDUCATION SPENDING, ESPECIALLY AT THE FEDERAL LEVEL	SCHOOL CHOICE, ESPECIALLY VOUCHERS AND SUPPORT FOR PRIVATE SCHOOLS	BLOCK GRANTS AND OTHER FORMS OF CONSOLIDATION OR DECENTRALIZATION
1. Business entrepreneurs Individuals: William Kolberg of the National Alliance of Business, Ed Rust of State Farm, Louis Gerstner of IBM Organizations: Business Roundtable, National Alliance of Business, Committee for Economic Development, Business Coalition for Education Reform Allies: President Bill Clinton, President George W. Bush, Representative William Goodling, Representative John Boehner	Yes	Yes	Yes, if funds are spent on reforms. Do not support efforts to equalize education spending.	Yes on charter/magnet schools; divided on vouchers and support for private school choice	Do not support block grants; support consolidation
2. Civil rights entrepreneurs Individuals: Kati Haycock, William Taylor, Dianne Piché, Marshall Smith Organizations: Citizens' Commission on Civil Rights, Education Trust, National Council of La Raza Allies: President Bill Clinton, President George W. Bush, Representative George Miller, Senator Edward Kennedy	Yes	Yes	Yes. Support using federal authority to leverage spending equalization, but willing to drop this demand to preserve standards and accountability.	Yes on charter/magnet schools; no on vouchers and support for private schools	No

3. Educational liberals Individuals: Mary Futrell, Edward McElroy, Monty Neill Organizations: National Education Association, American Federation of Teachers, other major organizations representing teachers and administrators; FairTest, Committee on Education Funding Allies: Senator Paul Wellstone, Representative William Ford, many congressional Democrats	Yes	Skeptical to opposed	Yes. Equalization of spending is major priority.	Skeptical to opposed on charter/magnet schools; no on vouchers and support for private schools	No
4. Educational conservatives Individuals: Chester E. Finn Jr., Diane Ravitch, Lamar Alexander, William Bennett Organizations: Educational Excellence Network (Thomas B. Fordham Foundation), Heritage Foundation, American Enterprise Institute, Hoover Institute, Empower America, Focus on the Family Allies: Representative Richard Armey, Senator Judd Gregg, many congressional Republicans	Skeptical to opposed	Yes, if states and localities are given wide discretion on how to do them	Yes, if funds can be used at state discretion. Do not support efforts to equalize education spending.	Yes	Yes
5. Organizations representing state elected officials Individuals: N/A Organizations: National Governors Association, National Conference of State Legislatures Allies: in practice, many Republicans	Skeptical to opposed	Yes, if states and localities are given wide discretion on how to do them	Yes, if funds can be used at state discretion. Do not support efforts to equalize education spending.	Yes on charter/magnet schools; divided on vouchers and support for private school choice	Yes

higher standards in schools throughout the land. Although they generally favor expanded investment in education at all levels in order to raise the quality of education, they have not advocated prescriptive efforts at the federal level to promote the equalization of education spending across districts and schools (also known as "opportunity to learn" standards) on the grounds that this would take the focus away from efforts to promote school quality and would incite intractable redistributive battles at the state and local levels.

Business entrepreneurs might also be expected to rally to measures promoting private school choice (such as school vouchers) and other "marketizing" reforms; in reality, however, the business community has often been divided or ambivalent about these initiatives, in no small part because such reforms are unusually controversial and thus threaten to crowd out other priorities. Business entrepreneurs have favored efforts to consolidate myriad federal education programs into a more manageable number of grants, but they have questioned the efficacy of block grants because they fear giving states and localities a discretion that might be used by opponents of standards, testing, and accountability to thwart reforms. Generally speaking, business entrepreneurs have been more closely allied with Republicans than Democrats, but they have also worked with Democrats such as Presidents Clinton and Obama.

Like business entrepreneurs, *civil rights entrepreneurs* from organizations such as the Citizens' Commission on Civil Rights, the Education Trust, the National Council of La Raza, and the Leadership Conference on Civil Rights have been strong, consistent supporters of federal efforts to promote rigorous standards, testing, and accountability policies in education. (It is important to note that the term "civil rights entrepreneurs" denotes a particular *faction* of the broader civil rights movement, the members of which were especially committed to standards, testing, and accountability policies. Not all members of the civil rights movement have been advocates of these reforms.) Civil rights entrepreneurs have viewed standards, testing, and accountability reforms as civil rights measures that would draw attention to the underachievement of historically disadvantaged students and thus create political pressure to improve the schools serving these students. In light of a long history of fighting with state and local governments on civil rights matters, these entrepreneurs favor federal leadership, believing that, in the absence of federal pressure, states and localities would not work to improve schools serving disadvantaged students. Additionally, these entrepreneurs have advocated expanded federal education spending, as well as federal efforts to promote greater equity in education spending, as ways to improve educational conditions for disadvantaged groups. However, civil rights entrepreneurs have proved willing to moderate their spending demands—and jettison demands for "opportunity to learn" standards entirely—in order to maintain and expand standards and accountability initiatives.

In general, civil rights entrepreneurs have favored public school choice, but have expressed the view that private school choice measures will undermine public schools, promote segregation, and intensify inequities of access to educational resources. Also, and again due to their skepticism of state and local treatment of disadvantaged students, civil rights entrepreneurs have questioned the efficacy of block grants and other methods of political decentralization. Civil rights entrepreneurs have generally allied with Democrats; however, on standards, testing, and accountability issues, they have proved willing to work with Republicans such as George W. Bush.

Educational liberals have historically been closely linked with—and have strong representation within—the Democratic Party. In terms of numbers and political resources, the most influential educational liberal organizations are the two major teachers unions, the National Education Association and the American Federation of Teachers, and major education administrator groups such as the American Association of School Administrators, the National Association of State Boards of Education, and the Council of Chief State School Officers. However, some civil rights organizations, especially venerable organizations such as the National Association for the Advancement of Colored People and the National Urban League, have often joined them. These groups have always been strong proponents of federal involvement in education. In fact, they were at the forefront of efforts to promote the federal role in education through programs such as the Elementary and Secondary Education Act and the Education for All Handicapped Children Act and institutions such as the Department of Education. However, unlike business and civil rights entrepreneurs, educational liberals have usually viewed lack of resources (especially for disadvantaged students), rather than low standards or an absence of accountability for results, as the cause of the most serious problems facing American schools. Undoubtedly, this stance reflects the desire among school personnel to increase educational resources and avoid accountability; but it also reflects skepticism of the methodology of test-based accountability, as well as ideological opposition toward incentive-based systems that can create "winners and losers" and thereby harm some students.[71] Educational liberals have thus advocated vigorous federal efforts to expand education spending and channel additional resources to disadvantaged students, including through the propagation of "opportunity to learn" standards.

In addition to increased (and more equal) spending, educational liberals have preferred reforms that empower school personnel, especially teachers, to educate children, such as increased flexibility within the terms of federal and state regulations and expanded support for professional development (of course this is not surprising, especially from teachers and administrators who value their autonomy). Because they are strong proponents of—and often employees of—public schools, educational liberals have been staunch critics of market reforms, which they view as an existential threat to public schools. Educational liberals have also argued, similar to the view expressed by civil rights entrepreneurs, that marketizing reforms tend to encourage resegregation and foster other educational inequities. On the issue of block grants, educational liberals are strong opponents, fearing that such decentralizing measures will weaken federal educational commitments, erode resources for favored programs, and encourage states and localities to divert resources from historically disadvantaged groups.

Educational conservatives, well represented by organizations such as the Thomas B. Fordham Foundation, the American Enterprise Institute, the Hoover Institute, and the Heritage Foundation, have a set of preferences quite different from that of business entrepreneurs, civil rights entrepreneurs, or educational liberals. Like business and civil rights entrepreneurs, educational conservatives have consistently expressed support for high standards, accountability for results, and teacher quality, viewing such measures as means for improving economic competitiveness and strengthening moral and civic values. However, unlike business and civil rights entrepreneurs, educational conservatives have generally preferred to limit the role of the federal government to voluntary or promotional activities. Rather than work through federal channels, educational conservatives have generally called on states and localities to voluntarily implement such reforms, along with vouchers and other marketizing measures, to improve schools. Indeed, unlike business and civil rights entrepreneurs or educational liberals, educational conservatives view measures promoting private school choice, such as school vouchers, as an integral component of effective education reform, both because they believe these policies give parents more choices in education and because they think these policies use market mechanisms to promote greater efficiencies in schooling.

Consistent with their general distaste for taxation, especially redistributive taxation, educational conservatives have tended to view debates about "opportunity to learn" standards as a diversion from the primary challenge of improving school quality, as well as a threat to state and local "control" of education. Conservative ideology and interest also inform educational conservatives' approach to block grants and decentralizing measures. Believing that state and local leaders are best positioned to evaluate the educational needs of their constituents— and skeptical of liberal educational priorities that tend to centralize power in the federal government—educational conservatives have perennially advocated block grants and other initiatives to devolve authority to state and local governments. Rarely has support for educational conservatism extended much beyond the Republican Party base.

Because states possess constitutional responsibility for education, no discussion of education politics can neglect *organizations representing state elected officials*, especially those of governors (the National Governors Association) and state legislators (the National Conference of State Legislatures). For the most part, state elected officials have expressed strong support for standards, testing, and accountability in education. Like business entrepreneurs, many state leaders have perceived that raising standards and holding schools accountable for results are keys to improving human capital and thus strengthening American economic competitiveness (and, in particular, the competitiveness of their own states). While they are strong supporters of measures to raise education standards, state elected officials have almost always sought to preserve their policymaking discretion and limit outside intervention in state and local educational affairs. From the perspective of organizations representing state elected officials, state (and local) institutions are best situated to respond effectively to the unique educational demands of their constituents. Additionally, state and local leaders perceive that it is in their electoral interest to retain the flexibility to bend federal policies to the needs of their most powerful constituents. Thus, the major organizations representing state elected officials have generally opposed new prescriptive federal rules in education, regarding such measures as obstacles to state innovation and responsiveness to local needs. For the same reasons, they have advocated reforms that would reduce federal grant conditions and otherwise devolve decision-making. Organizations representing state elected officials have generally favored increases in education spending, but only if new funds can be obtained without the imposition of new regulatory requirements.

Federal elected officials have an important part to play in the analysis as well, particularly as the allies of these groups. Political entrepreneurs provided much of the impetus for policies such as the Improving America's Schools Act, No Child Left Behind, and Race to the Top, framing policy ideas, disseminating policy proposals, and building coalitions of support. But allies in the executive branch and Congress helped shepherd these policies through the legislative process, broker compromises among contending factions, and pressure skeptical representatives to provide their votes. This perspective recognizes the important contributions of political allies while giving the most credit to political entrepreneurs.

The interaction among business entrepreneurs, civil rights entrepreneurs, educational liberals, educational conservatives, and state leaders—mediated by existing institutions and shaped by changing budgetary and public opinion dynamics—has defined the trajectory of the federal role in education policymaking over the past thirty years. In the early 1980s, business entrepreneurs and civil rights entrepreneurs were joined by educational conservatives and state leaders in critiquing extant educational arrangements and offering new proposals to reform the nation's schools. Over the past several decades, however, business and civil rights entrepreneurs have provided much of the impetus for the expansion of federal authority in the realm of education standards, testing, and accountability, while educational liberals, educational conservatives, and state officials have most often sought to check this development while at the same time offering their own distinct agendas. Over time, these contending forces have fostered the development of an expansive, but ungainly, federal presence in America's schools.

Plan of the Book

The following chapters trace the development of education politics and policy-making from the 1980s up to the present day, in a roughly chronological fashion. Given my theoretical framework, this approach is appropriate, indeed necessary. Institutionally bounded entrepreneurship is a historical process, in which the ongoing interaction of entrepreneurial innovation and institutional constraints produces a bounded pattern of change that unfolds over time. In order to adequately grasp the direction and intensity of these changes, therefore, it is necessary to examine how these developments played out in sequence.

Chapter 1 provides a brief overview of the organization of education policy in the United States prior to 1980. Chapter 2 examines the initial bout of educational entrepreneurship that gave rise to a new focus on education reform, especially at the state level, during the 1980s. Chapters 3 through 6 provide detailed analyses of the evolution of institutionally bounded entrepreneurship during four periods punctuated by expanding federal involvement in education: 1989–92, which saw debate over George H. W. Bush's America 2000 initiative (chapter 3); 1993–94, which witnessed enactment of the Goals 2000: Educate America Act and the Improving America's Schools Act (chapter 4); 1995–2002, which was bookended by the "Republican Revolution" against big government and by the passage of No Child Left Behind (chapter 5); and 2003–11, which encompasses reaction against No Child Left Behind as well as the Obama administration's ambitious initiatives (chapter 6).

Beginning with chapter 3, each chapter follows the same organizational schema, which is designed to highlight institutionally bounded entrepreneurship within a given historical period and identify institutional developments that set the stage for entrepreneurship at later moments in time. Each begins with an examination of how existing institutions and interests bounded the entrepreneurial innovations analyzed at length in the previous chapter. Next, they each detail how educational entrepreneurs reacted to these developments, and show how their new entrepreneurial activities shaped debates about how to improve schools within the period under investigation. Legislative deliberations are then analyzed in detail to show how coalition building (or failed coalition building) influenced policymaking outcomes. Throughout, the goal is not merely to pro-vide a step-by-step historical account but to reveal the more general process of institutionally bounded entrepreneurship within each historical episode. Each chapter concludes with a brief discussion of the broader theoretical lessons of the episode, along with a preview of the action contained in the subsequent chapter.

The conclusion assesses the evidence in favor of my argument and discusses the implications for future efforts to improve the nation's schools. Stepping away from the case of education, it also considers the lessons of this study for our broader theories of institutional change.

THE STRUCTURE OF AMERICAN EDUCATION POLICY BEFORE 1980

The substantial federal involvement in the areas of education standards, testing, accountability, and teacher quality embodied in programs such as Race to the Top and the No Child Left Behind Act marks an important departure from the traditional federal role in education. Behind these important changes, however, no less important continuities remain. Because these programs build on a long-standing federal education aid program, the Elementary and Secondary Education Act (ESEA) of 1965, which provides categorical aid to states and localities to implement compensatory education programs, they necessarily delegate to states and localities primary responsibility to put reforms into action. In practice, this has meant that ambitious reforms have been reshaped, and often diluted, in the process of implementation. This bounded style of institutional change, which has invited churning intergovernmental conflict for control of school reform, is at the heart of American educational development today. In the following chapters I trace the institutionally bounded expansion of federal authority in education since the early 1980s. To provide a context and a sense of the terrain on which new reforms were enacted, in this brief chapter I describe the structure of American education policy up to 1980.

Any discussion of education policymaking in the United States must begin with an appreciation of the influence of federalism on the governance of schooling. For most of the nation's history, education policymaking was a very decentralized affair. The U.S. Constitution does not mention education, and policymakers at all levels of government interpreted this silence to mean that states and, especially, localities should take responsibility for organizing and managing schools.[1] Even the coming of the New Deal, which revolutionized federal involvement in many areas of social policy, almost completely bypassed elementary and secondary education; well into the 1950s, in fact, the propriety of any federal involvement in schooling remained an issue of contention. It was only after the 1954 *Brown v. Board of Education* decision that federal involvement in education gradually began to take shape. Inspired by the civil rights movement, the landmark Elementary and Secondary Education Act of 1965 sought to provide greater economic and social opportunities for historically disadvantaged children through more equal access to better-funded schools. ESEA provided federal categorical aid to state and local governments throughout the nation to design compensatory education programs for students disadvantaged by race and poverty. Spurred on by the civil rights movement—as well as by the advocacy of a powerful constellation of education interest groups, led by the National Education Association and the American Federation of Teachers—ESEA also became the model for other compensatory education programs serving groups such as disabled students and English-language learners. By the end of the 1970s, the most important, and most expensive, federal education programs were geared to providing aid to the economically, physically, and educationally disadvantaged. These federal grant programs were bolstered by laws, regulations, and judicial decisions designed to eliminate racial and sexual discrimination and to promote student rights and the rights of the disabled. This system was bolstered not only by public support for the principle (if not the reality) of educational equity, but also by the ongoing advocacy of educational liberals and by the interest of members of Congress in channeling federal largesse to their districts.

While these developments stimulated a growing federal presence in education, the reality was that these federal policies had little influence on the school programs serving non-disadvantaged students; for a variety of reasons, in fact, federal programs evolved in ways that tended to reinforce, rather than reduce, the separation between the compensatory and regular school programs. Furthermore, despite decades of concerted effort by proponents of public education to dramatically expand federal spending, the federal contribution remained modest. Given their limited scale, federal education programs sent the implicit message that the vast majority of students and schools were performing adequately, and that the primary responsibility of the federal government was to remediate the special challenges facing disadvantaged groups.

Emulating the federal example, state governments began to intervene in schools in a much more extensive fashion after the 1960s in order to promote greater educational equity for historically disadvantaged students. Despite these changes, however, most states continued to delegate core decisions about curriculum, standards, and personnel to local governments. State governments set minimum requirements for students and teachers and provided funding for schools, but generally refrained from regulating curricular, assessment, and training decisions in detail. In any case, state education agencies possessed limited capacity to oversee thousands of schools in far-flung districts. Consequently, two scholars concluded in a 1992 evaluation of "the relations between governance and instruction" in education that "the general pattern [in educational governance] was extensive *delegated* state power" well into the 1980s.[2] The United States' federal system added another wrinkle to the organization of educational governance prior to 1980. While state education regimes were broadly similar, they varied in terms of their preparedness for the major political, fiscal, and administrative challenges presented by the rise of concern surrounding standards, testing, and accountability in the decades after 1980. This set the stage for serious conflicts between states and localities, on one hand, and proponents of coordinated standards, tests, and accountability, on the other.

In retrospect, the American education system in 1980 exhibited a curious blend of institutional embeddedness and potential political vulnerability. On one hand, the combination of targeted federal involvement, decentralized implementation, broad geographic dispersion of benefits, and strong interest-group support seemed to offer something for everyone, and thereby encourage institutional stability over time. On the other hand, the regime's comparative inattention to matters of educational performance—exemplified by federal evaluations that suggested that the ESEA had modest effects on the academic achievement of aid recipients—threatened to become a liability as spending at the federal and state levels increased dramatically, and as economic and political conditions became less welcoming for educational liberalism in the mid-to-late 1970s.[3]

The Halting Expansion of Federal Involvement in Education prior to 1965

There has almost always been a federal "role" in elementary and secondary education in the United States, but for most of the nation's history federal involvement occurred at the margins. Beginning with the Ordinance of 1785 and the Northwest Ordinance of 1787, the federal government subsidized the expansion of public education by setting aside proceeds from the sale of unsettled U.S. lands to fund public schools. In all, the federal government granted 98.5 million acres to the states for the purpose of supporting public education. After the Civil War, Congress went a step further, requiring that all new states admitted to the Union establish "free, nonsectarian public schools."[4] Additionally, with the Morrill Acts of 1862 and 1890, the federal government began to "fund…new land-grant colleges for the expansion of agricultural extension and provided for mechanical-vocational training," as historian Hugh Davis Graham has noted.[5] Several schemes to establish more-expansive federal aid to elementary and secondary education failed in the postbellum years; but between 1914 and 1917, with the passage of the Smith-Lever and Smith-Hughes acts, the federal government began to provide annual appropriations to support agricultural, industrial, and home economics education in secondary schools.[6]

Still, well into the twentieth century, "the day-to-day management of schools, including such matters as personnel, curriculum, and pedagogy, remained in the hands of local authorities, with state and federal governments having little influence," as Patrick McGuinn notes.[7] Even as the New Deal dramatically expanded federal involvement in many areas of society and economy, the federal role in elementary and secondary education remained modest, largely relegated to the support of school construction and improvement projects through the Works Progress Administration (or Work Projects Administration after 1939) and the provision of aid for needy high school students through the Civilian Conservation Corps and the National Youth Administration.[8]

If the 1940s witnessed a growing awareness of the importance of education for economic development—as well as an expanding effort by civil rights activists and teacher advocates to increase educational opportunities for disadvantaged students—significant obstacles to a more vigorous federal role remained.[9] As historian Gareth Davies notes, efforts to augment the federal role in education were usually constrained by the "three R's" of federal education politics: "race, religion, and reds." Supporters of African American civil rights were reluctant to endorse federal education bills that benefited segregated school districts, while southern politicians opposed any initiatives requiring districts to desegregate as a condition of receiving federal aid. The issue of religion pitted "advocates of strict church-state separation, public school interests, and anti-Catholic nativists," who opposed federal aid for parochial schools in any form, against "Catholic schools and bishops, [as well as] legislators with large Catholic constituencies," who preferred no federal aid if such assistance excluded parochial schools. The other "R," "reds," signified many Americans' enduring concern about federal control of education. The difficulty of reconciling these competing demands repeatedly scuttled efforts to channel federal aid for elementary and secondary education between 1945 and 1964.[10]

The major exceptions to this trend—a series of "impact aid" programs established between the early 1940s and the mid-1960s, and the National Defense

Education Act (NDEA) of 1958—proved the rule. Impact aid—begun with the Lanham Act of 1941—provided federal assistance to districts where local property tax revenues for education suffered as a result of the presence of federal installations, which could not be taxed. Although the program had a policy rationale, at least in theory, its political popularity was due in significant part to the fact that its funding formula was constructed so that federal aid would flow to the vast majority of congressional districts.[11] (The distributive educational politics initiated by the impact aid programs would later become a staple of federal education policy, easing the expansion of federal involvement by spreading money to as many districts as possible.) The NDEA, which provided categorical aid to states to improve math, science, and foreign-language instruction, was largely a response to public fears, precipitated by the Soviet Union's launch of the Sputnik satellite in 1957, that the nation's education system was lagging the Soviets' in the race for technological supremacy.[12] Even after enactment of the NDEA and impact aid programs, however, the federal role remained modest, constituting less than 2 percent of all education spending.

But changes in federal education policy—driven largely by racial struggle— were on the horizon. In 1954, in response to a lawsuit brought by the NAACP, the Supreme Court declared that the segregation of public schools by race was unconstitutional. In concluding that "in view of our decision that the Constitution prohibits the states from maintaining racially segregated public schools, it would be unthinkable that the same Constitution would impose a lesser duty on the Federal Government," the Court seemed to set the stage for vigorous federal efforts to eliminate segregation and promote greater racial equity in access to educational opportunities.[13] In the short term, however, such hopes were not realized. The so-called *Brown II* decision in 1955 declined to set firm deadlines for ending segregation and failed to lay out methods for desegregating schools. Rather than submit to *Brown,* southern whites engaged in "massive resistance" against the decision, taking the form of legal and administrative shenanigans, as well as intimidation and violence, to block the desegregation of southern schools. Meanwhile, the Eisenhower administration exhibited little energy in enforcing *Brown.* As a result, in many southern states "*Brown* had almost no immediate direct impact on desegregation," observes legal scholar Michael Klarman: "Across the South as a whole, roughly 0.16 percent of school-age blacks were attending school with whites in 1959–1960 and 1.2 percent in 1963–1964."[14]

Nonetheless, the *Brown* decision and the burgeoning civil rights movement slowly forced social inequities—including educational inequities—to the top of the public's consciousness, preparing the way for more significant federal involvement to promote educational equity for disadvantaged groups.

The Elementary and Secondary Education Act and the Rise of "Equity in Education"

Whereas John Kennedy made little headway on federal education policy during his truncated term of office, his successor, Lyndon Johnson, presided over a sea change in the federal role in education. Gaining momentum from a wave of public support in the wake of Kennedy's assassination, the infusion of large liberal majorities into Congress after 1958, and the political energy provided by the civil rights movement, Johnson advocated a major expansion of federal involvement in education in order to promote educational opportunities for groups historically disadvantaged by racism and poverty. Linking education to his broader "War on Poverty," Johnson explained that "our war on poverty can be won only if those who are poverty's prisoners can break the chains of ignorance....We must give our best the chance to do their best."[15] Johnson's view that extending educational opportunities would alleviate poverty and promote economic equality reflected a broader faith shared by many social scientists, foundation executives, and policymakers—as well as by civil rights activists—in the 1960s.[16]

Johnson won a smashing electoral victory in 1964, carrying 61.1 percent of the popular vote. Congressional Democrats reaped the gains of Johnson's victory, as well; at the start of 1965, Democrats enjoyed better than two-thirds majorities in both the House and the Senate. Nonetheless, Johnson and his advisers realized they had to negotiate treacherous political shoals if they were to enact major education legislation. The first of the three R's, race, had been alleviated by the enactment of the Civil Rights Act of 1964, which barred the provision of federal aid to institutions practicing racial discrimination; but the other two R's remained. The Elementary and Secondary Education Act was constructed in ingenious fashion to mitigate these potential controversies. To navigate the political minefield of federal aid to parochial schools, Johnson and his allies invoked a "child-benefit theory," recently endorsed by the Supreme Court, which held that it was constitutional for public funds to be used to aid children in private schools as long as the schools themselves did not directly benefit.[17] Administration officials addressed fears of federal "control" of education by structuring the ESEA as a *categorical* granting program, which provided federal funds to states and localities for the fairly limited purpose of designing compensatory education programs for students suffering from the effects of poverty and discrimination, rather than as a program of *general* education aid, as advocates of federal education spending had long sought. Building on the political lessons of the popular impact-aid program, the ESEA was designed to disburse federal largesse by a formula that spread federal assistance to virtually every congressional district. Over and beyond the political ideals embedded in the program, the geographically generous funding formula dramatically expanded the appeal of the ESEA among lawmakers and their constituents.[18]

Having built consensus among elite social scientists and policymakers and forged compromises with important education interest groups, Johnson rode herd on Congress, pushing his Democratic allies to enact legislation, without major amendments, while political conditions favored reform.[19] Ultimately, the legislation was supported by large majorities in both houses of Congress; in the House, the bill passed on a 263–153 vote, while in the Senate lawmakers voted 73–18 for enactment. Policymakers thus established a new role for the federal government in elementary and secondary education—providing resources to states and localities to expand educational opportunities and equity for disadvantaged groups.[20] Funded at more than $1.3 billion, the ESEA more than doubled the federal investment in elementary and secondary education overnight.

Over the next fifteen years, the ESEA budget expanded at an exponential rate, and numerous additional legislative "Titles" and programs were added. In 1965 the total federal budget for elementary, secondary, and vocational education was just over $2.6 billion dollars; by 1979 it had climbed to more than $16.6 billion (both dollar amounts are in constant 2008 dollars), approaching 10 percent of all spending on elementary and secondary education.[21] In a classic case of "policy feedback," the ESEA's appropriations and programs helped stimulate the emergence of new interest groups and the growth of existing ones, which in turn lobbied effectively for higher appropriations and more programs. Indeed, explain education scholars Harvey Kantor and Robert Lowe, the ESEA "not only created new groups of service providers and service recipients but also generated a broad constituency of support…from interest groups like the National Education Association," as well as the National Advisory Council for the Education of Disadvantaged Children, the NAACP, and the Lawyers Committee for Civil Rights under Law.[22] In another example of policy feedback, ESEA programs that bolstered the capacity of state departments of education (discussed in greater detail below) helped create a class of state-level administrators who also became their staunch advocates. Meanwhile, the broad geographic scope of the ESEA institutionalized bipartisan support in Congress by giving many policymakers a stake in its continuation and expansion. Whereas Democrats initially spearheaded the growth of federal investment in education, by the mid-1970s, Davies notes, "rather than fight the expanded federal role, Republicans increasingly sought a share of the political credit."[23]

The ESEA also became the model for subsequent efforts to promote educational equity for historically disadvantaged groups, especially English-language learners and the disabled. By the late 1970s, following enactment of laws such as the Bilingual Education Act of 1968 and the Education for All Handicapped Children Act of 1975, it could fairly be said that servicing disadvantaged groups—what many would call the "educational equity" agenda—had become the overriding mission of federal education policy.[24] Meanwhile, in a further reflection of the broader "minority rights revolution" of the 1960s and 1970s, federal court decisions related to desegregation, student rights, and the treatment of disabled and English-language learners led to further federal involvement in schooling. These decisions tended to reduce the discretion of state and local officials in addressing the concerns of these groups, and often required them to increase spending in order to meet students' special needs.[25]

It is very important not to overstate the expansion of federal involvement in elementary and secondary education in the decade and a half following enactment of the ESEA, however. Federal responsibilities grew within tightly delimited bounds. In a nod to the prerogatives of state and local policymakers, the ESEA and its progeny delegated substantial discretion to states and localities to design and implement compensatory education programs. Federal regulations sought to ensure that federal education funds reached the students for whom the programs were intended, but they did not hold state and local governments accountable for actually raising the achievement of eligible students. Rather, as Paul Manna notes, "policymakers...relied on state and local judgments about how to meet the particular needs of disadvantaged students."[26] With federal regulators focused on school districts' spending patterns and compliance with federal rules, federally funded but locally administered programs varied tremendously in their administrative practices and academic rigor.[27]

Furthermore, federal programs and their recipients were largely isolated from the regular school program and nonprogram recipients.[28] In part in order to comply with federal accounting rules, state and local policymakers often designed their compensatory education offerings as "pull-out programs," in which disadvantaged students were removed from regular classes and provided with separate, special instruction by federally funded instructors. This approach made it easier for federal regulators to track federal funds; but it also limited the overall impact of federal programs on schools, while fragmenting the education of recipients of federal aid.[29] Finally, because federal funding formulas spread federal funds across a very large number of districts—and because the number of students eligible to receive aid always exceeded available funds—the impact of federal categorical assistance was diluted. Indeed, many deserving students in poorer districts never received aid, even as wealthier districts continued to receive federal largesse.[30] In consequence, the structure of the ESEA and its progeny ensured that, even as rules and regulations proliferated, "the federal government exert[ed] little or no direct influence on such fundamental educational decisions as the length of the school year or school day, class size, teacher hiring, or acquisitions of textbooks or buildings."[31]

Evaluations of the ESEA conducted during the 1970s and early 1980s suggested that the program's effects on recipients' academic achievement were modest, and concentrated on lower-order skills.[32] Given the heterogeneity of local programs and the inefficiency of ESEA spending, such outcomes were not surprising. Despite its limitations, however, the ESEA remained politically popular, drawing support from civil rights advocates, teachers and administrators, and Democrats and Republicans alike.

The State and Local Roles in Education Governance

The policy trajectory just traced at the federal level was mirrored at the state and local levels. For much of their history, state governments had delegated most decision-making authority to local school districts and communities, even though they possessed constitutional responsibility for education.[33] In essence, state laws and regulations provided a broad framework of rules in which local governments were to operate: states created compulsory attendance laws, established minimum graduation expectations (usually in terms of number and distribution of credits), instituted minimum requirements for teachers, structured and consolidated school districts, authorized regional administrators to oversee local schools, and provided "foundation funding" to assist impoverished school districts. To be sure, the state role in funding education gradually expanded between 1900 and midcentury. Within this broad framework, however, "most school boards...assumed primary control over hiring and firing, curricula, the length of the school day and year, and the observation of holidays," as well as responsibility for financing public education, according to political scientist William Howell.[34] Concomitantly, most state education agencies were poorly funded and staffed, and lacked the capacity to oversee educational practices in far-flung classrooms.[35] Thus, as educational historian Thomas James describes the state of state educational authority at the end of World War II, "States...did not enumerate what had to occur within the production process of schooling itself. They did not, and could not, exercise direct control over the decisions that most directly shaped the educational experience of students within local school systems."[36] One major consequence of the limited capacity and influence of state governments in education was remarkable variation *within* states on such core matters as curriculum, staffing, accountability, and school finance.

Between 1945 and 1980, however, policy analysts spied a "Growing Role of the States in American Education."[37] In part, this was driven by the quest for rational management and standardization that permeated virtually all areas of public policy from the Progressive Era onward. State policymakers mounted consolidation campaigns to reduce the number of school districts and bring about a more centralized system of public schooling. Between the Great Depression and the 1970s, the number of school districts nationwide fell from almost 120,000 to fewer than 20,000; the average membership size of a local school board also declined dramatically.[38]

Perhaps more consequential for state involvement, however, was the rise of equity in education as the dominant educational agenda in the United States. While states had long turned a blind eye to educational inequities, the civil rights movement and the concomitant expansion of federal interest in schools spurred a quantum increase in the level of state involvement in education.[39] Desegregation litigation following the *Brown* decision, as well as lawsuits challenging state and local treatment of racial and linguistic minorities and disabled students, pressured state policymakers to take positive actions to address these students' needs and, more self-interestedly, head off future suits. Beginning in the late 1960s and early 1970s, in fact, many states began to mirror the activities of Congress, establishing categorical education programs that provided special assistance to disadvantaged groups of students.[40] Furthermore, as Paul Manna has noted, federal education policies often compelled states to exercise oversight over localities, and provided states with funds to modernize their administrative infrastructure.[41] As a result, state policymakers, especially state education departments, began to take a more active role in monitoring localities' decisions, especially in matters related to the treatment of historically disadvantaged groups. Indeed, many state department of education staff were "federal proxies," according to a major education textbook of the day, tied by interest and ideology to federal educational policies and purposes.[42]

In the realm of school finance, state efforts to promote greater educational equity actually outpaced those at the federal level. In the 1973 *San Antonio Independent School District v. Rodriguez* decision, the Supreme Court ruled that there was no federal constitutional right to an adequate education, undermining efforts to constitutionally redress, at the federal level, grievous finance inequalities between wealthy and poor school districts. But legal demands for greater equity in school finance prospered in the states during the 1970s and 1980s, as judges in dozens of states proved willing to invalidate state education finance systems on the grounds that extant financing schemes—which relied heavily on local property taxes for school revenues—violated *state* constitutions by discriminating against poorer districts and schools.[43] Reading the handwriting on the wall, other states preemptively reformed their school finance regimes in order to head off lawsuits. By 1980 as many as thirty states had made notable adjustments to their finance systems, in significant part by increasing state expenditures on education.[44]

Thus, like the federal government, state governments expanded their responsibilities from the 1960s onward in an effort to promote educational equity for historically disadvantaged groups. Even so—and in another parallel with federal policy—most state systems of education remained highly decentralized in important respects in 1980.[45] In an implicit acknowledgment of many citizens' desire for local control of education, core decisions related to standards, curriculum, and teaching remained primarily in the hands of local governments. Of course, there was some important variation among states, with New England states tending to devolve the most authority and southern states adopting more centralized education arrangements. On the whole, however, "until the 1980s, most states left curriculum decisions largely to local discretion, satisfied to specify a few required courses and issue advisory curricular frameworks for local consideration," according to education scholar Michael Kirst.[46] Additionally, few states closely regulated how prospective teachers were educated, or how (or whether) in-service teachers were evaluated. While most states required prospective teachers to complete a credentialed education program, they left the programmatic details to colleges of education. State examinations of the knowledge and pedagogical skills of prospective teachers were uncommon in the 1970s: indeed, as late as 1982, only eighteen states required, or had planned to require, that prospective teachers pass a test of their pedagogical or subject-matter knowledge.[47] Finally, accountability for results—so common today in discussions of education policy—was a rarity in the late 1970s and early 1980s. Systematic monitoring of student academic performance, or the linking of student performance to districts, schools, and teachers, was almost entirely unheard of. While there were standardized examinations, most were "norm-referenced" tests that merely compared students to one another, as opposed to some external set of expectations for achievement. In any case, as education historian Thomas Timar notes, "Proscriptions about student suspension generally outnumbered those for student academic achievement."[48]

Thus, similar to developments at the federal level, new state policies presumed that most students were achieving at adequate levels, and that new, more intensive educational interventions could be focused on disadvantaged students. Consequently, growing state involvement in education did little to orient schools to matters of educational performance. Not only was accountability for performance unusual; it was difficult even to ascertain whether students or schools were performing adequately. However, according to contemporary polls, this was not seen as a major problem; in fact, lack of discipline, use of drugs, and lack of proper financial support, not low standards or an absence of accountability, topped Americans' views of the biggest problems facing community schools. Moreover, a strong plurality of citizens continued to give the public schools in their community a positive evaluation.[49]

State and Local Diversity: Implications for Subsequent Education Policymaking

Thus far, I have been describing broad trends in federal and state education policymaking. However, an adequate understanding of the politics of education in the United States requires attention to the complexities fostered by the nation's diverse federal system. A venerable literature in political science and sociology has documented the wide variation in economics, demographics, and politics among the American states. Some states are wealthy, while others are poor; some are politically liberal and most frequently governed by Democrats, while others are bastions of Republican conservatism; some are racially and ethnically diverse, while others have more homogeneous populations. These differences help account for the divergent policy choices of state governments across a wide range of areas, including education.[50]

Indeed, it is important to remember that beneath broad educational similarities, states vary in crucial ways, reflecting their different political cultures, economic environments, and demographic circumstances. First, there were significant differences between states in the level of investment in elementary and secondary education. In the 1979–80 school year, average per-pupil spending in elementary and secondary education was $4,171; however, per-pupil expenditures ranged from a low of $2,890 in Arkansas to a high of $8,679 in Alaska, with considerable variation in between.[51] Furthermore, in spite of the infusion of federal aid from the 1960s onward, state departments of education differed considerably in their degree of professionalization, administrative capacity, and resources. Some state departments possessed ample resources and staff; in other states, however, education agencies were routinely hampered by inadequate budgets and staffing.[52] State laws allocating responsibility and authority among important political actors also varied in important ways. In some states, for example, authority in education is more concentrated in the governor or the state legislature, whereas in others, state boards and/or education agencies possess greater autonomy and control.[53] In much the same way, the political strength of teachers unions (which generally negotiate collective-bargaining arrangements at the *local* level) varies across states, with their influence greatest in more urban and non-southern states.[54]

These variations among states, which have endured across the decades, have had important implications for the implementation of standards, testing, and accountability policies. Whatever else they may do, standards, testing, accountability, and teacher-quality policies, especially when promoted at the federal level, attempt to induce greater policy consistency across geographic space. Furthermore, these policies presume that state and local policymakers possess considerable policy knowledge and administrative resources. As the foregoing suggests, however, states and localities differ considerably in their political, social, and economic environments, as well as in resources and capacity that can be brought to bear on education policy issues. In consequence, the receptivity to standards, testing, and accountability reforms varies across geographic space. These facts portended significant administrative and logistical difficulties for advocates of standards, testing, and accountability reforms. As we shall see in the following chapters, the tensions between the ambitions of standards, testing, and accountability reformers and the will and capacity of state and local officials helped contribute to a churning, inchoate style of institutional development over time.

The roles of the federal and state governments in education were transformed between 1954 and 1980. Education policymaking was profoundly influenced by the rise of the educational equity agenda, which underscored the special challenges facing poor, minority, disabled, and English-language learning students, and sought to provide these students with expanded educational opportunities and resources. This agenda gave rise to heightened federal and state involvement in education. Between the 1950s and the end of the 1970s, both the federal government and the states developed new programs and regulations designed to assist historically disadvantaged groups, impinging in important ways on the authority of lower-level governments. These policies were supported by an array of civil rights groups, educational interest groups, and state education bureaucrats, as well as by elected officials who gained politically from channeling new educational resources to their districts.

Nonetheless, while the federal and the state roles in education grew notably during this period, the responsibilities of governments at both levels remained quite limited. Operating primarily through categorical grant programs and regulations pertaining to the treatment of disadvantaged students, neither the federal government nor most state governments intervened vigorously in core educational decisions relating to curriculum, staffing, and accountability. Responsibility for the "regular school program" serving most students remained lodged in local school districts and schools. This state of affairs likely reflected public preferences; indeed, in 1980, 68 percent of Americans maintained that the "local school board" should have the greatest influence over what is taught in the public schools.[55] More broadly, the decentralization of core curricular, staffing, and accountability decisions reflected policymakers'—and citizens'—assumptions that most students were performing adequately and that intervention by higher-order governments should be concentrated on helping disadvantaged students improve academically.

Beneath the apparent stability of existing education policies, however, potential political vulnerabilities lurked. Perhaps most notably, the dearth of attention to the issue of academic performance was a liability making the system potentially susceptible to criticism, especially as education budgets increased and political conditions began to change in ways that eroded the political and economic foundations of the equity-in-education agenda. In the ensuing decades, proponents of standards, testing, and accountability pushed the federal government and the states to adopt new legal and administrative arrangements that focused education policy on academic performance. These reformers, however, had to negotiate an embedded system organized around very different assumptions and practices, bolstered by powerful constituencies and, to an important extent, supported by public opinion. Rather than wholly recast the organization of education policymaking, therefore, reformers were forced to take this system into account in structuring their own proposals. As the following chapters will show, the result of this dynamic was a bounded style of institutional change that altered, without erasing, prior institutions and interests.

A NEW DIRECTION IN AMERICAN EDUCATION POLICY, 1980–1988

The early 1980s witnessed a sea change in the rhetoric surrounding—and, to a lesser extent, the institutions composing—the American education system. The conventional wisdom surrounding education shifted decisively toward a new paradigm, often described as "excellence in education." This ideational framework put the focus on several novel interrelated themes: that low student achievement was *pervasive* and threatening to the nation's economic and social well-being; that *many* of the nation's schools were failing to provide an adequate education; that new public policies to make schooling rigorous would remedy educational deficiencies and address the challenges facing the nation; and that disadvantaged students would benefit disproportionately from efforts to strengthen academics. Each of the themes of this framework departed substantially from the previously dominant equity-in-education paradigm, stimulating important departures in education politics and policymaking. Attention to excellence in education, and education issues more generally, intensified substantially among elected officials, education interest groups, and the public, leading to a wave of school reform throughout the land. Whereas education was once the provenance of a relatively closed community of education policymakers, education professionals, and federal and state education bureaucrats, the 1980s opened schools to a host of new actors, including business entrepreneurs, civil rights entrepreneurs, educational conservatives, and federal and state elected officials. Consequently, state governments, though not yet the federal government, began to engage in more vigorous efforts to influence standards, curricula, testing, and teacher quality.

The rhetorical and institutional developments of the 1980s were pivotal because they set the tone for education policy up to the present day. On one hand, excellence in education generated many of the educational motifs that character- ize contemporary education discourse. When President Obama links the per- formance of schools to the future of the American economy and calls on states and localities to adopt high academic standards and accountability for results, he harks back in many ways to the ideas and policy proposals that originated in the 1980s. On the other hand, excellence in education set the stage for major institu- tional changes in schooling—in particular, for more muscular and prescriptive involvement by state and federal governments in education. These changes were not all of a piece; indeed, the progress of education reform, especially at the federal level, has been halting, uneven, and subject to reversals. Yet the ideational shifts heralded by excellence in education have significantly altered the way educational authority is organized in the United States, gradually fostering a more central- ized, and somewhat more standardized, form of educational organization.

Why did excellence in education begin to dominate the discussion of educa- tion policymaking in the United States in the 1980s after a long period of rela- tive neglect? How did policymakers, governments, and education interest groups respond to the emergence of this agenda? I argue in this chapter that the entre- preneurial behavior of four major groups—business entrepreneurs, civil rights entrepreneurs, educational conservatives, and organizations representing state officials (especially governors)—was pivotal to the emergence of the excellence- in-education agenda and the shifting politics of education in the United States. Whereas these groups later split into rival factions (business entrepreneurs and civil rights entrepreneurs versus educational conservatives and state leaders) over the issue of federal involvement in school reform, in the 1980s they worked together to promote major changes to education at the state and local levels. Exploiting the opportunity created by poor economic conditions, flagging stu- dent achievement, rising deficits, and sagging public enthusiasm for the political status quo, these four groups developed and disseminated overlapping policy proposals centered on the theme of "excellence in education." This agenda firmly established the set of ideological claims linking national interests, educational institutions, and the rhetoric of reform. It also presumed new institutional rela- tionships in which states would assume greater responsibility and oversight of core educational matters. The agenda-setting by these groups played a pivotal role in moving the debate on education policymaking, driving state govern- ments, national elected officials, and important educational interest groups to alter their agendas to reflect "excellence" concerns.

In analyzing the origins of excellence in education, I also establish a baseline for interpreting the subsequent development of the politics of school reform in the United States. Institutionally bounded entrepreneurship is a dynamic model, illustrating how entrepreneurs' agendas (and, ultimately, public policies) evolve in response to their interaction with existing institutions and political developments. By understanding the initial themes and ideas of the entrepreneurs who promoted versions of excellence in education in the 1980s, we can better appreciate how these ideas developed as the politics of school improvement played out over time. I highlight two components of excellence in education that came under increasing pressure over time: an assumption that states would take the lead in reforming schools and that the federal government would have a minimal role; and an assumption that simply making each area of education policy more rigorous would suffice to improve schools. The way these assumptions were contested—and altered—over time had profound consequences for the ultimate development of the federal role in education.

Finally, this chapter begins to flesh out my claims about what the politics of school reform tells us about social policymaking in the United States in the post-Reagan era. The convergence of diverse groups on excellence in education at an early date belies claims that this agenda embodied a fundamentally conservative turn in education politics; it also holds the key to understanding the long-term political durability of ideas promoted by these actors. As my institutionally bounded entrepreneurship approach suggests, the fact that excellence in education served as the "common carrier" of diverse ideologies and interests explains a great deal about its enduring vitality over the past three decades.

I begin by briefly discussing some of the contextual factors attending the emergence of excellence in education in American education politics, suggesting how they provided an environment in which the excellence-in-education agenda could flourish. I then show how business entrepreneurs, civil rights entrepreneurs, educational conservatives, and state leaders mobilized to promote a vision of excellence in education. Next, I analyze key themes of the excellence-in-education paradigm, illustrating how these four groups linked extant political conditions, educational challenges, and school practices in a narrative that legitimated new forms of government involvement in schools. In the final section of the chapter I examine how elected officials, state governments, and educational liberals responded to the rise of the new agenda.

The Context of Excellence in Education

As the new decade dawned, the nation experienced major economic and political tribulations that unsettled the institutions and interests that comprised the educational equity regime described in the previous chapter. Destabilizing existing institutions, eroding extant coalitions, and shaking up the conventional wisdom, these developments helped pave the way for excellence in education. Foremost among these developments was the economic crisis of the 1970s and early 1980s. After a long period of vigorous growth, the American economy began to enter a prolonged period of economic instability in the 1970s. By the end of the decade, "stagflation"—a combination of economic stagnation and rapid inflation—gripped the economy, undermining the economic security of millions and casting conventional economic prescriptions into doubt.[1] The struggling economy, coupled with the costs of the Vietnam War, also contributed to the erosion of the nation's fiscal position, threatening existing social policy commitments and weakening the capacity of the federal government and state governments to undertake new public projects.[2] Attending the economic crisis was a realignment in American ideological and partisan politics. Even as the economic environment and the budgetary situation deteriorated, bitter cultural conflicts over civil rights, crime, abortion, and women's liberation helped efface many Americans' commitment to the Great Society liberalism that had undergirded the educational arrangements of the equity-in-education regime. Indeed, a powerful conservative movement, which crested with the election of Ronald Reagan in 1980, issued a vocal challenge to the federal role in education, calling for devolution of authority to state and local governments and for greater governmental support for private and religious schools.

These interrelated developments destabilized existing policy commitments in education no less than in other areas of government investment and involvement. In a nation that has traditionally called on schools to provide young people with the skills needed to build the economy, poor economic conditions seemed to cast schools' competence in this role in doubt. While frustration with the Great Society was probably not centered on education—though busing for the purpose of school desegregation undoubtedly contributed to public disaffection—the generally declining fortunes of modern liberalism threatened the stability of education programs deemed central to the Great Society vision. What really made these broader economic and political developments reverberate in education policy, however, was their coincidence with educational trends that reflected poorly on school institutions. As figure 1 shows, some, though not all, measures of educational performance fell noticeably from the late 1960s through the late 1970s or early 1980s. At the time, careful analysts realized that some of this apparent decline was due to changes in the composition of the nation's student population; but they also acknowledged that some of it appeared to reflect a real downward shift in student achievement.[3] Many Americans were alarmed by the apparent stagnation of student achievement, and the popular press was filled with accounts of "failing" schools. Furthermore, the apparent correspondence

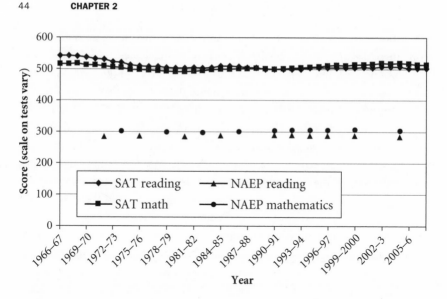

FIGURE 1.   Performance of high school students on SAT and NAEP tests, 1966–2006. Source: National Center on Education Statistics, U.S. Department of Education. The SAT scores are those of "college-bound seniors," while the NAEP scores are of a nationally representative sample of seventeen-year-olds. The Department of Education has rescaled all SAT scores so they are directly comparable over time.

between the nation's economic travails and American students' soft performance created a plausible prima facie case that schools might be responsible for the poor state of the economy.

Mobilizing to Promote Excellence in Education

In a context of considerable economic, cultural, and educational foment, prevailing educational arrangements—especially their modest attention to performance—were increasingly likely to be seen as a liability rather than as a virtue. Starting as early as 1980, a sprawling collection of groups mobilized to transform these conditions into a durable movement for excellence in education. While *A Nation at Risk*, a famous report issued by the National Commission on Excellence in Education on April 26, 1983, is often credited with providing the impetus for excellence in education, it makes more sense to think about that report in the context of a broader political movement that both preceded and elaborated on it.[4] Well before publication of *A Nation at Risk*, in fact, various political entrepreneurs were already providing energy and direction for excellence in education.

Indeed, aside from their other activities, these figures contributed to no fewer than *nine* "major reports on education" published in 1983, as counted by the Education Commission of the States.[5] Furthermore, because federal commission reports have a checkered history in eliciting major policy change, especially in education, focusing on the ongoing activities of business entrepreneurs, civil rights entrepreneurs, educational conservatives, and state officials helps explain the sustained enthusiasm for excellence in education in the long years—indeed, decades—after 1983.[6]

In the proceedings of employer association meetings, the pages of trade journals, and the speeches of prominent corporate leaders, evidence of business dissatisfaction with the education system mounted in the early 1980s. At a 1980 conference at Wesleyan University organized by employers, business entrepreneurs bewailed what one manager called an "inescapable crisis" of low educational achievement, especially in mathematics.[7] In the pages of *Industry Week*, an important business publication, expressions of disappointment and concern began to appear on a regular basis. A 1981 *Industry Week* headline thundered that "Education Is Failing Industry"; two 1982 *Industry Week* opinion piece headlines warned business leaders, "We'd Better Do Something about Science Education" and "Business Must Shore up Education."[8]

Business entrepreneurs could draw on impressive organizational resources, strengthened in the late 1970s and early 1980s to promote their interests on tax, regulatory, and labor issues, to advance the campaign to "shore up" schools. Venerable business organizations such as the National Association of Manufacturers, the Committee for Economic Development, and the American Chamber of Commerce revitalized their membership bases, fundraising, lobbying, and communications. Equally important, the one hundred largest American corporations created the Business Roundtable, which by virtue of its prestigious membership, economic power, and aggressive lobbying tactics wielded extensive influence in state and national politics. Both the older business associations and the newer ones such as the Business Roundtable organized state and local chapters, creating organizational networks through which ideas and information about education policy could flow. These corporate organizations also had literally hundreds of millions of dollars at their disposal, which could be deployed to shape the political debate on education policy. A substantial portion of these investments went to direct corporate efforts to shape public opinion through media appeals.[9] Considerable sums were also invested in lobbying and political campaigns: the number of corporate PACs grew exponentially during the 1974–80 period, from 89 to 1,251, and the cash flow to congressional candidates expanded from $8 million to $39 million between 1972 and 1980.[10] Finally, business organizations unloaded their overflowing coffers into foundations and think tanks, which in turn developed policy ideas that resonated with business objectives.[11]

Joseph Alibrandi of Whittaker Corporation of California exhorted business leaders in mid-1983 that "if we can sell the world on a 'Coke and a smile,' we should certainly be able to sell our own hometowns on the importance of good public schools."[12] As an initial foray in efforts to promote excellence in education, corporate leaders in major cities forged "compacts" with local schools, agreeing to hire local high school graduates who achieved specific educational goals. The New York City Partnership, led by Richard Munro, president of Time Inc., was established in 1979 to promote business projects in support of the city's school system. In another prominent example of a business-education partnership, business leaders joined with Boston school and city officials to create the Boston Compact in 1982, in which business leaders pledged to reserve entry-level jobs for Boston high-school graduates if schools raised attendance and curricular standards.[13] By December 1982, such cooperative agreements between businesses and community schools had formed in Michigan, Georgia, Colorado, California, Wisconsin, New York, Arizona, and Alabama, according to the National Association for Industry-Education Cooperation.[14]

Soon, however, business entrepreneurs began to break from exclusively local efforts to focus on influencing state policy. Some spearheaded legislative campaigns to institute novel reforms. For example, starting in 1982 the Minnesota Business Partnership, representing major corporate organizations such as 3M, General Mills, Pillsbury, Honeywell, and Northwest Airlines, began an intensive study—funded with more than $250,000 of cash and in-kind contributions—of the state's education system. The partnership's report, which recommended sweeping changes to promote academic rigor in the state's schools, helped shape Minnesota governor Rudy Perpich's education reform plan.[15] Spurred by the view that, in Alibrandi's words, "California's public school system has now deteriorated from one of the best to one of the worst in the United States," California business entrepreneurs also moved to reform the state's education system.[16] From 1982 on, the California Business Roundtable, led by Cornell Maier of Kaiser Aluminum and Chemical Corporation, lobbied vigorously on behalf of school reform policies, including a longer school day and school year, the adoption of standards requiring students to take English, science, mathematics, history, and other "basic" courses before they could graduate from high school, and tougher disciplinary and attendance rules.[17] In perhaps the most prominent example of business entrepreneurship on behalf of excellence in education, billionaire businessman H. Ross Perot of Electronic Data Systems used his appointment in 1983 as chairman of a Texas education reform panel appointed by the governor to champion an array of school reforms. Spending large amounts of his own money and using his own staff, Perot succeeded in pressuring state legislators to accept major reforms, including an examination to test teacher competence, a provision barring failing students from participation in extracurricular activities, an increase in state graduation requirements, and a mandated state testing program including a high school exit exam.[18]

Entrepreneurs such as Maier and Perot received the lion's share of media attention, but other business entrepreneurs worked behind the scenes to promote excellence in education. Between 1983 and 1985 business entrepreneurs participated extensively on state task forces throughout the United States charged with examining state education systems and offering recommendations about how to improve schools. As two scholars report, business entrepreneurs "constituted almost 25 percent of the membership of these task forces: 9 percent of the participants on task forces sponsored by educators *but 31 percent on task forces sponsored by governors and state legislators.*"[19] According to education journalist Thomas Toch, the vigorous involvement of business entrepreneurs in discussions of excellence in education tilted the policymaking debate in favor of this agenda, especially by bringing fiscal conservatives to the table. "When chambers of commerce and leading corporate executives came out in favor of increased appropriations and tax hikes for education," Toch explained, "the opposition of their budget-minded allies on city councils and in state legislatures began to dissipate."[20]

Reflecting on excellence in education in a 1993 speech before the Conference Board, an organization of top corporate executives, prominent education scholar Ernest Boyer similarly credited business entrepreneurs with turning the tide in favor of excellence in education in many states: "It's fair to say that reform simply would not have occurred on the scale that it did in the 1980s without the active involvement and encouragement of business. In state after state, as governors and legislators struggled to pass landmark reform bills...business leaders were often among the most stalwart allies."[21]

Business entrepreneurs' state legislative campaigns were accompanied by broader efforts to shape the policy debate. For example, thirteen elite business leaders, including the presidents or chairmen of RCA, AT&T, Xerox, Dow Chemical, and Ford Motor Company, joined hands with twelve governors in December 1982 to report on the state of the nation's schools; their high-profile report, *Action for Excellence* (released in May 1983), declared that "our ability to compete is threatened...by a shortage of skilled engineers and scientists—and, perhaps, more seriously, by a lack of general scientific and mathematical literacy; forms of literacy which will be essential if our citizens are to support a technologically advancing economy."[22] Subsequently, these business leaders worked with the gubernatorial signatories of the report on a multistate effort to "personally lobby state officials and conduct a media campaign for education reform in states where action has been slow," according to *Education Week.*[23] In 1982 a Business-Higher Education Forum task force, co-chaired by Robert Anderson, chairman of the board and chief executive officer of Rockwell International Corporation, and David S. Saxon, president of the University of California, began to study the nation's economy with a view to recommending actions to the president to improve economic performance. The forum issued a fifty-one-page report in May of the following year, which warned that "a growing body of evidence indicates that many American workers lack fundamental skills in mathematics, science, critical thinking, and verbal expression—primarily because of a shortage of well-trained faculty in the nation's public schools."[24] Business entrepreneurs played a critical role in sustaining enthusiasm for excellence in education in the years following the publication of *A Nation at Risk*. For example, beginning with its influential 1985 statement, *Investing in Our Children*, the Committee for Economic Development aggressively promoted excellence in education with media blitzes, congressional testimony, and organized letter-writing campaigns.[25] In 1987 the Committee for Economic Development's second report, *Children in Need*, drew extensive press attention, as well as the commendation of members of Congress.[26] In short, as *Education Week* reported with some hyperbole in 1990, "business leaders have helped write virtually every reform report written in this decade. As a result, they have become both the strongest critics and the staunchest advocates of public education."[27]

Even as business entrepreneurs worked through various channels to promote excellence in education, certain civil rights entrepreneurs mobilized to champion school reforms for disadvantaged students. Frustrated with what they viewed as the slow pace of academic improvement among historically disadvantaged students, the limited ability of existing programs to assist these students, and the low expectations of staff within schools serving them, these entrepreneurs believed that excellence in education for *all* students was necessary to ensure that poor and minority students were taught to high standards. To be clear, not all civil rights activists believed that excellence in education was the best way to improve schools; some took the classical educational liberal perspective that expanded resources for schools, as well as increased investments in health and social services, were the keys to school reform. However, according to Cynthia Brown, who had served as assistant secretary for civil rights in the Department of Education during the Carter administration and was working at the Council of Chief State School Officers' Resource Center on Educational Equity during the mid-1980s, "It was just natural for those of us who worked on the equity agenda [to take up the "excellence" agenda]....There were some folks in the civil rights movement who said you couldn't have equity and excellence at the same time—there was a lot written about that—and people like me were saying, 'Yes, you could.'"[28]

In the 1980s this group included figures such as Ronald Edmonds of Harvard University and Michigan State University; Ernest Boyer of the Carnegie

Foundation for the Advancement of Teaching; John Goodlad of UCLA; Marshall S. Smith of the University of Wisconsin (and later Stanford University); Cynthia Brown and David Hornbeck of the Council of Chief State School Officers; Phyllis McClure of the NAACP Legal Defense Fund; Kati Haycock of the Achievement Council; and William Taylor and Dianne Piché of the Citizens, Commission on Civil Rights. Although these figures were situated in diverse institutional settings, they were familiar with each other and often conversed on education topics. Some, such as Boyer, Smith, and Brown, had worked together in the Department of Education during the Carter administration. Those three, along with McClure, Hornbeck, and Taylor, had formed part of the tight-knit federal education policy community, working on desegregation, affirmative action, and educational equity issues throughout the 1970s. These ties were reinforced through numerous conferences and networking events—some geared to "spreading the gospel of school improvement to thousands of the nation's educators and policymakers," in the words of *Education Week*—which drew these figures together to share ideas and strategies.[29]

One of the earliest efforts among civil rights entrepreneurs to promote school improvements for disadvantaged students was the "effective schools" movement, led by Ronald Edmonds. Edmonds and his colleagues began in the mid-1970s to examine urban schools with histories of success in raising the achievement of disadvantaged students. In findings that would strongly influence subsequent research and advocacy among civil rights entrepreneurs, Edmonds and his colleagues found that certain school characteristics—especially strong administrative leadership, high academic expectations, a focus on educational performance, a collegial and work-focused climate, and frequent student evaluations—were associated with higher achievement among poor and minority students. In a 1979 article titled "Effective Schools for the Urban Poor," Edmonds argued that "(a) we can, whenever and wherever we choose, successfully teach all children whose schooling is of interest to us; (b) we already know more than we need to do that; (c) whether or not we do it must finally depend on how we feel about the fact that we haven't so far."[30] By 1982, urban districts in New York City, Milwaukee, Chicago, Saint Louis, and New Haven, Connecticut, were attempting to introduce reforms consistent with Edmonds's "effective schools" model.[31] "Effective schools" research also penetrated the professional discussion about improving the lot of disadvantaged students; in March 1983, a literature review cited dozens of studies on the subject.[32]

In another prominent—and early—example of efforts to strengthen the academic orientation of schools, esteemed psychologist James Comer engaged in efforts throughout the 1970s to strengthen schools serving impoverished (and primarily African American) students in New Haven, the site of his university appointment at Yale University.[33] Like Edmonds's approach, Comer's was grounded in the belief that "all children, regardless of ethnicity or socioeconomic status, can learn and succeed." Funded by sympathetic foundations, Comer's program sought to build stronger relationships between parents, students, and school staff, in order to build consensus support for reforms to promote student achievement.[34] By 1990, programs based on Comer's ideas were under way in eight states.[35]

These early efforts to promote "effective" or "excellent" schools for disadvantaged students had an important impact on the trajectory of school reform. As the *New York Times* explained in early 1984, "Implicit in the calls for reform [signaled by the National Commission on Excellence in Education and the other reform commissions] are some fundamental assumptions, which the effective schools movement was created in the 1970's to dignify: that schools differ in their effectiveness, that the differences are not accidental and that schools are worth reforming in the first place."[36] In subsequent years, other civil rights entrepreneurs worked to promote excellence in education, embracing many of the themes—if not the specific campaigns—of these pioneers. Buoyed by sympathetic philanthropic foundations such as the Twentieth Century Fund, the Carnegie Foundation for the Advancement of Teaching, the Carnegie Corporation, and the Ford Foundation, civil rights entrepreneurs contributed significantly to excellence in education by publishing academic treatises targeted to policymakers and more accessible reports geared to a mass audience. Robert Wood, political scientist and secretary of housing and urban development during the Johnson administration, helped formulate the Twentieth Century Fund's influential 1983 report on American education, *Making the Grade*.[37] The following year, former Carter administration official Ernest Boyer published his *High School* report, which presented a dismal picture of American secondary schools. The Carnegie Foundation, which underwrote Boyer's study, later produced an Academy Award–nominated documentary film based on the report.[38]

Other civil rights entrepreneurs trained the spotlight on the special need for excellence in schools serving disadvantaged students. In 1983, Kati Haycock, formerly a director of outreach and affirmative action for the University of California system, established the California Achievement Council to promote excellence in education for disadvantaged students. The next year the Achievement Council published *Excellence for Whom?* which called on the state to improve school accountability for performance, implement a rigorous curriculum for all students, and develop new programs to train teachers to teach historically disadvantaged groups.[39] The Achievement Council became, for Haycock, a platform to national prominence: after several years' work in California, Haycock took a senior-level position with the Children's Defense Fund, from which she continued to advocate for high standards and accountability for results. Similar to the Achievement Council, the National Commission on Secondary Education for Hispanics, led by civil rights activist and former ambassador to Honduras Mari-Luci Jaramillo, excoriated what it viewed as the culture of low expectations permeating schools serving Hispanic students and recommended that "states and accrediting agencies focus on the improvement of student achievement, retention, and other schooling performance factors as the basis for accreditation, in addition to the present emphasis on access to facilities, teacher certification, library books, etc. Systems of rewards and penalties should be instituted, but not as systems that would promote pushing out students in order to maintain standards."[40]

Funded by mainstream foundations and written by figures associated with the Democratic Party, such manifestos helped spread excellence in education to circles less susceptible to the calls of business entrepreneurs, providing the foundation for broader Democratic support for sweeping school reforms. These reports also helped extend attention to excellence in education after the initial fervor over *A Nation at Risk* and the other reports of 1983 had abated. In 1985, for example, Michigan State professor and former U.S. Commission on Civil Rights member David K. Cohen coauthored a report, *The Shopping Mall High School*, which castigated secondary schools for diluting their academic standards and channeling poor and minority students into "tracks" that failed to prepare them for college or the world of work.[41] Rather than celebrating efforts since 1983 to promote excellence in education, *The Shopping Mall High School* questioned the efficacy of these reforms and pushed for renewed exertions to strengthen schools serving disadvantaged students. As educator Larry Cuban explained in a 1985 review of the book, "Governors, legislators, and federal policy makers who have celebrated the upturn in academic performance and public confidence in the schools should gulp a few Excedrin. This book will surely give them a headache."[42]

Of equal importance, some civil rights entrepreneurs used their positions in public office to raise the prominence of the school improvement agenda. Perhaps foremost among these advocates was David Hornbeck, chief state school officer of Maryland, prominent activist in (and president of) the Council of Chief State School Officers, and future president of the Children's Defense Fund, who ardently defended the principle of excellence in education for all students. To promote excellence reforms, Hornbeck called a conference bringing together civil rights luminaries such as William Julius Wilson, Gary Orfield, Marian Wright Edelman, and James Comer, as well as respected education scholars Patricia Albjerg Graham, Herbert Walberg, and Henry Levin.[43] Based on these discussions, Hornbeck persuaded the Council of Chief State School Officers in 1987 to advocate legal reforms that would give disadvantaged students a legal right to sue for access to a rigorous curriculum and high-quality teachers.[44] William Taylor, who helped draft Hornbeck's proposal, contends that the plan "helped influence the course of public school reform in states around the country over the next few years."[45]

From its origins, excellence in education exhibited a striking plasticity, appealing to adherents of diverse ideological and political perspectives. If civil rights entrepreneurs viewed excellence in education as a new way to promote educational equity for historically disadvantaged groups, educational conservatives saw excellence as an antidote to the alleged "excesses" unleashed by Great Society education policymaking. Applying conservative ideas to analyze school institutions, these intellectuals argued that the educational liberalism promulgated by the Democratic Party in the 1960s and 1970s corroded schools' commitment to academics, authority, competition, and morality and installed undesirable values such as self-expression, personal development, equality of outcomes, and moral relativism.[46] Adherents of these arguments included William Bennett, chairman of the National Endowment for the Humanities during the first Reagan administration and secretary of education during Reagan's second term; Chester E. Finn Jr., professor of education and public policy at Vanderbilt University; Diane Ravitch, professor of education at Teachers College, Columbia University; Joseph Adelson, professor of psychology at the University of Michigan; Nathan Glazer, professor of sociology and education at Harvard University; and Andrew Oldenquist, professor of philosophy at Ohio State University.[47]

Educational conservatives began to publish briefs favoring excellence in education prior to, and immediately following, the election of Ronald Reagan in 1980 (and well before publication of A Nation at Risk). In 1980 and again in 1981, Chester Finn published highly influential manifestos castigating the educational status quo and issuing a ringing call for excellence in education. The product of ten years' work, Diane Ravitch's The Troubled Crusade, published in 1983, presented an unflattering portrait of the trajectory of education since the 1960s.[48] Departing from the writings of many educational liberals—which tended to laud schools while castigating society for failing to provide adequate support—these early tracts gave powerful voice to the view that schools were failing and that policy changes were needed to bring about improvement. Beyond this work, individual educational conservatives had a hand in shaping some of the major excellence-in-education reports of the early 1980s. For example, both Ravitch and Finn contributed to the Twentieth Century Fund's influential study Making the Grade. Finn also assisted Ernest Boyer in the development of Boyer's High School report, offering advice and comments on drafts of the study.

Unlike civil rights entrepreneurs, who could draw on networks established through prior government service or collaboration on civil rights and education policymaking, educational conservatives were relatively isolated figures at first, issuing calls for excellence in education from far-flung locales (often university positions). Believing that supporters of their brand of excellence in education would have more influence if they worked in concert, Finn and Ravitch sought to build a new network linking sympathetic scholars, journalists, and activists.[49] As Finn later recalled, "Diane and I each knew a few academics who agreed with us about the makeover that K–12 education needed, plus a smattering of sympathetic education leaders and state officials, but these people were scattered and seldom in touch. Sensing that there might be safety, camaraderie, and perhaps influence if we found a way to band together, we decided to create a "network" of like-minded folks."[50] Grants from the Olin and Mellon foundations and the National Endowment for the Humanities (secured by Bennett while he was serving as its chairman) allowed them to establish the Educational Excellence Network (EEN) in 1981.

Though it claimed fewer than one thousand members in its early years of existence, the Educational Excellence Network boasted prominent members with the capacity to influence the terms of the debate: in addition to Ravitch and Finn, it included famous Harvard sociologist James Coleman; Harvard political scientist Paul Peterson; University of Virginia English professor and proponent of "cultural literacy" E. D. Hirsch; University of Massachusetts (Boston) arts and sciences dean Richard Freeland; and California State Board of Education chairman Michael Kirst, among others. In its earliest years EEN operated primarily as a clearinghouse of excellence ideas and information, disseminating "News and Views" (as its newsletter was called) to its members. These efforts helped build solidarity and shared perspectives among EEN members, generating the political capital for more-ambitious initiatives. Indeed, after the publication of *A Nation at Risk* in 1983, the organization made vigorous efforts to reach out to other reformers and extend the political life of excellence in education. The EEN held academic conferences that brought together various proponents of excellence in education, as well as members of the broader education policy community and government agencies such as the National Endowment for the Humanities, to debate the challenges facing schools and develop recommendations for addressing them. In 1984 the EEN released its first book (a product of a 1983 conference on the subject), *Against Mediocrity: The Humanities in America's High Schools*, which railed against a perceived decline in the humanities curriculum and proposed reforms for reviving the disciplines of history, English, and social studies. This report was followed almost immediately by *Challenges to the Humanities* (1985), another effort to strengthen the quality of education in the humanities.[51] Two years later Finn and Ravitch's *What Do Our 17-Year-Olds Know?*—a devastating exposé of high school students' limited knowledge of American history, jointly sponsored by the National Assessment of Educational Progress and the National Endowment for the Humanities—appeared in print to much popular controversy.[52]

If educational conservatives initially felt excluded from the halls of power, they quickly gained access, largely thanks to the entrepreneurial behavior of Terrel Bell, Reagan's first secretary of education. Even before publication of *A Nation at Risk*, Bell's Department of Education fostered excellence in education by publishing articles by sympathetic business leaders, educational conservatives, and policy analysts.[53] *A Nation at Risk*, however, was Bell's most important contribution to excellence in education. Stymied by hostile Reagan administration officials in his efforts to create a presidential-level commission to examine the public schools—Reagan and his top advisers preferred to focus on the messages of eliminating the Department of Education and establishing tax credits for tuition at private schools—Bell established the National Commission on Excellence in Education on his own authority in 1981. The strident and sharply critical tone of the National Commission's report, *A Nation at Risk*, initially surprised Bell, but he embraced it in the hopes that the report would stimulate renewed public investment in education.[54] After the National Commission released its famous report in April 1983, Bell fanned the flames of excellence in education by holding a series of high-profile forums throughout the nation to draw attention to the report and by making at least 140 speeches about excellence in the year following its publication.[55] Bell's effective use of the bully pulpit, along with the efforts of other proponents of excellence in education to foster a change of direction in the educational debate, put the Reagan administration's education policy on a new trajectory. Realizing the increasing salience of excellence in education, Reagan altered his agenda to reap the political dividends of *A Nation at Risk* and the other reform reports in circulation.[56] Indeed, according to Gareth Davies, "Such was the coverage [of *A Nation at Risk* and the other reform reports of the day] that Reagan's reelection staff...[decided] to make education one of the principal issues of the campaign. Reagan, having paid almost no personal attention to education during the first two and a half years of his presidency, now embarked on a nationwide speaking tour."[57] Following the 1984 election, Bell stepped down from his position as secretary of education, but his replacement, William Bennett, was equally enthusiastic about promoting excellence in education in the political sphere. Not only did Bennett use his many speeches and public appearances to stump for school reform; he hired Finn, along with other similarly minded figures, to staff top Department of Education positions.[58] With Bennett at the helm, Reagan's Department of Education became a megaphone for (state-led) excellence-in-education reform, publishing reports on "What Works" in education and publicly ranking the states in terms of educational quality.

Educational conservatives viewed states and localities as the proper sites of excellence-in-education reforms, arguing that the federal government's usurpation of educational authority had undermined school performance. This preference for state and local leadership put educational conservatives in natural alliance with state leaders—especially from the South—eager to bring excellence to ailing education systems while strengthening their hands over one of their states' largest budget items. In fact, during his time at Vanderbilt University, Finn closely advised Tennessee governor Lamar Alexander, one of the earliest gubernatorial proponents of excellence in education. Alexander and other entrepreneurial southern governors such as William Winter of Mississippi, Bill Clinton of Arkansas, Richard Riley of South Carolina, James Hunt of North Carolina, and Bob Graham of Florida were eager to shed the legacies of Jim Crow and modernize their states' economies. Southern governors also faced sharp pressure from business entrepreneurs, who were frankly negative in their evaluations of southern schools. Working through southern regional organizations such as the Southern Regional Education Board and the Southern Growth Policies Board—which drew together governors, state legislators, business leaders, and education officials to discuss education policymaking—these figures developed an approach that viewed school reform as the key to economic and social reform. The efforts of these governors, like those of business entrepreneurs, civil rights entrepreneurs, and educational conservatives, substantially antedated publication of A Nation at Risk. Indeed, in its influential 1981 report, The Need for Quality, the Southern Regional Education Board declared an "imperative need…to work together to improve the quality of education at all levels."[59] Bill Clinton reaffirmed the SREB's view in his inaugural gubernatorial address in Little Rock on January 11, 1983, declaring that "over the long run, education is the key to our economic revival and our perennial quest for prosperity."[60]

Individual southern governors raised attention to excellence in education by conducting major legislative campaigns within their states. In 1983 Clinton fought a highly visible and ultimately successful battle with the state's teachers union to tie a salary increase to a testing program for educators.[61] Following this policy victory, Clinton recalls, "Arkansas began to get a lot of positive national coverage for our education reforms, including praise from Secretary of Education Bell."[62] Other southern governors led similar crusades within their states. Lamar Alexander of Tennessee began an "intense promotional campaign" (in the words of Education Week) for merit pay in early 1983, ultimately convincing the state legislature to enact a version of his proposal the following year.[63] Mississippi governor William Winter's campaign to foster education reform began somewhat earlier, after his election in 1979. Cognizant of the state's abysmal educational performance, Winter proposed a reform agenda calling for mandatory kindergarten, a stronger attendance policy, increased teacher pay, and expanded education spending. When his school improvement bill was defeated by voice vote on the last day of the 1982 legislative session, Winter organized a grassroots campaign that successfully pressured the state legislature to enact a version of his reform in a special legislative session in December of that year.[64] In another example of southern gubernatorial entrepreneurship, Richard Riley of South Carolina "was instrumental in implementing tough, new standards for promotion and high school graduation," according to the *Journal of Blacks in Higher Education*. Riley sponsored an ambitious package of reforms, including teacher salary increases, investments in school buildings, expansion of professional development, and school accountability for students' academic achievement.[65] Though the efforts of Clinton, Alexander, Winter, and Riley may have received the most extensive attention, the *New York Times* reported in March 1983, a month before the publication of *A Nation at Risk*, that "sweeping changes in education policy are being pursued throughout the South by a growing number of political leaders who assert that the ability of their states to attract growth industries hinges increasingly on the educational depth of the work force."[66]

Southern governors' emphasis on excellence in education helped foster significant changes in the policies of southern states. In June of 1983, the Southern Regional Education Board approvingly reported that since the publication of *The Need for Quality*'s education recommendations in 1981, "various Southern states have moved decisively on a number of those recommendations, even in the face of severe budgetary constraints.... The Southern governors and many legislators have played a major role in focusing on the improvement of education as the underlying prerequisite for economic development."[67] Southern governors' entrepreneurship also helped foment a cascade of gubernatorial attention to the subject in states outside the South, leading noted education journalist Fred Hechinger to exclaim in March 1983 that "American governors have embarked on a national campaign to give all levels of education the highest priority."[68] Echoing southerners' attention to the "need for quality," twenty-three of forty-eight governors surveyed by *State Government News* emphasized education reform as one of the top priorities in their state of the state messages in 1983. In 1984 the number had risen to thirty out of forty-eight. By 1985 ten governors had asked for both more education funding and more reforms, while twenty others requested one or the other.[69] Education reporters commented on the noticeable shift in gubernatorial rhetoric, exclaiming that, in many cases for the first time, governors were "call[ing] school improvement a top priority."[70]

Southern governors also led efforts to mobilize existing gubernatorial organizations, such as the Education Commission of the States and the National

Governors Association, in order to build excellence reform coalitions and carry their message to broader audiences.[71] Of the twelve gubernatorial representatives on the panel responsible for *Action for Excellence*, published by the Education Commission of the States, seven were from southern states. Following publication of *Action for Excellence*, the Education Commission of the States (under the chairmanships of governors James Hunt of North Carolina, Pierre du Pont of Delaware, Charles Robb of Virginia, Thomas Kean of New Jersey, Bill Clinton of Arkansas, and John Ashcroft of Missouri) re-created itself as a clearinghouse for excellence in education, disseminating reform ideas, as well as technical advice, to policymakers. Southern governors also led the National Governors Association's initial effort to promote excellence in education; the initiative leading to the publication of *Time for Results*, the NGA's influential 1986 report, was spearheaded by Alexander, Clinton, and Riley (in all, southern governors made up three of the panel's eight members and controlled its chairmanship and one of its two co-chairmanships). Throughout the 1980s the NGA played a critical role in disseminating school improvement ideas by "translating relevant research into information useful to policymakers; recommending specific policy directions...; and generally, encouraging state action by publicizing information about those states that had already formulated a reform agenda," according to education scholars Lorraine McDonnell and Susan Fuhrman.[72]

Excellence in Education: The Critique and the Program

If proponents of excellence in education had failed to develop an impressive justification for their cause, their political exertions would likely have come to naught. However, excellence in education wove together broad political and economic developments and educational trends into an effective narrative that revealed educational failures as the cause of the nation's larger ills and prescribed school improvements as the key to national rejuvenation. By creating a compelling story that fit the facts and synthesized themes in a way that appealed to diverse audiences, these entrepreneurs provided a strong foundation for important policy changes in education.[73]

The central tenet of the excellence movement was that the nation's various economic and social difficulties issued from pervasive deficits in the intellectual and moral abilities of American citizens, especially the nation's younger people.[74] In a departure from the previously dominant view that most schoolchildren were performing adequately to meet the nation's economic needs, advocates of excellence in education alleged that widespread underachievement threatened the performance of the American economy and weakened the ability of the nation to compete in global markets.[75] Thus, according to *A Nation at Risk*, "Our once unchallenged preeminence in commerce, industry, science, and technological innovation is being overtaken by competitors throughout the world.... The educational foundations of our society are presently being eroded by a rising tide of mediocrity that threatens our very future as a Nation and a people. What was unimaginable a generation ago has begun to occur—others are matching and surpassing our educational achievements."[76] As technological sophistication progressed and global competition stiffened, the disadvantages of American workers would only multiply, proponents of excellence in education warned. The National Governors Association counseled that "the twenty first century worker will not be able to compete using twentieth century skills."[77]

Moving beyond economic justifications, the various proponents of excellence in education tapped the social and cultural foment sweeping the country by attributing allegedly pervasive ethical failings among young people to inadequate education. Educational conservatives enjoyed carping on this issue. Andrew Oldenquist, for example, contended that "it is not 'late capitalism,' Laws of History, or worn-out DNA that is making our children stupid or bad citizens, but educational philosophy and policy regarding how young humans must be trained in order to be competent, civil, productive, and relatively satisfied members of their societies."[78] Joseph Adelson agreed, arguing that young people had imbibed "modernist" and "egalitarian" values that "scorned the pursuit of success," embraced moral relativism, and celebrated sexual hedonism.[79] From his various positions in the Reagan administration, William Bennett did much to propagate this view in his numerous speeches, television appearances, and interviews.[80] Nonetheless, figures unassociated with the political right—including Ernest Boyer and academics Arthur Powell, Eleanor Farrar, and David Cohen—sounded similar themes in their own examinations of schooling in the United States. As these analysts contended, American students were often apathetic, ill-informed, and unprepared for the responsibilities of American democracy. Enervated citizens, these critics feared, threatened to undermine the functioning of American institutions and erode the nation's civic life.[81]

By framing the nation's challenges as problems of pervasive student underperformance, the various supporters of excellence in education established grounds for an agenda focused on thoroughly reforming school institutions, rather than merely providing supplemental programs for historically disadvantaged groups. They elaborated on this by developing narratives that linked young people's unsatisfactory intellectual and moral skills to specific educational institutions and practices. Proponents of excellence in education agreed that school leaders had failed American youths by setting low standards for students, teachers, and themselves.[82] "We have let our entire educational system dissipate before our eyes," moaned businessman Don L. Gevirtz.[83] The chief criticism was that academic standards had declined: throughout the nation, these critics claimed, graduation requirements were minimal, homework and testing demands were modest, grades were inflated, course content was diluted and diverted from core academic concerns, and moral values were deprecated or ignored.[84] Minimal expectations in schools resulted in poorly educated and weakly disciplined youth, the various exponents of excellence in education explained, because students adapted themselves to the expectations presented to them. As Diane Ravitch argued, "Pupils respond to teachers' expectations, and constant reinforcement of high expectations can contribute to good behavior and to increased academic effort....Some current practices, which have become widespread in recent years, communicate low expectations and low standards."[85] Furthermore, teaching standards were flaccid: supporters of excellence in education charged that teachers lacked adequate content knowledge and pedagogical skills, and in some cases suffered from illiteracy and innumeracy.[86] The incapacity of teachers undermined the transmission of knowledge and skills to students, thus retarding their academic progress.[87] In addition, too many schools and districts organized themselves inefficiently, handled youngsters impersonally, and monitored students' performance inadequately, according to reports such as *Action for Excellence*.[88]

If pervasive educational deficiencies were at the root of the nation's social and economic crises, and *if* these inadequacies were due to systematic school failures to set high standards for students and teachers, then educational excellence—that is, the enhancement of educational standards for students, teachers, and schools—was the logical remedy for schools and in turn for the nation. Anticipating the primary theme of the dozens of reform reports that would appear in the following years, Chester Finn proclaimed in a September 1981 article in *Change* magazine that "the time has come to form a new national consensus whose unifying idea is educational quality."[89] To achieve this objective, the myriad groups advocating excellence in education offered a dizzying array of recommendations. In order to make schooling more academically rigorous, many recommended higher graduation requirements, increased homework, and a more demanding academic curriculum; but some also suggested an increased emphasis on science and mathematics coursework within the curriculum, while others advocated the elimination of traditional divisions between academic subjects entirely in order to focus on "higher order" learning skills. Proposals to improve teaching included such diverse offerings as performance-based pay, career ladders, special salaries to attract science and math teachers, across-the-board salary increases, career entry and continuation tests, increased academic rigor in teacher education programs, elimination of teacher education programs, and alternative entry into the education profession. At the organizational level, some studies emphasized the importance of small class sizes and personalized instruction, while others called for longer school days and years, and still others recommended enhancing the authority and autonomy of school principals and school staff. Finally, some exponents of excellence in education—especially educational conservatives such as Chester Finn—proposed to marketize the entire education system by permitting parents to use public funds to purchase educational services from the provider of their choice, be it public, private, or religious.

Skeptical of the new agenda, and fearful that it would displace the equity-in-education agenda they had long championed, educational liberals often lambasted excellence in education for failing to attend to the special challenges facing disadvantaged students.[90] As Elizabeth Duncan Koontz of the Citizens' Council on Women's Education declared in October 1984, "Americans will not condone a drive for educational excellence that is purchased at the expense of equity.... Excellence without equity is elitism."[91] But those charging that excellence in education was insensitive to the challenges facing disadvantaged students arguably failed to appreciate how proponents of excellence in education viewed these problems and proposed to address them. In essence, these proponents argued that ensuring an excellent education for all students would realize the promise of equity for disadvantaged students. As John Goodlad averred in his influential study, *A Place Called School*, "The struggle for equality of access to public schools is not over, but a new era in that struggle will turn more attention to what and how students learn in schools.... The central problem for today and tomorrow is no longer access to school. It is access to knowledge for all. The dual challenge is that of assuring both equity and quality in school programs."[92]

Nor was this merely a rhetorical sop offered by educational conservatives to disguise their "true" purpose of privatizing education or punishing teachers and students. Proponents of excellence in education—led by civil rights entrepreneurs—claimed that disadvantaged students were the greatest victims of existing school practices. In this view, many schools reduced expectations for minority and disadvantaged students based on the belief that they were not cut out for academic subject matter. This belief became calcified in "tracking" systems, in which students were shunted into curricula of varying academic rigor based on perceived abilities and interest in ways that reinforced racial and economic inequities.[93] Even as schools plied disadvantaged students with opportunities and resources, they tracked them into "vocational, commercial, and general classes, in which academic demands were modest at best," according to David Cohen and his colleagues.[94] These practices were inequitable because they failed to provide disadvantaged students with the knowledge and skills necessary to meet the challenges posed by contemporary economic and social conditions. Existing educational practices thus consigned poor and nonwhite students to diminished economic prospects and second-class citizenship.

Fortunately, many proponents of excellence in education argued, disadvantaged students would benefit disproportionately from a new emphasis on excellence. Jeannie Oakes of UCLA—hardly a paragon of educational conservatism—called for the elimination of tracking and the creation of more uniformly academic educational experiences in order to expand access to a more equal education:

> It seems likely...that the reorganization of schools so that the predominant pattern becomes the use of heterogeneous groups could equalize students' educational experiences in several ways. First, if students were given a common curriculum, ideally comprised largely of the high-status knowledge now primarily reserved for students in high tracks, the closing off of students' access to future opportunities would be considerably postponed and perhaps lessened. All students would be at least exposed to those concepts and skills that permit access to higher education. And if some students do not grasp the concepts as quickly or comprehensively as others, they will have been given a beginning, a chance.[95]

Similarly, Susanna Navarro of the Mexican American Legal Defense and Educational Fund (MALDEF) argued in favor of rigorous graduation requirements for all students because "my hope is that the grade schools and junior high schools will be changed substantially enough so they can gear up the students to meet those requirements."[96] Fortified with expanded knowledge and skills, the proponents of excellence in education argued, disadvantaged students would be better prepared to face the heightened demands imposed by economic and social changes, and thus better positioned to share in the promise of American life.

Though excellence in education was championed by a national network of diverse policy entrepreneurs, virtually all assumed that state governments would take the lead in promoting reforms (with the assistance of local governments). Historically speaking, this approach envisioned a much more muscular role for state governments in education.[97] However, the emphasis on state leadership was also perceived by observers as shifting policymaking momentum away from the *federal government*, which had been the primary impetus behind traditional educational equity programs.[98] Remarks by Diane Ravitch, made in 1984, spoke volumes about the expectations of many proponents of excellence in education in the early 1980s. "There has been a decisive, if not permanent, shift" in the locus of decision-making from the federal to the state level, she declared.[99] For some—especially educational conservatives and state leaders—state primacy was celebrated as an antidote to overweening federal involvement, which had (in this view) perverted school priorities. Chester Finn, for example, pilloried Great Society–style education initiatives that exhibited boundless confidence in the federal government but failed—in his judgment, at least—to bolster school quality, and suggested that loosening federal mandates would contribute to school improvement.[100] For others, most notably business and civil rights entrepreneurs, a focus at the state level probably reflected more pragmatic considerations. These entrepreneurs likely realized that, given Reagan's strident criticism of federal involvement in education, the expansion of federal authority in schooling was unlikely to occur in the foreseeable future.[101] Even if the president's opposition could somehow be overcome, the looming $200 billion budget deficit in 1983 seemed likely to hamstring any significant federal involvement in school reform.[102] Whether due to an ideological preference or a pragmatic concession to political reality, proponents of excellence in education looked to state capitals to provide the momentum for school reform.

Excellence in education was rhetorically powerful and analytically plausible, contemporary observers realized, but it also suffered from notable blind spots. How reforms would actually work in practice—how they would be implemented by states, districts, schools, and teachers, and how they would perform in concert to raise educational standards—was often poorly explained.[103] Two prominent education analysts complained at the time that prominent reform commissions "made simplistic recommendations and failed to consider their ramifications. They proposed increasing time without altering pedagogy, instituting merit schemes without describing procedures, and adopting the 'new basics' without changing old definitions."[104] In a similar critique, political scientist Paul Peterson wrote in 1983 that reformers offered "wholesome entrees," but did not provide much guidance on how to "cook" them. As Peterson emphasized, "*The problem is that no one has written any reliable recipes for producing the desired results.* Schools are such complex institutions that policy-makers at the national, state, and local levels have been unable to produce, everywhere and anywhere, the management, school discipline, and homework assignments they want."[105]

Though the ambiguity surrounding implementation of excellence in education would haunt the paradigm in subsequent years, the excitement these ideas produced led to major changes in education politics and policymaking in the 1980s. Responding to the broad enthusiasm for excellence in education, state officials, members of Congress, and important education interest groups shifted their positions and actions to take excellence into account. These strategic moves reinforced the excellence-in-education agenda, consolidating its status as the new predominant education paradigm.

Excellence in Education Sweeps the Nation

State policymaking—the target of most proponents of excellence in education—was roiled by the rise of the new educational agenda. During the 1970s, some states (especially in the South) had made modest efforts to improve their education systems, usually by instituting "minimum competency" standards and high school exit examinations; but most observers, citing the debility of these earlier initiatives, viewed the post-1983 reforms as a sea change in education policymaking.[106] As one Parent Teacher Organization representative exclaimed in 1985, "The excellence movement has hit the states hard."[107] Between 1983 and 1985, every state in the union convened at least one commission on the issue of excellence in education; in all, over three hundred state-level reform commissions assembled.[108] This commission activity set the stage for an unprecedented wave of state-level lawmaking during the 1980s. All told, the states adopted more than seven hundred statutes related to graduation requirements, standards, testing, and teacher quality between 1984 and 1986—more than they had in the previous twenty years—and continued to adopt additional policies through the end of the decade. By the end of 1984, according to one review of state-level policy activity, "43 states had raised their high school graduation requirements, 37 states had acted to institute statewide assessments of students, and nearly 30 states had made changes in teacher certification procedures, including the enactment of a teacher competency test." This assessment continued by noting that "many [states] revised textbook selection procedures, updated curriculum guides or prescribed the objectives and the content of the curriculum taught in the local schools."[109] Thus, as prominent commentators on American education recognized, the post-1983 reforms "signaled an unprecedented level of state activity" and "addressed core educational functions that had not previously received much attention by governors and legislators."[110]

Underlying these policymaking changes were profound shifts in the rhetoric surrounding education at all levels of government. Striking changes can be documented even at the federal level, where little policy activity was forthcoming in the 1980s. In a major departure from the 1960s and 1970s—when educational equity dominated the educational landscape—excellence in education was becoming a much more prominent issue on the federal agenda in the 1980s. Figure 2 shows that attention to excellence in education, as measured by the hearings on the subject as a proportion of hearings on all education issues, increased dramatically in the 1980s, especially after 1983. Indeed, congressional attention reached levels unmatched in the previous two decades. Sustained by the enthusiasm of the various proponents of excellence in education, members of Congress heard testimony on subjects such as the alleged shortage of mathematics,

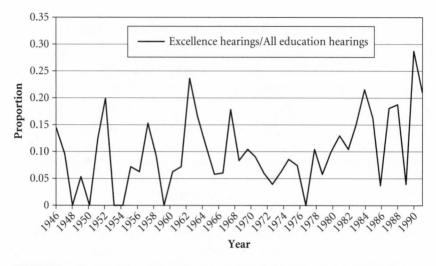

FIGURE 2. Congressional attention to excellence in education: hearings on education, 1946–90. Analysis by the author, using data from the Policy Agendas Project (www.policyagendas.org).

science, and engineering students, the efforts by reformers to improve the quality of elementary and secondary school curricula, and proposals to create a national system for accrediting teachers.

We see a similar, if more exaggerated, trend if we examine presidential rhetoric. In response to the Sputnik crisis, President Dwight Eisenhower made excellence a central concern of late 1950s-era addresses. Eisenhower was the exception, however; like members of Congress, most postwar presidents, especially after Lyndon Johnson, were primarily concerned with issues related to desegregation and compensatory education. After the proponents of excellence of education, strengthened by publication of *A Nation at Risk*, pushed Reagan's hand, however, presidential attention to excellence in education began to expand dramatically. Both Reagan and his successor, George H. W. Bush, attended frequently to excellence in education, often raising attention to the issue in their speeches. Presidents Bill Clinton and George W. Bush were even more enthusiastic exponents of school reform, dedicating considerable policymaking, as well as rhetorical, attention to the subject (see figure 3, for years up to and including the presidency of George H. W. Bush).

Educational liberals were far more ambivalent about excellence in education and responded in a much more complex manner to the growing prominence of the new agenda. The major teacher unions, along with groups representing school administrators, school boards, and state departments of education, as well as some civil rights organizations, had played a pivotal role in expanding

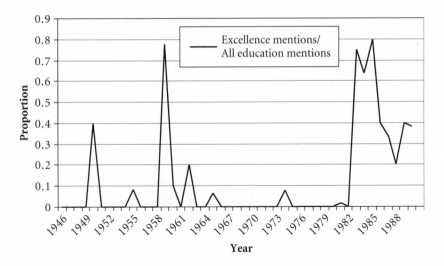

FIGURE 3.   Discussion of excellence in education in presidential State of the Union addresses. Analysis by the author, using data from the Policy Agendas Project (www.policyagendas.org).

the federal role in education and establishing the U.S. Department of Education in 1979. Believing that the most pressing problems in education stemmed from social conditions that undermined students' ability to learn, and from a lack of adequate educational resources to deal with these issues, these groups tended to view education policy primarily through the lens of funding. In its 1982–83 Handbook, the National Education Association, the nation's largest teachers union, reaffirmed this approach by declaring an expansion of general federal aid for education—with an ultimate goal of "one-third federal funding of public education"—its top legislative priority.[111] Although this position had a long history in liberal thinking, it also dovetailed almost perfectly with the NEA's material interest in reducing class sizes and increasing teachers' salaries and benefits.

The excellence-in-education paradigm, which traced students' intellectual and civic deficits to the failings of school institutions and practices, challenged educational liberals' primacy in the making of education policy. At a more material level, the merit pay, teacher testing, and accountability proposals being considered by proponents of excellence in education also potentially challenged core teacher union principles such as solidarity, seniority, and tenure. As excellence in education gained credence in the halls of power, therefore, educational liberals had to make decisions about how to respond to the new agenda. The two largest education organizations, the National Education Association and the American

Federation of Teachers, initially responded in different ways to excellence in education. At first, the NEA struck a defiant tone. In his report to the association's 1983 national convention, NEA president William McGuire thundered, "What must we do, then, in response to all these most recent quick-cure plans, including those which make no educational sense? The first thing we must do is not be defensive. We are not the problem. We must not allow ourselves to be intimidated into acting as if we were."[112] McGuire called for better teacher training and stronger licensing standards, as long as they were accompanied by higher salaries, smaller class sizes, and expanded administrative support. However, he strongly opposed efforts to test teachers already in service, and ridiculed teacher merit-pay proposals as "magic elixirs" that proposed to "solve all of education's problems today" by "isolating a few teachers for receipt of a few more coins."[113] In contrast with McGuire's defiance, American Federation of Teachers leader Albert Shanker made a strategic decision to embrace the language of excellence in education, despite the misgivings of his advisers who viewed the paradigm as a mean-spirited attack on the public schools.[114] If the AFT did not rally behind the banner of excellence in education, Shanker warned, the prospects for public education were grim: "If these leaders of government and industry after having invested time, effort and prestige on a program to rebuild American education find their efforts frustrated [by the teachers unions], there is no question as to where the tilt of public policy will go. We will lose the support we now have. There will be a massive move to try something else, and it will be all over."[115] To avert this catastrophe, Shanker argued, the union must move beyond collective bargaining and focus more on issues of teacher and school quality, both to guarantee its professional survival and to ensure that teachers influenced the content and implementation of reforms. In his public statements and his *New York Times* column, "Where We Stand," Shanker endorsed measures, such as teacher testing and peer review, that the NEA was resisting.

The NEA's apparent intransigence toward excellence in education drew widespread criticism from the press, while Shanker's careful positioning garnered the AFT's leader a reputation for educational statesmanship. However, under pressure from the media—as well as from President Reagan, who exploited the opportunity to intensify his rhetorical assault on the union—the NEA moved grudgingly toward positions already adopted by the AFT. During the presidency of Mary Futrell, the NEA ended its official opposition to teacher testing and to the idea of a national teacher accreditation board.[116] Furthermore, in a series of carefully worded booklets published in December 1983, the NEA averred its support for the general principles of excellence in education, while explaining objections to specific policies such as merit pay.[117]

To be sure, the major teacher organizations reserved the right to support or oppose specific reforms on a case-by-case basis, depending on their resonance with teachers' interests. Of equal importance, the NEA and AFT argued that expanded education spending was inextricably linked to efforts to improve school quality. In its 1984 "Open Letter to America on Schools, Students, and Tomorrow," the NEA declared that "every school should establish clear, significant, appropriate, and achievable expectations for students. Schools must provide the resources that will enable students to know their subjects."[118] Similarly, even as the AFT lauded some excellence-in-education policies, it savaged the Reagan administration for cutting federal support for education; indeed, the AFT's 1983 report, "The Three R's (Reagan, Rhetoric, and Reality)"—written in cooperation with the AFL-CIO, the AFT's organizational partner—called Reagan "the most anti-education President we've ever had."[119]

Nonetheless—and even if the NEA and AFT were less than enthusiastic about (if not avowedly hostile to) excellence in education—the strategic accommodation of the two teachers unions with the ascendant agenda had the effect of reinforcing the legitimacy of the paradigm in public discourse, even though many classroom teachers felt "dispirited" or "disempowered" by reforms, according to contemporary surveys.[120] By failing to counter excellence in education with a clear, compelling narrative that resonated with the politics of the times or appealed to multiple audiences, the major teachers unions (especially the NEA) were forced to fight a rearguard action to ensure that excellence encompassed some core union objectives. Ironically, however, this effort had the consequence of further strengthening excellence in education. Indeed, each of the two unions was advancing its own vision of school reform by the end of the 1980s.[121]

While some educational liberals—especially academic critics located in education schools—continued to characterize excellence in education as a conservative ideological attack on educational equity or a corporate takeover of schooling, such figures were hardly at the center of the education debate.[122] To be sure, major political fights over policy enactment and implementation continued in subsequent years. After 1983, however, discussion about excellence in education largely focused on matters of technique, rather than broader questions about whether the proponents of excellence in education had correctly identified problems or developed adequate solutions.

The excellence-in-education agenda exploded to the forefront of the education debate in the early 1980s. This paradigm was grounded in four central claims: that schools were in significant part to blame for the social and economic challenges facing the nation; that schools had failed because they had allowed academic standards to slip; that policies to make schooling more rigorous would remediate their failings and thereby address the problems facing the country; and that efforts to improve education for all students would redound to the benefit of disadvantaged students. Each of these claims departed in significant respects from the equity-in-education agenda that had previously animated education policymaking, heralding a novel movement in education policymaking to shape core processes of teaching and learning in schools throughout the nation. This policy program also presumed that state governments would take on much more active roles in strengthening school institutions and practices.

The rise of excellence in education was made possible by the activities of a diverse bloc of political entrepreneurs. Whereas business entrepreneurs and civil rights entrepreneurs would later break from educational conservatives and state leaders over the issue of federal involvement in standards, testing, and accountability, in the 1980s they converged on a shared agenda to reform the nation's schools. These figures succeeded in leveraging popular frustration with extant political and economic conditions to craft a powerful policy agenda that justified new departures in education policymaking. The key contribution was a powerful political narrative that linked together stagnating economic conditions, widespread social disaffection, and student test score trends in a coherent account that revealed educational problems as the source of broader social difficulties and pointed the way to educational—and hence, social—reform. This agenda also benefited from its synthesis of themes that were attractive to diverse audiences. Entrepreneurs' rhetorical innovations and efforts at mobilization helped transform the education policy environment, yielding important changes in state policymaking patterns and policymakers' discourse. At a broader, and more subtle, level, entrepreneurs' framing of educational problems and setting of the policy agenda challenged the relatively closed policymaking environment that had characterized pre-1980s education policy, opening the policy system to a host of new actors who had previously played a relatively marginal role.

Indeed, excellence in education, from its inception, served as a common carrier of diverse political and economic interests. The underlying ideologies and interests of business entrepreneurs, civil rights entrepreneurs, educational conservatives, and state leaders were not the same; but the members of each group worked, sometimes in collaboration with members of other groups, to advance a common vision (or set of overlapping visions) of excellence. The fact that support for excellence in education crossed partisan and ideological lines suggests that the lineages of contemporary policies such as those embodied in No Child Left Behind and Race to the Top—policies that draw heavily on excellence themes—are much more complex than often believed.

This chapter has focused primarily on the entrepreneurial side of institutionally bounded entrepreneurship. In the next chapter, we begin to see how institutions, and broader political dynamics, may conspire to constrain the expansion of entrepreneurial agendas. Rather than halt the expansion of excellence in education, however, these institutional and political obstacles pushed entrepreneurs to recalibrate their agendas. As various proponents of excellence in education struggled to implement their favored policies at the state level, many increasingly came (in some cases, to their own surprise) to support federal involvement—and more-coordinated "standards-based reforms"—as ways to improve education.

FEDERAL SCHOOL REFORM BUILDS MOMENTUM, 1989–1992

The politics of education changed fundamentally with the emergence of "excellence in education" in the early 1980s. From 1989 to 1992, excellence in education was itself transformed, leading to important shifts in the politics of education reform in the United States. First, a novel "standards-based reform" paradigm, which proposed to strengthen education systems by aligning them around coordinated standards, testing, and accountability policies, rose to prominence in discussions about how to improve schools. "Standards-based reform" was an elaboration of the excellence-in-education agenda, continuing the emphasis on academic achievement while refining the means for reaching this goal. Second, federal officials began to weigh serious efforts to promote school reforms informed by standards-based reform ideas.[1] In 1989 President George H. W. Bush agreed with the nation's governors on the adoption of six National Education Goals, which detailed performance expectations that schools and students were supposed to meet by the year 2000. Then Bush proposed, and Congress debated, the "America 2000" initiative, which called on the federal government to support the establishment of voluntary national standards and voluntary national tests, and to promote private school choice options.

Although developments during this period were halting—in the end, America 2000 was not enacted into law—momentum built for federal involvement in education revolving around coordinated standards, testing, and accountability for results. Growing enthusiasm for greater federal involvement was largely due to the effective efforts of business entrepreneurs, civil rights entrepreneurs, educational conservatives, and state leaders in building institutions and relationships capable of maintaining and expanding their agendas. In this early period of federal involvement—when the scope of federal engagement remained modest and ill-defined—these four groups continued to work in parallel (and sometimes in concert) to promote similar reforms. Continuing their work as political entrepreneurs, each of these groups engaged in extensive extra-governmental agenda setting, organizational maintenance, and coalition building to reinforce the cause of school reform at the state and federal levels. The importance of policy knowledge and professional networks was on full display, as entrepreneurs leveraged their expertise, personal relationships with policymakers, and access to foundation funding to influence policy. These processes set the stage for major shifts in education policymaking in subsequent years, dramatically expanding the federal role in education in the United States.

In this chapter I highlight the interplay between institutional constraints and political entrepreneurship, central to my account of institutionally bounded entrepreneurship, to explain the rise of the standards-based reform agenda and the expansion of federal interest in education, as well as the ultimate failure of America 2000. First, I show how existing institutions conspired to limit the consolidation of excellence in education in the 1980s. As we might expect in a federal system, excellence in education diffused in an uneven and fragmented fashion among the states, defying reformers' hopes for thoroughgoing policy changes. Second, the chapter reveals that this pattern of policy development reshaped entrepreneurs' beliefs and strategies, stimulating the further evolution of education policy. On one hand, the standards-based reform paradigm—which animated many subsequent efforts to improve schools—emerged as an effort by various proponents of excellence in education to address the silences on implementation matters characteristic of excellence and cope with states' fragmented response to that paradigm. On the other, many of these entrepreneurs concluded that federal leadership was needed to compensate for the unevenness and incoherence of state and local reforms, leading them to champion the policy ideas that ultimately found expression in the America 2000 strategy. Articulating new ideas, developing new institutional networks (and elaborating old ones), and building alliances with administration officials and members of Congress, these entrepreneurs worked to persuade policymakers in both parties to endorse more-ambitious reforms than they had initially anticipated.

These entrepreneurs' efforts drove federal leadership of standards-based reforms to the top of the national education agenda in 1991 and 1992. But the Bush administration's failure to secure a diverse supporting coalition obstructed enactment of major education legislation during the president's tenure. In a bid to satisfy conservatives within his own party and expand the role of markets in education, Bush insisted that national standards and tests be tied to an ambitious program to promote private school choice. Educational liberals in the Democratic Party—which controlled both houses of Congress during Bush's tenure—refused to accept these controversial proposals, and sought to link federal standards-based reforms to a dramatic expansion of federal education aid. Neither the administration nor the Democratic Congress proved willing to compromise, leading to the demise of Bush's education strategy in the final months of his presidency.

In the first part of this chapter I examine the response of the states to excellence in education, showing how federalism promoted an uneven and fragmented response to excellence policies touted by business entrepreneurs, civil rights entrepreneurs, educational conservatives, and state leaders. Next, I illustrate how the various proponents of excellence in education responded to these trends, and how these reactions shaped the subsequent development of education policy in the United States. The following part of the chapter reviews the political debate surrounding America 2000, to show that Bush's failure to rally a cross-partisan coalition accounts for its unhappy legislative denouement. In spite of the fracas over America 2000, the conclusion suggests, the events that transpired between 1989 and 1992 prepared the ground for federal standards, testing, and accountability reforms in the future. Having developed powerful organizations and network ties, the proponents of standards-based reform were well positioned to shape the progress of education policymaking during the Clinton presidency.

Institutional Constraints on the Expansion of Excellence in Education

According to two scholars surveying the terrain of excellence in education in 1989, "The visibility of the education reform movement is manifest in the intensity of policy activity. Since 1983 the states have generated more rules and regulations about all aspects of education than in the previous 20 years. Nationwide, more than 700 statutes...were enacted between 1984 and 1986."[2] These findings have led scholars such as Paul Manna to suggest that pervasive commitment to excellence in education at the state level paved the way for subsequent federal involvement by providing federal officials with political legitimacy and administrative capacity on which they could draw.[3]

However, while the states' responses to excellence in education were impressive in historical perspective, a focus on aggregate measures (such as total number of laws passed) ignores more subtle trends. First of all, as we might expect in a diverse federal system, there was considerable variation in the attentiveness of individual states to the new agenda. Some states adopted many policies advocated by the proponents of excellence in education, but others took a much more modest course. One study analyzing patterns of state adoption of policies in seven areas—heightened teacher-certification requirements, reformed teacher compensation practices, extended school days and years, increased graduation requirements, expanded student testing, revised curriculum materials, and enhanced school financing—found that almost 60 percent of states (twenty-nine states) adopted policies in between two and four of these domains between 1980 and 1987.[4] Ultimately, the U.S. Department of Education concluded in 1988, "[state education reforms] vary considerably in their design, largely reflecting the unique historical and political circumstances of each State."[5] As a general rule, excellence in education reforms advanced most rapidly in southern states, while states in the Great Plains and Mountain regions tended to lag behind.

Furthermore, even as states adopted various policies touted by supporters of excellence in education, they did not necessarily synchronize these initiatives in a way to promote student achievement. In significant part, this was due to silences in the excellence-in-education paradigm itself: as the last chapter showed, in their zeal to critique existing arrangements, proponents of excellence in education largely ignored the challenges of policy design and implementation. Reflecting these silences, many states adopted reforms without working out how these policies would interact and jointly affect the education of students.[6] In a review of the reforms of the 1980s, a group of policy analysts concluded that "reforms that are designed as coherent packages with mutually reinforcing parts have the greatest impact. Each part facilitates the other, and the entire package sends a coordinated message to local educators. *As a rule, though, the recent round of reforms lacked such coherence. The most common problem was not that specific provisions conflicted, but that they were often unrelated.*"[7]

This policy "incoherence," as it was often labeled by its critics, found its way into many areas of state and local education policy. One analysis found that state graduation requirement policies often failed to provide clear guidance about the kinds of knowledge and skills students were expected to learn.[8] Other studies argued that state tests, which relied heavily on generic commercial exams, only occasionally gelled with state graduation requirements, statements of learning expectations, or instructional materials.[9] Yet another report concluded that in many states "there is little relationship between teacher preparation programs and state curricular goals."[10]

Meanwhile, educational achievement trends provided little to cheer about. The National Assessment of Educational Progress (NAEP), the respected,

nationally representative assessment that tracked the performance of nine-, thir-
teen-, and seventeen-year-olds over time, revealed that student achievement was
only marginally better in 1988 than it had been a decade earlier. Perhaps even
more worrisome, close observers of excellence in education fretted that state and
local policy changes did not seem to alter the abysmal educational conditions
facing many poor and minority students. According to the NAEP Long Term
Trend in Student Achievement (in reading and mathematics), achievement gaps
between blacks and whites and between Hispanics and whites did not shrink in a
uniform fashion between 1980 and 1990: at some age levels there were significant
signs of progress in each subject; but at others, gains were much more modest.[11]
Although many factors contributed to the patterns of NAEP achievement, these
trends did not reflect well on an excellence-in-education paradigm often touted
as a panacea for the challenges facing the disadvantaged. In any case, a rigorous
effort by the U.S. General Accounting Office to examine the impact of typical
excellence-in-education policies on the achievement of disadvantaged students
in four large school districts in four states found that these policies had limited
effects.[12] Thus, Marshall Smith, a strong proponent of both improved educational conditions for disadvantaged students and excellence in education, worried that "the reform emphasis on more challenging content and skills either has
not had much of an effect [on the achievement of disadvantaged students] or the
effect is not reflected on the NAEP tests."[13]

Given these trends, we might presume that federal elected officials would be
eager to take action to improve the nation's schools. But, at least at first, the
Bush administration articulated only a very modest agenda for education. On
the campaign trail, Bush had made the memorable promise that he would be
an "education president" if elected, raising attention to the plight of the schools
and impinging on an issue traditionally owned by Democrats. Once installed in
office, however, top administration officials took the position that, in the words
of domestic policy adviser Roger Porter, "many of these changes [that need to
take place in education] must be brought about by state and local governments,
and by the involvement of parents, teachers, business organizations, and other
community groups."[14] In a 1989 memo titled "The Education President: Outlining the Education Agenda," Ken Yale, executive secretary to Bush's Domestic
Policy Council, counseled that the president's primary role in education reform
was rhetorical rather than programmatic:

> Education is one policy domain where the President's most important
> role is to influence the ideas and expectations of those who make the
> important policy decisions and spend most of the money: state and
> local officials and American families. To exercise Presidential leadership

in education is preeminently a matter of using the personal and moral authority of the office-holder to publicize what works in education—what is successful, what is being done well—and to argue that success can be repeated elsewhere.[15]

This programmatic modesty was in evidence in Bush's initial education proposal, dubbed the "Educational Excellence Act of 1989." The proposal featured a hodge-podge of small grants to promote magnet schools and alternative certification, and reward schools, teachers, and students for academic performance. This strategy was not deeply informed by the standards-based reform paradigm, nor did it promote big-ticket items, such as national standards and tests, that would later become central to the administration's agenda.

Rebuffed on this modest measure by the Democratic Congress, Bush sought to work outside legislative channels by promoting a series of "National Education Goals" in cooperation with state governors.[16] Agreement on these goals was secured in late 1989. But the administration subsequently lost interest in education policymaking, dedicating little energy to the issue in 1990.[17] The low priority given by the administration to education policy was signaled by its retention of Lauro Cavazos as secretary of education through the end of 1990, despite the fact that he was almost universally perceived as inept in education policymaking circles.[18] When it came to standards, testing, and accountability, then, Bush was no entrepreneur. Instead, the energy for these reforms came from the unelected advocates of excellence in education, who continued to refine their agenda and promote new mechanisms for strengthening the nation's schools.

Institutionally Bounded Entrepreneurship and the Rise of the Standards-Based Reform Paradigm

The intellectual authors of "excellence in education" were forced to come to grips with disappointing policy developments in the states and localities and the absence of policy leadership in the White House. Part of this readjustment involved proponents of excellence in education elaborating a more sophisticated policy agenda under the banner of standards-based reform.[19] The standards-based reform agenda—a self-conscious effort to address the blind spots of excellence in education and remedy the fragmentation endemic to state-level reforms—became a point of convergence for business entrepreneurs, civil rights entrepreneurs, educational conservatives, and state leaders alike.[20] While each group made independent contributions to standards-based reform, it is also important to appreciate that the paradigm's development, and especially its success, were in significant part due to collaboration by members of these groups.

Business entrepreneurs were vocal in their criticisms of state efforts to institute excellence in education in schools. In a 1988 feature in *Industry Week*, industry journalist William Miller declared that employers continued to "wrestle with 'dumb' kids." Miller's text caricatured an inarticulate adolescent to make his point: "Too many kids in Amerrica don't know how to spell rite. They can't reade real good neither. They don't know when the Civill war okurred, where the Pacific Oshun is on a map, they find understanding fracshuns is too awesome for them—really!—and they don't…like…you know…express there thots too good."[21] Adopting a more measured tone, the Business Roundtable declared in 1989 that "the nation still lacks the world-class education system needed to prepare our children for the 21st century."[22] Foremost in business entrepreneurs' minds was the fear that state and local education reforms suffered from fragmentation and incoherence. "There is no educational problem that is not being successfully addressed somewhere," the National Alliance of Business intoned in a 1989 tract. "[But] we lack a coherent approach to define, monitor, measure, and publicize the quality of education nationally."[23]

With its *Essential Components of a Successful Education System*, published in 1989, the Business Roundtable made an early and influential contribution to the emerging view that the fragmentation of existing state and local policies proved that policies affecting education needed to be coordinated so that they worked in concert to promote student achievement. "No single improvement will bring about the systemic change that is needed," the Roundtable publication explained. "The effort requires a comprehensive approach that utilizes the knowledge and resources of broadly based partnerships in each state."[24] Anchoring such a system, the Roundtable suggested, was a coordinated regime of standards expressing expectations of what students should know and be able to do; assessments capable of gauging students' progress toward the standards; and measures rewarding or sanctioning schools based on their record of raising student achievement. While responsibility for standards, tests, and accountability would be centralized, local administrators and teachers would be given more authority to make school-level decisions. Roundtable members insisted that only *coordinated* reform efforts that sought to align entire education systems would overcome the fragmentation endemic to contemporary state education strategies: "Adopting some [reforms] while ignoring others will not result in a system capable of raising the achievement of all students to world-class levels," the Roundtable warned.[25] Following intra-business discussions about how to improve education (which led to the creation of a pan-business Business Coalition for Education Reform in 1989), other major employer associations, including the National Alliance of Business, the Committee for Economic Development, the U.S. Chamber of Commerce, the National Association of Manufacturers, and the Conference Board, ratified the Roundtable's agenda.[26]

While states struggled to institute excellence in education reforms, business entrepreneurs drew on existing networks—and established new institutions and practices—to disseminate standards-based reform ideas to schools throughout the land. For example, Business Roundtable firms committed in 1989 to a ten-year effort to lobby state and local governments to implement coordinated standards, testing, and accountability reforms. Over the next ten years, Roundtable firms worked to promote the *Essential Components of a Successful Education System* in almost every state in the union, organizing hundreds of business education coalitions, lobbying public officials, and stimulating grassroots involvement. To be sure, these efforts were uneven: state Business Roundtables racked up impressive policy victories in some states, while in others Roundtable organizations could point to few successes.[27] Nonetheless, looking back on this effort in 1999, Edward Rust, chairman and CEO of State Farm Insurance and chairman of the Business Roundtable's Education Task Force, suggested that "although the job is far from finished, there is much to show for our work with governors, legislators, educators and other business leaders."[28] In addition to these state-by-state lobbying activities, the Business Roundtable contracted with private organizations to operate "educational retreats" for governors and CEOs to inform them about standards-based reform ideas and recommend strategies for achieving reforms.[29]

At the same time, under the leadership of William Kolberg, a vocal advocate of standards-based school reform, the National Alliance of Business instituted a "Corporate Action Agenda," which provided information and resources to members to "foster collaboration, networking, and information dissemination designed to make business leaders effective advocates and action agents for education improvement and reform." The National Alliance of Business also provided technical advice on standards, assessments, and accountability and organized speakers series and seminars to educate members about how to advocate for school improvements.[30] Complementing the National Alliance of Business's efforts to organize and mobilize grassroots employers were its new initiatives to expand the coalition of support for standards-based reforms. In April 1990 the National Alliance of Business established a Center for Excellence in Education dedicated to "help forge long-term coalitions between business and education."[31] The Center for Excellence in Education recruited an impressive array of education stakeholders, including the presidents of both the National Education Association and the American Federation of Teachers, the president of the Council of Chief State School Officers, and the executive director of the National Governors Association, to discuss ways to promote standards-based reforms and expand federal efforts to improve schools.[32] Given the wide diversity of ideologies and interests involved, consensus on these issues was hardly forthcoming. But by early January 1991, Kolberg was reporting to the center's board that progress was being made: indeed, "most of the Board members attending the December [1990] meeting agree that our country needs to develop national standards defining what we expect our children to learn in our schools."[33]

Business entrepreneurs also gave their imprimatur to broad-based policy statements, increasing the legitimacy of these documents and opening them to a wider audience. For example, prominent business leaders, including Badi Foster of the Aetna Institute for Corporate Education, John Hurley of Chase Manhattan, and Peter Pestillo of Ford Motor Company, contributed to the important 1990 report by the Rochester-based National Center on Education and the Economy (NCEE), *America's Choice: High Skills or Low Wages!*, which called on the nation to adopt explicit skill standards and qualifying assessments as means for raising the quality of the nation's human capital.[34] Though the report had also been endorsed by prominent intellectuals, union leaders, and civil rights groups, business entrepreneurs, led by William Kolberg of the National Alliance of Business and William Lurie of the Business Roundtable, made the National Center's proposals their own, advocating the NCEE's agenda in testimony before Congress in 1990.

Participation in the development of *America's Choice* also allowed business entrepreneurs to strengthen intellectual and personal ties with civil rights entrepreneurs and important figures in Democratic Party councils—ties that later bore fruit in efforts to shape education policy (as we shall see in subsequent chapters). Led by Marc Tucker, the National Center on Education and the Economy was closely affiliated with prominent civil rights entrepreneurs such as David Hornbeck, William Taylor, and Marshall Smith, as well as with prominent political operatives such as the Clintons (Hillary Clinton served on the center's board).[35] These civil rights entrepreneurs already shared many of business leaders' concerns about the institutional "incoherence" plaguing state efforts to institute excellence in education. Building on conversations with Hornbeck, Taylor, and others, as well as the scholarly analyses of the Consortium for Policy Research in Education (CPRE, an interuniversity education research outfit), Marshall Smith, who was associated with CPRE, developed a powerful critique of extant state education reforms—and, by association, the excellence in education agenda—blaming policy failures on "the lack of a coherent strategy for allocating the resources we do have or for overcoming problems in both quantity and quality when they arise."[36] In his seminal 1990 article, "Systemic School Reform," coauthored with graduate student Jennifer O'Day, Smith argued that this "incoherence" could be remedied with comprehensive state efforts to improve schools. This vision—which paralleled the Business Roundtable's *Essential Elements of a Successful Education System* in significant respects—would "provide a coherent direction and strategy for educational reform throughout the system" by elaborating clear standards of what students would be expected to know and do, devising assessments that would gauge students' progress toward these standards, and implementing mechanisms for holding schools and districts accountable for ensuring that students reached the standards.[37] Teacher training, accreditation, and professional development would also be coordinated with state standards so that teachers were prepared to educate students to the standards. In Smith's view, this "systemic" approach would not only improve the performance of education systems generally, but increase the likelihood that disadvantaged students benefited from school reforms by strengthening citizens' commitment to funding schools and (perhaps) providing disadvantaged students with legal grounds to demand better treatment.[38]

Smith's approach, like that of business entrepreneurs, suggested a path for addressing the policy incoherence endemic to the excellence-in-education paradigm and abetted by the nation's diverse, decentralized education system. While the approach seemed to invest policymaking power primarily at the state level, its emphasis on centralized standard-setting and evaluation implicitly sketched an agenda for federal involvement, one that would be taken up shortly. As Maris Vinovskis notes, Smith's article "circulated widely" in the scholarly community.[39] But Smith also worked hard to disseminate standards-based reform ideas in the education policy community. Most important—and in a parallel action with the National Alliance of Business's Center for Excellence in Education—Smith secured funding from the Pew Foundation to establish a Forum on K–12 Education Reform in 1991, which brought together diverse policy intellectuals to, in his words, "think through standards based reform ideas" and determine how to implement them in practice.[40] The forum's members discussed contemporary articles and scholarly studies, traveled to school sites to examine effective practices, and debated policymaking proposals. Bringing together many of the same figures and organizations active in the Center for Excellence in Education, Smith's forum helped reinforce understanding and support for standards-based reforms among figures active in education policy, including some who would shape policy in the first Bush administration (Chester Finn) and the Clinton administration (Smith, Michael Cohen of the National Governors Association, and Thomas Payzant of the San Antonio Unified School District). Indeed, especially during the Clinton administration, forum members played a central role in formulating federal education policy. As the forum would report to its members in June 1994, "Many of the ideas previously discussed by the Forum are now addressed in federal legislation. While it's not possible to determine the extent to which the Forum influenced the passage or content of the legislation, it is clear that Forum members played a leading role. At one point, three of the leaders in the Department of Education were Forum members."[41]

Another venue from which Smith could spread the gospel of standards-based reform was the Consortium for Policy Research in Education. Smith's interaction with consortium colleagues, and his interpretation of CPRE studies of state excellence reforms, had informed his version of the standards-based reform paradigm.[42] In any case, many CPRE colleagues were enthusiastic about Smith's proposals, going so far as to make one of the organization's three institutional research goals the conducting of "research that will lead to *greater coherence* of state and local program and finance policies that promote student learning."[43] Through its various activities—organizing conferences, publishing books, and circulating "policy briefs" summarizing standards-based reform ideas—CPRE helped build support for the standards-based reform paradigm.[44] These works were widely read and discussed in the education policy community, leading many to believe that Smith and CPRE deserved primary credit for the success of the paradigm. Reflecting this view, *Education Week* observed in 1992 that "the commonalities in language and thinking [on standards, assessments, and accountability] generally reflect the influence of a small circle of educational scholars, including Mr. Smith and his colleagues at the Consortium for Policy Research in Education."[45]

Smith's close colleague David Hornbeck, another strong believer in standards-based reform, made critical policymaking contributions to the expansion of this agenda. Having worked throughout the 1980s at the Council of Chief State School Officers to promote school improvements, Hornbeck had come to view coordinated standards-based reforms as essential: if the nation wanted to educate all its children, especially disadvantaged students, he declared in 1990, "it will be necessary for states to implement a system that is based on rich outcomes, driven by meaningful rewards and sanctions, with the school as the unit of measurement and managed by a school staff who have appropriate technical and financial resources."[46] Hornbeck was given his shot to realize this vision in practice when the Kentucky Supreme Court invalidated much of the state's education system in 1989. Hired by a task force appointed by the Kentucky state legislature to develop a plan to respond to the court's decision, Hornbeck designed what *Education Week* described as the "linchpin" of the plan—a system that held schools accountable for reaching educational standards set by the state.[47] The Kentucky Education Reform Act (KERA), enacted in April 1990, was viewed by standards-based reform advocates as a flagship example of comprehensive school reform, and received considerable attention in education policy circles and in the education press.[48]

A participant in Smith's Forum on K–12 Education Reform and leading exponent of educational conservatism, Chester Finn had already begun to develop a version of standards-based reform consistent with educational conservative principles, in the mid-to-late 1980s. Finn's complaints about the incoherence of state excellence-in-education reforms echoed those of the Business Roundtable, the National Alliance of Business, and civil rights entrepreneurs such as Smith and Hornbeck. Declaring in a 1989 article in *Commentary* magazine that the United States was a "Nation Still at Risk," Finn argued that a principal threat to the progress of school reform was that "our reform efforts to date have lacked any coherent sense of exactly what results we are seeking to achieve."[49] Finn's 1991 opus, *We Must Take Charge* (which built on his earlier writings), was an extended brief for coordinated standards, testing, and accountability as a solution to the problem of fragmented educational governance that he believed plagued contemporary schools. Indeed, Finn averred that "clear goals, accurate information feedback on the attainment of those goals, and consequences tied to success or failure—these are the essence of 'accountability' and of effective management."[50] Putting an educational conservative "spin" on standards-based reform that pleased conservative Republicans but did not appeal to many others, Finn contended that school choice—especially forms of choice that permitted students in failing schools to attend private schools at public expense (so-called vouchers)—would help stimulate improved performance in public schools and serve as the ultimate weapon of educational accountability.

Finn and other sympathetic educational conservatives realized that their approach, which heralded a more centralized turn in education policy, could potentially put them at odds with the most strident antigovernment educational conservatives in the GOP's congressional wing. But they argued that centralizing some aspects of education policy would ease the realization of other values—especially accountability for government bureaucracies and teachers unions—close to educational conservatives' hearts. Additionally, as just noted, educational conservatives such as Finn always coupled more centralizing measures related to standards and assessments with radically decentralizing ones, such as proposals advancing private school choice, thereby blunting the potential divisions in the conservative camp.

Finn and other well-known educational conservatives such as Diane Ravitch used their prominence in the education community to promote standards-based reforms. As the Educational Excellence Network reported in "Network Accomplishments (Fall 1988 to Winter 1991)": "It's difficult to make a tidy separation between Ravitch's and Finn's various writing-and-speaking activities (and their service on sundry boards and panels) and the work of the Network. They each do quite a bit of this sort of thing.... Ravitch, for example, is a weekly columnist for the *New York Daily News* and Finn does a fortnightly education commentary distributed by Radio America."[51]

They also parlayed their eminence into funding from prominent foundations to promote their version of standards-based reform. Drawing on support from such diverse patrons as the W. J. Hume Trust, the Phil Hardin Foundation, the Lyndhurst Foundation, and the Mobil Foundation, the Educational Excellence Network undertook numerous activities to promote standards-based reform and school choice. The network published a legislative handbook on restructuring, school choice, and accountability—the product of a conference drawing together reformers, education experts, and state policymakers—called *Education Reform in the '90s*. Additionally, with grants from the John D. and Catherine T. MacArthur Foundation, the Joyce Foundation, and the Gates Foundation, the network collaborated with the National Conference of State Legislatures "to inform state legislators about current policy options in the reform of public education," focusing on "three key school reform domains: restructuring, parent enabling (including choice), and assessment/accountability." Teaming up with the Bradley Foundation, the network sponsored the development of a model history curriculum, *Building a History Curriculum: Guidelines for Teaching History in the Schools*, which anticipated national education standards.[52]

State officials, especially the education governors who had contributed to excellence in education in the 1980s, were also gearing up to promote standards-based reforms. As Gordon Ambach, who was serving as executive director of the Council of Chief State School Officers at the time, later explained, state chief executives were coming to the realization that "states didn't have a clear sense of what expectations should be.... The term 'standards' wasn't really used much at the state level in the 1980s."[53] The Southern Regional Education Board, which in 1981 had produced the influential excellence-in-education report *The Need for Quality*, was one of the first organizations to draw the attention of state officials to the institutional incoherence of state excellence reforms and make the case that revisions to the excellence in education agenda were necessary. Led by former South Carolina "education governor" Richard Riley (and featuring the involvement of Hillary Rodham Clinton), the SREB Commission for Educational Quality began in 1987 an examination of the progress of southern state education reforms. According to Riley, the SREB's investigation—summarized in 1987's *A Progress Report and Recommendation on Educational Improvements in the SREB States*—revealed that "very few states had gotten into the standards movement.... This was seen by us as a big problem, because you can't have accountability without standards."[54] As a first step toward establishing a standards-based education system, Riley's team recommended in its 1988 report, *Challenge 2000*, that SREB states adopt a series of student achievement goals around which their education systems might be aligned. To reach the goals, states would undertake many of the familiar standards, testing, and accountability reforms advocated by other entrepreneurs.[55]

The SREB's arguments gelled with those being offered by business entrepreneurs, civil rights entrepreneurs, and educational conservatives. This consistency of language and themes with the activities of these groups was no happenstance: they met regularly throughout the late 1980s and early 1990s, on an informal basis, to share ideas and build consensus around the standards-based reform paradigm. As Education Commission of the States chairman (and governor of Maine) John McKernan later reported on these meetings, "We were pleased, and somewhat surprised, to find remarkable consistency about what principles should guide reform efforts, what reforms are needed, what types of policies will support them and what strategies will bring them about."[56]

In a reflection of this budding consensus, the SREB's recommendations—along with the parallel analyses being offered by business entrepreneurs, civil rights entrepreneurs, and educational conservatives—quickly came to define the governors' approach to reforming schools. Indeed, the 1988 report of the National Governors Association, *Results in Education*, echoed the SREB, arguing that "states and schools must define their goals and objectives, develop, implement, and monitor new practices and programs, and then adjust them as required. States can help by defining central education goals and by measuring their progress toward those goals."[57] These early activities provided state policymakers, led by entrepreneurial governors such as Riley, Clinton, Alexander, and Hunt, with a basis for promoting the standards-based reform agenda on a broader scale. The National Governors Association produced a series of reports evaluating the progress of state reforms, which contained pointed criticisms of states' modest progress in coordinating standards, tests, teacher training, and other facets of their education systems. These reports also provided a clear vision of standards-based reform to which states could peg their approaches.[58] The Education Commission of the States also released policy briefs, with titles such as "Introduction to Systemic Education Reform," "Bringing Coherence to State Policy," and "Creating Visions and Standards to Support Them," that both reflected the growing consensus and advanced grassroots efforts to promote standards based reforms.[59]

The late 1980s and early 1990s thus witnessed a crucial intellectual shift among business entrepreneurs, civil rights entrepreneurs, educational conservatives, and state leaders, that would significantly alter the course of education policymaking. Realizing that the inattention of excellence in education to matters of policy implementation invited states to undertake what they viewed as flabby and ill-conceived reforms, these figures developed a standards-based reform paradigm self-consciously designed to address these failures and strengthen education. This paradigm infused these advocates' proposals for state—and increasingly federal—policymaking in the ensuing years, legitimating the more centralized policymaking that has come to characterize education politics.

Institutionally Bounded Entrepreneurship and the Expansion of Federal Involvement in Education

Burgeoning consensus among business entrepreneurs, civil rights entrepreneurs, educational conservatives, and state officials on the necessity of standards-based reforms was joined in the late 1980s and early 1990s to growing enthusiasm for limited, but significant, federal involvement in reforming schools. Just as these entrepreneurs saw standards-based reform as a remedy for the "incoherence" of state "excellence" reforms, so did they view expanded federal leadership as a cure for the uneven progress of school improvement and the unsteadiness of leadership within individual states. Complaints about the slow progress of state-level improvement among proponents of standards-based reform were legion. Reflecting on the "new concern about the workforce needs of the coming years, *and the slow pace to date of efforts to achieve systemic change in education*," the Conference Board reported in 1988 the growing sentiment that "the problem is now so immense that it requires the attention of the President.... While the first wave of education reform was centered in the state capitols and in the leadership of governors, either on their own or in concert with the Education Commission of the States, it is apparent that the third wave will look to Washington and national leadership."[60] Revealingly, given educational conservatives' usual skepticism of federal involvement in schools, Chester Finn embraced a similar line, reporting in 1989 that "mounting frustration" with the "decentralized, incrementalist approach" to school restructuring was ubiquitous among educational conservatives.[61] Even state officials, led by the nation's governors, were dissatisfied by the lugubrious pace of state-level education reforms. A 1988 National Governors Association report groused that "in the future, intellectual flexibility will be valued highly. Students must be able to communicate complex ideas, respond to novel situations, and learn new skills....Yet such higher order skills are not measured in most state testing programs. Consequently, states must move to give adequate attention to assessing these skills."[62]

State governors' frustration with the slow pace of state education reforms motivated them to push a reluctant Bush administration to endorse its first major education initiative: the National Education Goals of 1989. During the 1988 presidential campaign, Bush had promised to meet with the nation's governors to discuss education issues, but he foresaw the meeting as a media event to showcase existing state-level strategies rather than a policymaking event that would result in a joint statement of national educational objectives (in fact, Bush had never mentioned the subject of national goals during the campaign).[63] Frustrated with the slow pace of state-led improvement, however, the NGA had other ideas. In December 1988, NGA education staffer—and future Clinton administration official—Michael Cohen advised NGA chief executive Raymond Scheppach that the education summit should focus on the subject of National Education Goals.[64] In Cohen's view, a national statement of academic goals would energize the school reform movement and provide the nation with an explicit statement of objectives against which progress could be judged. Joined by prominent governors such as Bill Clinton of Arkansas, Scheppach lobbied the administration to use the summit as a platform for publicizing national statements of expectations about what students should know and be able to do.[65] This unexpected lobbying effort shifted the Bush administration's views about the purposes of the proposed summit. After expressing some misgivings about national goals earlier in the month, the White House agreed in mid-September 1989 to organize the summit around national goals. Nonetheless, reflecting a characteristic hesitance to expand federal involvement in education, administration officials insisted—as domestic policy adviser Roger Porter advised Chief of Staff John Sununu just prior to the opening of festivities—that the summit should "demonstrate the importance of education and of strengthening our Nation's educational system *while recognizing that it is at the state and local levels where education is provided and where reforms and change must occur.*"[66]

At the summit, the president and the governors agreed in principle to the creation of a series of National Education Goals. Over the course of the following months, administration officials and gubernatorial representatives, led by Bill Clinton and South Carolina governor Carroll Campbell, hammered out an agreement on six national goals, to be met by the year 2000. The president and the governors agreed that by this deadline all children would start school ready to learn; that 90 percent of all students would graduate from high school; that American students would demonstrate "competency" in English, mathematics, science, history, and geography; that U.S. students would be "first in the world" in science and mathematics achievement; that American adults would strengthen their knowledge and skills; and that every school would be free of drugs and violence.[67] However, at the request of the Bush administration, which remained fearful of excessive federal involvement in schooling, the statement announcing the national goals was extremely vague on the matter of how the states and the federal government would work to make the goals a reality.

Despite the president's initial ambivalence, the National Education Goals helped generate momentum for federal promotion of national standards and tests. Having devised national goals, the governors and the president realized the need for an organization to monitor the nation's progress toward them. A National Education Goals Panel (NEGP), a nongovernmental partnership organization composed of gubernatorial and administration representatives, was created in 1990 for this purpose. At first, as Maris Vinovskis has noted, the Bush administration still declined the opportunity presented by NEGP's establishment to launch more-expansive federal education initiatives; indeed, the administration's position seemed to be one of benign neglect (over the objections of congressional Democrats, who wanted to expand federal involvement in schooling, administration officials had insisted that the NEGP remain nongovernmental so as not to overly implicate the federal government in standards-based reforms).[68] However, under the leadership of Governor Roy Romer of Colorado, NEGP became an important forum in which various proponents of national involvement in education, including civil rights entrepreneurs Marc Tucker of the National Center on Education and the Economy and Marshall Smith of Stanford University and CPRE, discussed proposals to establish national standards and tests.[69] In late March 1991, prior to the announcement of America 2000, "the National Education Goals Panel…unveiled a plan to create a national assessment system to measure progress toward the national education goals for the year 2000."[70] These developments converged with advocacy efforts of business leaders and conservative intellectuals simultaneously under way.[71] In fact, when educational conservatives Lamar Alexander, Chester Finn, and Bruno Manno submitted the draft America 2000 initiative in early April 1991, administration officials insisted that its standards and testing proposals be harmonized with the NEGP's work.[72] Gubernatorial interest in a system of national standards and tests thus served as a catalyst for the Bush administration's embrace of more-vigorous federal involvement, helping pave the way to America 2000 and subsequent federal education reforms.

Business entrepreneurs matched the enthusiasm of state leaders for expanded national involvement in education, focusing their energies on efforts to promote national standards and examinations. The Business Roundtable spearheaded this agenda, calling for national education standards and national testing as early as 1987, as the 1988 presidential campaign was getting under way.[73] Dissatisfied with Bush's vague educational pronouncements in the 1988 presidential campaign, business entrepreneurs made concerted efforts to persuade administration officials to embrace national standards and tests.[74] In June 1989 the Business Roundtable invited President Bush to a meeting of its CEOs in order to lobby him on the issue.[75] John Akers, chairman and CEO of IBM and member of the Roundtable's Education Task Force, followed up the meeting with a personal letter to the president enclosing a Roundtable publication that reaffirmed the organization's commitment to national objectives.[76] Even as business entrepreneurs lobbied the Bush administration to commit federal resources and authority to national standards and tests, they put pressure on teacher organizations— especially the "subject matter" associations claiming authority over particular academic subjects—to articulate national expectations of student achievement that could help advance the discussion. In 1989, Shirley M. Frye, president of the National Council of Teachers of Mathematics, observed that her organization's much-lauded statement of mathematics standards responded in significant part to the criticisms of business leaders, who argued that schools had failed to produce workers who could think mathematically and solve problems.[77]

These efforts made an important impression on the Bush administration's education agenda. In response to entreaties from the Business Roundtable and the Business Coalition for Education Reform, in 1989 Bush established a President's Education Policy Advisory Committee (PEPAC), which, Bush explained, would "bring together leaders from business and labor, educators at every level, state and local government officials and the media in a partnership to improve our schools."[78] Paul O'Neill, CEO of the Aluminum Company of America (Alcoa) and staunch proponent of federal activism in education, assumed the committee's chairmanship and was joined on the panel by corporate executives such as David Kearns of Xerox and John Akers of IBM. In large measure due to O'Neill's leadership, according to Chester Finn (who served on the committee), PEPAC recommended the establishment of voluntary national standards and examinations in early 1991.[79] Echoing the justifications uttered in earlier business publications, PEPAC defended national standards and testing proposals on the grounds that expanded national efforts were needed to compensate for the unevenness of state-level reforms:

> There are no tests based on absolute standards of content and proficiency by which each student, parents, teachers, school administrators, any level of government or the general public can judge student performance, compare that performance to other students, or aggregate results to make comparisons to other classes, schools, states or countries. *There are many tests for individuals available commercially or in a number of states, but they are not comparable to each other and none is derived from a national consensus on what children should know. Without such tests, the host of education strategies cannot be targeted effectively or judged properly on the basis of their results. Accountability systems remain judgmental, not objectively based.*[80]

Even as PEPAC deliberated, business entrepreneurs associated with the Business Roundtable, the National Alliance of Business, and the U.S. Chamber of Commerce undertook a comprehensive lobbying campaign on behalf of

national standards and testing. They pushed Bush to embrace a more prominent role for the federal government through a "Core Business Group," which
met with the president on a regular basis between 1989 and 1992.[81] In these
meetings—and in public statements to the press—business leaders such as William Kolberg of the National Alliance of Business stressed that "we need a clear
national strategy for addressing education reform, and we are concerned that
over time, ad hoc institutions not grounded in law may not be sufficient to
provide the pro-active national leadership that is necessary."[82] At the same time,
business leaders extended their campaign to the halls of Congress, calling, in
Kolberg's words, for "the establishment of a system of national standards, coupled with assessment, [that] would ensure that every student leaves compulsory school with a demonstrated ability to read, write, compute and perform
at world-class levels in general school subjects [as well as] to learn, think, work
effectively alone and in groups and solve problems."[83] The presence in Congress
of business entrepreneurs was such that *Education Week* was moved to report
in October 1991 that "business leaders, who once only appeared to testify on
trade and tax matters, have become star witnesses at hearings on such issues as
education reform, Head Start, and Chapter 1 [of the Elementary and Secondary
Education Act]."[84]

Business entrepreneurs' heavy lobbying on behalf of national standards
and tests—both in public venues and behind closed doors—clearly shaped the
administration's thinking. Top Bush administration officials, including Bush's
second education secretary, Lamar Alexander, acknowledged working closely
with business lobbyists on the content of America 2000, which, of course,
included measures to promote these business priorities.[85] Additionally, the
administration's America 2000 strategy delegated to business leaders the responsibility to raise funds for the New American Schools Development Corporation,
a nongovernmental agency tasked with funding school reform demonstration
projects throughout the United States.[86] Business entrepreneurs were not, by
any means, singly responsible for the legislation: in fact, many opposed America
2000's school choice component—widely viewed as a nod to the initiative's conservative supporters—as programmatically impractical and politically unwise.[87]
But the mark of business entrepreneurs on the legislation's national standards
and testing provisions was clear to contemporary observers. "In announcing the
[America 2000] plan," a reporter observed, "Mr. Bush chose to do so in the East
Room of the White House before an invited audience largely composed of—
yes—business leaders."[88]

The inside access offered to business entrepreneurs associated with the Business Roundtable, the National Alliance of Business, and the U.S. Chamber of
Commerce was also enjoyed by educational conservatives, who, in light of the

slow pace of school reforms to date, were increasingly coming to share business leaders' enthusiasm for national standards and tests. As early as 1988, in fact, William Bennett, Reagan's secretary of education, had unveiled a "model curriculum," the James Madison High School Curriculum, which, while entirely voluntary, was conceived as an effort to articulate "a shared body of knowledge" appropriate for all of the nation's students.[89] In 1989, well before Bush administration officials gave serious consideration to national standards and testing, Finn expressed strong support for "a national core curriculum" and suggested that "federal leadership could be immensely helpful in catalyzing the consensus-seeking process" in favor of such a curriculum.[90] Yet, consistent with their view of "standards based" education reform, educational conservatives emphasized that the federal government should do more to promote private school choice so that parents would have more leverage to hold schools accountable for results. Ultimately, educational conservatives such as Chester Finn believed that "if we can't/don't attain [our educational goals] in five years, we should declare national educational bankruptcy and give the parents the money to shop for a decent education wherever they think they can find one."[91]

In a testament to the entrepreneurial role played by these figures, the federal leadership strategies recommended by Finn, Ravitch, and other educational conservatives far outpaced what the Bush administration was willing to propose in 1989 and 1990. Indeed, the Educational Excellence Network complained in early 1991 that "we had no way of knowing that the Bush administration would prove so weak-kneed and inarticulate vis-à-vis education (with the important exceptions of the Charlottesville 'summit,' the national goals that followed and the recent appointment of Lamar Alexander as Secretary of Education)."[92] Important educational conservatives successfully advanced the agenda of national standards, national tests, and federal support for school choice within the Department of Education after Bush selected Alexander to replace Lauro Cavazos as secretary of education in December 1990, however.[93] Alexander, Finn, and Bruno Manno (with an assist from Ravitch, who had not yet been appointed to a position within the department) developed many of the main ideas contained in America 2000, drawing on concepts they had developed in discussions in venues such as the Pew Forum on K–12 Education Reform, PEPAC, and the Educational Excellence Network.[94] As Finn explained, "The whole idea [of America 2000] was worked out in the weeks before Alexander was confirmed as Secretary....We started working at Vanderbilt [in Tennessee, where Alexander and Finn were located] and brought it to the White House."[95] Consistent with educational conservative ideology, these figures did not presume that the federal government would dictate to states and localities how to improve schools, but they did believe that national authority could advance the cause of standards-based school improvement. As one America 2000 planning document put it, "Washington will never create better schools; that will only happen locally; but we can cause them to happen."[96]

The plan, which paired national standards and testing with proposals to advance school choice and foster "New American Schools," drew strong praise from top administration officials—and the president himself—no doubt because it largely conformed to the advice they were simultaneously receiving from gubernatorial advisers and business entrepreneurs (except on the issue of private school choice). According to Finn's notes from meetings with Bush's policy advisers, top officials heralded America 2000 as a "perfect blueprint to go forward," "the most aggressive education change plan," and "a fantastic proposal."[97]

In contrast to the contributions of business entrepreneurs, educational conservatives, and state governors, the contribution of civil rights entrepreneurs to the nationalization of the debate over federal education policy during George H. W. Bush's tenure is more difficult to discern, because these figures did not enjoy the same privileged access to the Bush administration's inner councils. In truth, civil rights entrepreneurs' taste for federal solutions to education problems sharply distinguished them from Bush's closest allies, making them unlikely collaborators. Nonetheless, civil rights entrepreneurs did play a part in advancing the debate on national involvement in the late 1980s and early 1990s. As early as 1988, Kati Haycock's Achievement Council and Phyllis McClure's Legal Defense Fund were issuing scathing critiques of states' failures to institute comprehensive reforms that benefited historically disadvantaged students, raising questions about the capacity of state and local governments to improve their schools.[98] Haycock's work with the Achievement Council helped catapult her to prominence in the education media, where her critiques of state curricular and teacher reforms were repeatedly quoted in the late 1980s.[99] In the same year—1988—David Hornbeck, along with Lester Salamon of the Institute for Policy Studies at Johns Hopkins University, began a project to raise national attention to the nation's "human capital problem." Drawing on support from the Ford Foundation, the Carnegie Corporation, and the William T. Grant Foundation, Hornbeck and Salamon assembled a group of prominent policy analysts and education specialists to consider how to strengthen the nation's students and schools. Converging on the conclusion that "these endeavors call for concerted efforts from all levels of government and from both the public and private sectors," the group expressed the "sense that vision, leadership, and a strong contribution to financial equity are called for at the federal government level."[100] At the same time, Marshall Smith's Forum on K–12 Education Reform worked from what the forum's founding document called the "driving assumption" that "the primary educational policy issue of the 90s will be how to structure state *and national* policy systems to provide the stimulation, focus, and coherence necessary to enhance the capacity of local districts and schools to provide very high quality instruction," considering national strategies (as well as state-based approaches) to promote standards-based reforms.[101]

Indeed, as early as 1986, Smith was proposing to transform the Elementary and Secondary Education Act into a program that required states and local education agencies to set achievement standards for the disadvantaged students they served and to be held accountable for their records in improving student outcomes.[102] This approach, augmented by the standards-based reform ideas that Smith and his colleagues subsequently developed, inspired Haycock, McClure, Hornbeck, Smith, and other civil rights entrepreneurs to band together to promote a standards-based reform overhaul of the ESEA. The next chapter shows that their Commission on Chapter 1, assembled in 1990, developed the policy framework that formed the basis of the Clinton administration's Improving America's Schools Act of 1994—the way station on the road to No Child Left Behind.

Political Conflict over School Choice and Education Spending, and the Failure of America 2000

The America 2000 proposal announced in April 1991 was widely viewed as an ambitious policy effort to improve education in the United States.[103] Although the plan included proposals that were supported in many sectors of the education community—most notably, proposals to promote voluntary national education standards and tests—it also included much more controversial initiatives. First, in a bid for the support of educational conservatives and conservative members of Congress, America 2000 placed private school choice at the center of efforts to improve schools. In addition to promoting federal school choice demonstration projects, America 2000 sought to weave private school vouchers into the fabric of the Elementary and Secondary Education Act by permitting students receiving ESEA assistance to use their allocations in private schools if they changed schools under a legal state or local program.[104] Second, America 2000's chief framers assumed, as did most educational conservatives and Republican members of Congress, that the primary challenges facing schools were institutional, rather than fiscal. Consequently, the tab for the administration's entire program was modest, at only about $600 million—well below what many members of Congress, especially educational liberals, were accustomed to budgeting for major education initiatives.[105]

These features of the administration's proposal antagonized congressional Democrats and their educational liberal allies. Educational liberals cast a wary eye on the administration's proposals to advance private school choice. Democratic senator Edward Kennedy of Massachusetts, who agreed to cosponsor the legislation in Congress in the spirit of cooperation with the administration, nonetheless argued that "the administration's proposal goes overboard on choice. By offering public dollars to private schools, including religious schools, the administration is opening the bitter and divisive policy and constitutional debates of the past about public aid to private schools."[106] Indeed, public school teachers and administrators feared that such reforms would threaten the integrity and fiscal stability of public schools, while many civil rights organizations (including, but not limited to, civil rights entrepreneurs) worried that private school choice would tend to encourage resegregation and further reduce disadvantaged students' access to good public schools. Furthermore, educational liberals insisted that school improvement initiatives be paired with expanded investments in education. In response to Bush's "Educational Excellence Act" in 1989, House Democrats (cheered on by educational liberal interest groups) had introduced a massive, $5.7 billion "Equity and Excellence in Education Implementation Act," which coupled some of Bush's proposals with a doubling of the administration's proposed increase for Head Start and a quadrupling of its recommended allocation for Chapter 1 of the Elementary and Secondary Education Act. A version of this legislation garnered overwhelming support from congressional Democrats *and* Republicans in the House, but foundered due to conservative Republican senators' opposition to a provision establishing a national board for professional teaching standards.[107] As the debate over America 2000 heated up, educational liberals continued to argue that expanded spending accompany school reforms. Adopting an approach it would champion for the remainder of the decade, the NEA called for more than $100 billion in new federal education spending, both to ensure that all eligible students gained access to existing programs, and to support initiatives on class-size reduction, teacher hiring, and school modernization.[108]

Electoral considerations also figured prominently in the calculations of educational liberals in Congress. Bush's popularity was waning as the economy slid into recession in 1991 and 1992. Eying the prospects of victory in the 1992 presidential election, educational liberals were loath to grant Bush a clear policy victory that he could trumpet on the campaign trail.[109] Rather than encouraging them to follow Bush's lead on education policy, the electoral situation persuaded educational liberals to pursue their own policy goals. If Bush accepted educational liberals' proposals, so much the better; if he did not, Bush and the Republicans would be blamed for the failure to enact education legislation.

These starkly different views about how to improve education—exacerbated by electoral considerations—set the stage for a showdown. Several scholars, including John Jennings, Patrick McGuinn, and Maris Vinovskis, have provided richly detailed descriptions of the legislative battle over America 2000, to which I refer interested readers; I sketch the outlines of the conflict here, to focus on how the administration's insistence on controversial measures undermined the chances of legislative compromise.[110] Spurred by the heavily lobbying of the major teachers unions and other education groups, Democrats in both the House and the Senate bucked Bush's priorities to focus on expanding federal investments in education.[111] Both chambers' versions of the legislation featured dramatically increased spending on existing federal education programs, as well as new proposals to finance efforts to coordinate school reforms with comprehensive health service initiatives. Consistent with their desire to protect public schools and maintain resources for teachers and school administrators, educational liberals in Congress also diluted the private school choice measures favored by the administration. The House legislation, which included language that would permit private school choice only if the local district wanted it and the policy conformed to state law, was negotiated in a compromise between top administration officials and House Democrats.[112] In the Senate, however, dialogue between the administration and the Democrats broke down completely, goading Senate Democrats to propose block-granting federal funds to states to design and implement their own education projects. This approach, which departed sharply from Democrats' usual insistence on attaching strong categorical conditions to federal education aid, was probably intended to frustrate the administration's emphasis on standards, assessments, and private school choice by giving states free rein over the use of federal dollars.

These developments led the administration to issue a veto threat, with Lamar Alexander decrying the legislation for "includ[ing] none of the President's proposals and promis[ing] so little in the way of real educational reform."[113] Nonetheless, in 1992 congressional Democrats went ahead with proposals that elevated education spending and denigrated the administration's standards, testing, and private school choice initiatives. The Senate bill passed that body in January 1992 on the strength of the Democrats' majority.[114] The Bush administration responded by reiterating its veto threat and directing Senate Republicans to block passage if a conference report including such language reached the floor in that chamber.[115] In a clear indication of how federal education policy had become an electoral issue, House Democrats voted to enact their version of the bill just before the start of the 1992 Republican National Convention, denying Bush the opportunity to paint the Democrats as obstructionists and clearing the way for a congressional vote on education legislation before the 1992 election.[116]

On September 25, 1992, the House and Senate conference committee agreed to the conference report on a "Neighborhood Schools Improvement Act" that jettisoned much of America 2000, and the House adopted the conference report by voice vote.[117] To save the administration the embarrassment of vetoing education legislation in the midst of the presidential campaign, Republican senators filibustered the conference report after it passed the House. The clock thus ran out on the 1992 congressional session without national standards, national testing, or school choice policies being enacted into law. Unfortunately for Bush, the clock ran out on his presidency as well. The 1992 elections elevated Democratic challenger Bill Clinton to the White House, thus denying Bush the opportunity to enact major education legislation into law.

The collapse of America 2000 in the waning days of the 1992 congressional session obscures developments of profound consequence in the history of American education policymaking. First, the standards-based reform paradigm, which viewed coordinated standards, tests, and accountability as the keys to effective school improvement, was embraced by business entrepreneurs, civil rights entrepreneurs, educational conservatives, and state leaders—and, in direct consequence, by important segments of federal elected officialdom—as the best strategy for improving the nation's schools. This approach subsequently inspired the most important education initiatives of the last two decades, including the Improving America's Schools Act of 1994, the No Child Left Behind Act of 2002, and the Race to the Top program of 2009–10. Second, in comparison with the Reagan years, enthusiasm for expanded federal involvement in efforts to strengthen schools grew significantly in the late 1980s and early 1990s, as evinced by the establishment of National Education Goals and the National Education Goals Panel, and the vigorous debate over the America 2000 initiative. In the ensuing years, confidence in the ability of the federal government to promote comprehensive school improvement burgeoned, producing a revolution in the organization of educational authority in the United States.

These developments were driven by the interaction of political entrepreneurship and institutional constraints central to my account of institutionally bounded entrepreneurship. The states' varied commitment to excellence in education defied reformers' hopes for a profound transformation of education policymaking. In truth, progress was hindered in significant part because advocates of excellence in education had crafted a critique rather than a coherent program or mechanism for implementing that program. Even so, the various proponents of excellence in education were encouraged to rethink their agenda because they were frustrated by what they viewed as the slow pace of progress in general, and by the poor coordination of state policies in particular. But they converged around standards-based reforms and federal leadership because they believed these innovations to be effective antidotes to the policymaking problems evident in many states and localities. This approach not only seemed to solve the substantive problems in the classroom; perhaps more important, it appeared to address an even knottier challenge—crafting a national policy in an area that had traditionally been dominated by intensely local perspectives, in a fashion that could appeal both to more liberal reformers (civil rights entrepreneurs) and more conservative reformers (business entrepreneurs, educational conservatives) without completely alienating state and local officials or public opinion. Developing and exploiting organizations, strengthening coalitions, and networking with elected officials, these figures played the central part in building support for the standards-based reform paradigm, expanding political support for federal leadership of school reform and persuading the Bush administration to adopt the initiatives that became America 2000.

Bill Clinton's elevation to the presidency set the stage for a major shift in federal education policy. Clinton was a strong proponent of standards-based reforms, an advocate of expanded federal involvement, and a close ally of reformers such as Marc Tucker, Marshall Smith, and David Hornbeck. As state and local efforts to improve schools continued to sputter, further frustrating efforts to raise student achievement and reduce achievement gaps, supporters of standards-based reform and federal leadership gained leverage to justify an expanded federal role in education. During Clinton's first term, these figures crafted a proposal to overhaul the federal role in education that formed the foundation of Clinton's legislative agenda and instigated a major shift toward the federal government in governing authority in education.

A NEW FEDERAL ROLE IS BORN, 1993–1994

Bill Clinton's first two years in office are often remembered as a series of defeats for the president and the Democratic Party: the collapse of the Health Security initiative, the row over "gays in the military," and the loss of the House of Representatives and the Senate in the "Republican Revolution" of 1994. But Clinton and the Democrats also enjoyed two stunning legislative victories in education, which, in the eyes of scholars, "enacted the first truly national education policy in U.S. history," "lay the foundation for a new accountability regime," and made "standards-based reform and its premise of 'high standards for all students' the centerpiece" of federal education policymaking for the first time.[1] The Goals 2000: Educate America Act established a process for creating national education standards and provided grants to states to adopt their own systems of aligned standards, tests, and school report cards. The Improving America's Schools Act (IASA) was even more ambitious, reconfiguring a venerable Great Society program, the Elementary and Secondary Education Act (ESEA), to require states to adopt education standards in math and reading, institute aligned tests, develop district and school report cards, and ensure that all students made progress toward the same high standards. Whereas federal education policy had previously concerned itself with providing aid for compensatory programs serving disadvantaged students, the new reforms brought the federal government into the business of requiring states to legislate standards-based education reforms for all students and all schools.[2] The two acts also established a new understanding of educational equity for disadvantaged students; within the terms of

Goals 2000 and the IASA, "equity" was conceived as equitable access to high standards and rigorous curricula, rather than merely more-equitable access to school resources.

Goals 2000 and the IASA thus anticipated the No Child Left Behind Act and the initiatives of the Obama administration, inaugurating a significant expansion of federal involvement in the politics of education. Even as the two laws extended federal responsibility, however, they reaffirmed the traditional mode of federal intervention in schools. Rather than establish a novel set of institutions to achieve their objectives, Goals 2000 and the Improving America's Schools Act worked through conventional categorical grants to the states and localities. This tendency was illustrated most clearly in the IASA, which layered new requirements atop traditional ESEA programs, without significantly altering the policy machinery used to achieve them. In practice, this mode of federal involvement devolved responsibility for many of the most important decisions about standards, tests, and accountability to states and localities, which varied widely in their enthusiasm and capacity for implementing standards-based reforms. Clinton's reforms thus combined new federal purposes with old institutions in an unwieldy mix, inviting intergovernmental struggles over the reach of federal involvement and the scope of standards, testing, and accountability reforms.

Framed by my theory of institutionally bounded entrepreneurship, this chapter explains the convoluted expansion of federal authority in education policy between 1993 and 1994. Though some states and localities hewed closely to the standards-based reform vision promoted by business entrepreneurs, civil rights entrepreneurs, educational conservatives, and state leaders, many continued to resist this approach. These developments spurred business entrepreneurs and civil rights entrepreneurs, who had spent the late 1980s and early 1990s building capacity to promote federal reforms, to intensify their efforts. Breaking from educational conservatives and state leaders, who preferred to limit federal leadership of school reform to efforts to encourage voluntary reforms at the state and local levels, business and civil rights entrepreneurs called on federal officials to revise the Elementary and Secondary Education Act to require states and localities to adopt standards-based reforms as conditions of receipt of federal education aid. Devising and disseminating policy proposals, building coalitions, and working closely with elected officials, these entrepreneurs ultimately succeeded in persuading policymakers to adopt sweeping reforms that put federal education policy on a new path. This marked an important shift of the politics of federal education reform toward a more involved federal role featuring efforts to regulate state and local policies related to standards, testing, and accountability.

However, the fact that business and civil rights entrepreneurs elected to rely on traditional modes of federal involvement in education—conditions on grants-in-aid—is an indication of the institutional obstacles to sweeping policy reform in the nation's fragmented political system. Hemmed in by established institutional commitments, tight budgets, and ambivalent public opinion, business and civil rights entrepreneurs adopted the path of least resistance, layering their reforms atop programs that already enjoyed broad political support and firm financial commitments. While politically astute, this approach had the practical consequence of delegating to states and localities—many of which were ambivalent about standards-based reforms—the responsibility to institute these policies. The reforms championed by business and civil rights entrepreneurs were further diluted in the legislative process; in order to win the approval (or at least the acquiescence) of important legislators and interest groups, entrepreneurs and their allies were forced to concede some of their more sweeping proposals, reinforcing this devolutionary trend. Exhibiting the bounded change characteristic of federal education reforms of the past few decades, the reforms that emerged from the legislative gauntlet were impressive in historical perspective but considerably more modest than business and civil rights entrepreneurs might have preferred.

Nonetheless, the victories were substantial, and were ultimately attributable to the success of business and civil rights entrepreneurs in building a diverse, cross-partisan coalition in support of their reform proposals. Beginning during the presidency of George H. W. Bush, and accelerating during the presidency of Bill Clinton, business entrepreneurs and civil rights entrepreneurs had developed cross-cutting organizations and networks that appealed to diverse constituencies. Working closely with President Clinton, business and civil rights entrepreneurs attracted the support of important Democrats and Republicans to their cause. These efforts succeeded in significant part because administration officials, business entrepreneurs, and civil rights entrepreneurs were able to present their proposals in diverse ways depending on the audience. These figures also avoided the controversial issues—most notably, efforts to promote equalization of school spending (otherwise known as "opportunity to learn" standards) and private school choice—that elicited the strongest political opposition. In contrast, neither educational liberals nor educational conservatives and state leaders succeeded in building such broad coalitions of support for their respective agendas. These groups continued to produce proposals that appealed primarily to their respective bases; in consequence they attracted relatively narrow, non-winning, coalitions of support.

The chapter begins by examining states' responses to the standards-based education reform agenda, illustrating how the decentralized policy responses of state and local governments continued to bound that agenda. Next, it traces the efforts of business entrepreneurs and civil rights entrepreneurs to induce federal officials to endorse a dramatic expansion of federal leadership of standards-based school reform. After suggesting how the agenda of business entrepreneurs and civil rights entrepreneurs was molded by the structure of existing institutions and interests, I show that this agenda nonetheless drew political sustenance from its relatively broad base of political support. The conclusion previews how the developments described in this chapter shaped the prospects for the subsequent evolution of education policymaking in the 1990s and early 2000s.

State Policymaking and the Bounded Expansion of Standards-Based Reform

While standards and tests foundered at the national level during George H. W. Bush's tenure in the White House, state and local governments were simultane-ously straining to institute so-called standards-based initiatives. Though some states forged ahead in implementing standards-based reforms, ambivalence about major changes in education, the technical challenges of instituting aligned standards, assessments, and accountability reforms, and the limited resources available for major policy changes all likely contributed to the uneven spread of standards-based reforms in the early 1990s. According to a review by Policy Studies Associates, a Washington research center, by 1993 only fifteen states had implemented curricular standards, eight had instituted performance standards, and thirteen had implemented assessments aligned to these standards, though more were planning such reforms.[3] Parallel surveys from the mid-to-late 1990s indicate that state-level "planning" activities did not bear immediate fruit in many states, however; indeed, as late as 2000, many states still declined to imple-ment comprehensive standards-based reforms.[4]

At the same time, trends in academic achievement continued to disappoint. According to the National Assessment of Educational Progress's Long Term Trend Assessment, average student achievement scores in both reading and mathematics were virtually unchanged at all age levels between 1988 and 1992.[5] New information about progress among academically disadvantaged students was sobering as well. Studies based on large-scale surveys of teachers and school administrators indicated that teachers often held lower expectations for disad-vantaged students; that these students were exposed to less-challenging materi-als; and that these youths were less satisfied with themselves and their school experiences.[6] Though it is doubtful that states and localities went out of their way to discriminate against disadvantaged children, it was evident (to business entrepreneurs and civil rights entrepreneurs alike) that reforms were still not radically altering conditions in schools serving these students. These developments were especially disturbing to proponents of federal standards-based reforms because policymakers had already made efforts to shore up the progress of historically disadvantaged groups with the 1988 Hawkins-Stafford Amendments to the Elementary and Secondary Education Act.[7] These amendments had required states and localities to track the educational progress of disadvantaged students in compensatory education programs and institute "program improvement" measures when performance lagged. As Maris Vinovskis notes, the ongoing academic struggles of disadvantaged students (and the failure of federal compensatory education reforms to alleviate them) raised questions about the adequacy of the Hawkins-Stafford reforms and helped stimulate ongoing discussion about how to strengthen federal education leadership.[8]

Heightened attention to education, fostered by the debate over America 2000, the National Education Goals, and the Elementary and Secondary Education Act, ensured that school reform would feature prominently in the 1992 presidential campaign. However, neither of the major parties' presidential candidates presented reform proposals that clearly anticipated the major reforms that would be enacted in 1993 and 1994. As the Republican nominee, Bush touted the argument, by then the conventional wisdom, that reforming the schools was essential to strengthening the nation's economy. "If we don't change education we're not going to be able to compete," Bush claimed. "Federal funding for education is up substantially, Pell Grants are up, but it isn't going to get the job done if we don't change K through 12 [education]."[9] Pointing to Bush's leadership of the National Education Summit and his sponsorship of America 2000, administration officials argued that the president had the best plan to improve the nation's schools. "President Bush is for lower taxes, less regulation, limiting excessive litigation in this country, a radical agenda for changing the schools of the nation," Secretary of Education Lamar Alexander insisted. "On all these issues, he is opposed by the interest groups that his opponent, Bill Clinton, will line up with. Governor Clinton stands for higher taxes, more regulation, limited changes in schools....Bill Clinton showed us what kind of education President he would be when he went out to the teachers' unions and told them what they want to hear."[10] The president also began to take a bolder stance on school choice.[11] To highlight his education leadership and reach out to educational conservatives in the GOP base, he trumpeted a new "GI Bill for Children," which would have advanced private school choice by giving low- and middle-income parents a $1,000 educational voucher to spend at the school of their choice.

Democratic contender Bill Clinton kept pace with Bush in making the reform of education a major theme of his candidacy. Like Bush, Clinton contended that comprehensive educational improvements were necessary to shore up the nation's economy. "We can't compete successfully in a global economy with a workforce that lacks the skills of our competitors," Clinton warned in a campaign document, "The Clinton Education Reform Plan: A New Covenant for Learning."[12] The Democratic contender also lambasted his opponent for failing to exercise leadership in promoting comprehensive reforms. "I think we need a real education president," Clinton argued on the campaign trail. "We need more than photo ops at schools, and rhetoric, and telling other people what to do. We need a real education policy."[13] Though he was undoubtedly motivated by his long involvement in the standards-based reform movement and his desire to help the nation achieve the National Education Goals, Clinton's emphasis on education was also an effort to remake the Democratic brand in an era of Republican dominance of presidential politics.[14] Focusing on education, and tying it to the issue of economic competitiveness, were part and parcel of his "New Democrat" strategy of repositioning the Democratic Party as a party of economic growth and social investment rather than the party of the "welfare state" and "tax-and-spend liberalism." As scholars such as Patrick McGuinn have suggested, Clinton hoped that this approach would make the Democratic Party more appealing to centrist voters, reviving the party's fortunes in presidential elections. Notably, the popularity of Clinton's appeal hinged on its resonance with the bromides of the excellence-in-education and standards-based reform movements of the 1980s and 1990s.

Though Clinton aspired to present a New Democrat approach to federal education policy, his agenda failed to anticipate many of the major themes that ultimately found expression in Goals 2000 and the Improving America's Schools Act. The major New Democrat statements on education tended to focus on ideas such as voluntary national standards and tests, a national apprenticeship program, and public charter schools, while pointing to the states and localities as the proper sites of most standards-based reforms.[15] Indeed, asked by campaign staff to comment on a document outlining Clinton's education agenda, Marshall Smith archly noted, "One problem is that much of this paper is indistinguishable from policies of the Bush administration." Smith also complained that Clinton's agenda appeared too much like a laundry list of programs without a unifying direction or theme, reproducing the errors that had plagued excellence in education and inspired the standards-based approach offered by business entrepreneurs, civil rights entrepreneurs, educational conservatives, and state leaders during Bush's presidency.[16]

Even in the aftermath of the 1992 election, which Clinton won with 43 percent of the vote in a three-way race (Bush received 37 percent of the vote, while independent candidate Ross Perot took home 19 percent), the new president's education agenda was slow in materializing. In particular, Clinton's transition planning for the reauthorization of the Elementary and Secondary Education Act suggests how dependent his administration was on unelected political entrepreneurs for what became the "Clinton education agenda." Transition guides written by close Clinton advisers in the immediate aftermath of the 1992 election contained only the sketchiest treatments of how the ESEA was to be reformed, declining to recommend that the program require states to adopt coordinated standards and tests and hold all children to the same high standards, as conditions of receipt of federal aid. Instead, these proposals tended to elaborate traditional Democratic education goals, such as increasing federal education spending and expanding compensatory education programs. Although increasing the "coherence" of federal education programs was also an important theme, transition materials provided little sense of how this was to be accomplished.[17] Ultimately, the inchoate nature of Clinton's education agenda suggests that the primary entrepreneurial impetus for Goals 2000 and the IASA lay outside the administration. Indeed, Clinton's election presented business entrepreneurs and civil rights entrepreneurs with a prime opportunity to focus federal education policy on their favored standards, testing, and accountability reforms.

Educational Entrepreneurship and the Origins and Development of Goals 2000 and the IASA

Business entrepreneurs' contributions to the Clinton education agenda had their origins in the battle over America 2000. For business entrepreneurs associated with the Business Roundtable, the National Alliance of Business, the Committee for Economic Development, and the U.S. Chamber of Commerce, the collapse of America 2000 in 1992 only heightened dissatisfaction with the pace of school improvements in the states and localities. "There was huge frustration with the states," Tom Lindsley of the Business Coalition for Education Reform recalls. "We wanted to insist that states would establish standards and consistent benchmarks, as well as assessments."[18] The difficulty of achieving standards-based reforms at the state level was put in bold relief for business entrepreneurs by the modest progress of the Business Roundtable's fifty-state effort to foster these policies. Despite working to promote standards, tests, and accountability measures in the states since 1989, Roundtable leaders feared that they had made relatively little progress by the conclusion of Bush's presidency: indeed, the "Plan to Pair Business with Government for Reform [was] Stymied in Many States," *Education Week* reported in February 1991.[19] Thus, according to one report published in 1993, Roundtable members believed that "although many states have adopted education reforms advocated by [the Business Roundtable], business leaders still have much work to do in the education-policy arena."[20]

Business entrepreneurs continued public campaigns to promote awareness of what they viewed as the dire state of American education. The "Help Wanted" Campaign of 1991 and 1992, spearheaded by the Business–Higher Education Forum, the Business Roundtable, and Public Agenda (a polling firm) and financed by IBM, Union Carbide Corporation, and the Charles Stewart Mott Foundation, developed a series of advertisements that warned Americans about the perils of poorly educated students and underperforming schools. "'Made in America' used to mean top-quality at a fair price," one "Help Wanted" ad intoned. "But now, people here and abroad want Japanese cars, Korean TV's, Scandinavian furniture and Italian shoes.... Second-rate skills mean a second-rate America. We've got a job to do."[21]

Of equal importance, they continued to refine and expand their organizational capacity to inspire business involvement in school reform and shape national education politics. For example, if the Business Roundtable's fifty-state strategy achieved only modest policy victories by 1993, the state-level networking and coalition building it stimulated helped shore up business entrepreneurs' enthusiasm for standards, testing, and accountability reform. As the organization later averred, "We asked our corporate members to create or join state coalitions of business leaders and others committed to improving schools.... Because of constant changes in political and business leadership, the organizations provide much needed continuity and stability over time."[22] The national Roundtable organization reinforced this by serving as a central clearinghouse for business information-sharing on education policy, disseminating examples of successful policymaking, as well as political tips, to members in states and localities throughout the nation.[23] Similarly, the National Alliance of Business's Center for Excellence in Education helped consolidate the commitment of business to standards-based reform through its many conferences, group discussions, and debates. As NAB president William Kolberg explained in mid-1993, "In some ways, in a systematic sense, we've learned how to do it.... There is a level of commitment there [by business leaders]. There is a sophisticated understanding about how long [reform] takes. I think the National Alliance of Business will be in the education-reform business for as long as it takes to be done."[24] Such organizational efforts sustained business support for standards-based reform, leading business entrepreneurs to "Say Commitment to Education Still Strong," according to *Education Week*.[25]

However, the combined experience of slow progress at the state level and the collapse of America 2000 at the national level led business entrepreneurs to the realization that more-focused federal policies were needed. At a December 1992 meeting of the National Alliance of Business's Center for Excellence in Education, business leaders urged that "in the area of systemic change and reform: [Congress should] support national goals and assessments; provide grants to states to set standards, develop curriculum frameworks and assessments, create school-focused and standards-driven professional development programs, undertake public outreach that involves the community in developing programs, begin the development of school delivery standards, and create accountability systems."[26] Although this program bore some resemblance to Bush's America 2000 program, its greater focus on standards-based reforms, support for "school delivery" (or opportunity to learn) standards, and emphasis on accountability systems—and its silence on private school choice—suggest its closer kinship with what would become Goals 2000.

In their efforts to firm up the Clinton administration's agenda, business entrepreneurs found a staunch ally in Richard Riley, Clinton's choice for education secretary. During his governorship of South Carolina, Riley had collaborated with business leaders on South Carolina's landmark 1984 Education Improvement Act. In subsequent years, especially due to interactions through the SREB and the NGA, Riley's familiarity with business entrepreneurs' ideas had grown. Consequently, it was to be expected that Riley would welcome business entrepreneurs with open arms after ascending to the position of secretary of education. Indeed, William Kolberg of the National Alliance of Business later crowed that "we have a very close relationship with the [Education] Department. [Secretary] Riley has really opened the doors and told us he wants to work with us."[27] Michael Cohen, a close ally of Clinton's and Riley's who moved from the National Governors Association to the Department of Education to become a top education adviser after the 1992 election, similarly recalls that the administration made the pitch to business leaders that "our agenda is your agenda."[28] This was no mere overstatement: recalling his views about the state of standards-based reforms when he took office in a 2002 article, Riley echoed the concerns articulated by business entrepreneurs when he argued,

> The idea of higher standards for all children was emerging, but only in fits and starts. Just a handful of states and communities were consistently engaged in pursuing high standards, and the progress was slow. Many people doubted or simply did not believe in the fundamental principle underlying the standards movement: that we should have high expectations for *all* children—including poor children, children with disabilities, and the many new immigrant children flooding into our nation's classrooms.[29]

As the administration worked closely with business entrepreneurs, its strategy evolved from merely seeking to pass the Democrats' "Neighborhood Schools Improvement Act" of 1992, as suggested in some transition memoranda, to a much more disciplined effort to induce states to adopt coordinated standards, testing, accountability for results, and "opportunity to learn" standards, as a means for achieving the National Education Goals.[30] In fact, the heart of the Goals 2000 initiative pitched by the administration—the program to fund state development of standards-based reforms—"presume[d] that every state will move to the adoption of more challenging standards, and will need to make substantial reforms to its education system in order for all students to achieve them," according to a memorandum from Michael Cohen to the president outlining the proposal. As Cohen explained, the granting program sought to "leverage system-wide change—change in how the 94% state and local dollars are spent."[31] Another important feature of the Goals 2000 legislation—the National Education Standards and Assessment Council, which would help develop voluntary national standards, tests, and "opportunity to learn" standards, review and certify state content and performance standards, and conduct research on standards-based reforms—also bore the mark of business influence. Such a panel had long been supported by the National Alliance of Business, which believed that a federally legislated body was needed to "have the continuing responsibility for developing and applying measures and standards for determining progress against the national goals."[32] Thus, as *Industry Week* later reported, "It's not surprising, given its participation in drafting them, that industry is pleased with the Goals 2000."[33]

The mark of business entrepreneurs on Clinton's education agenda was plain to see. In contrast, educational liberals perceived they had little influence on Goals 2000. Although Clinton officials had kept congressional leaders appraised of their plans, Gordon Ambach of the Council of Chief State School Officers, a close associate of Secretary Riley, warned the secretary in late March 1993 that among many Democrats "there is a sense that their work of last year [the Neighborhood Schools Improvement Act] has been largely, if not completely ignored in the new proposed bill [Goals 2000]....There is the problem of "no ownership" because the members believe they were not included in forming the content of the Administration bill."[34] Even after he had redrafted portions of the legislation in April 1993 to address some of the concerns of educational liberals, Riley reported to Clinton that many House Democrats "would prefer to not have this bill [Goals 2000] at all."[35] Nonetheless, the administration forged ahead with the Goals 2000 program, much to the delight of business entrepreneurs. For their part, business entrepreneurs promised to make every effort to help the administration pass the Goals legislation. As a Department of Education staffer reported to her superiors in March 1993, "members of the [Business Coalition for Education Reform]...are interested in assisting us in any way they can. We are to let them know if members of the coalition can be helpful with specific House members."[36]

Business entrepreneurs' contributions to the Clinton administration's education agenda were impressive. But they were arguably exceeded by those of civil rights entrepreneurs. While business entrepreneurs collaborated with Clinton officials on the substantively important, but (at around $400 million) fiscally modest Goals 2000 Act, civil rights entrepreneurs developed a radical new framework for the massive $9 billion Elementary and Secondary Education Act, which was subsequently adopted in large part by the Clinton administration. This remarkable achievement was made possible by civil rights entrepreneurs' careful advance work in securing financial support from sympathetic patrons, developing new programmatic ideas, fostering large and diverse policy coalitions, and building close working relationships with policymakers.

Like business entrepreneurs, civil rights entrepreneurs remained dissatisfied with the progress of standards-based reforms, especially with the failure of these reforms to reach poor children and children of color. In 1988 Kati Haycock of the Achievement Council complained that "into the education of poor and minority children, we put less of everything we believe makes a difference. Less experienced and well-trained teachers. Less instructional time. Less rich and well-balanced curricula. Less well-equipped facilities. And less of what may be most important of all: a belief that these youngsters really can learn. All in all, we teach poor and minority students less."[37]

Not content to issue lonely criticisms of the educational status quo, civil rights entrepreneurs joined forces to reinforce the resonance of their critiques, develop new policy solutions, and expand their capacity to influence the policy debate. As noted in the previous chapter, civil rights entrepreneurs gained strength through the networking and legitimacy afforded by organizations such as the Pew Forum on K–12 Education Reform and CPRE. These efforts remained robust at the dawn of Clinton's presidency. Even as it continued to host regular meetings of its members, geared to promoting shared views on K–12 education reform, the Pew Forum expanded its membership (to twenty-seven members), cosponsored conferences with organizations such as the Aspen Institute, the National Advisory Council for New Directions in Education, Columbia University's Teachers College, and CPRE, and sponsored books on professional development and the relationship between higher education and K–12 education reform.[38] Likewise, CPRE continued to serve as a major outlet of policy-relevant research and political analysis related to the cause of standards-based reform. In 1993, in fact, CPRE brought together prominent education policy scholars to publish

states to adopt the standards-based reforms civil rights entrepreneurs (and business entrepreneurs, as well) had been advocating since the late 1980s.[47] In order to be eligible for ESEA funds, each state would have to set high education standards for all students, as well as performance benchmarks that calculated student progress against the standards; develop rich assessments keyed to state standards that gauged all students' progress toward the standards; establish annual report cards that tracked all schools' yearly progress in raising *both* the achievement of all students and the performance of specific disadvantaged groups (such as poor children, English learners, and minorities); institute criteria that measured whether students' and schools' yearly academic progress was "adequate"; and implement mandatory accountability systems that rewarded or punished districts and schools based on their performance in raising all students to high levels of achievement. To further promote education restructuring, schools serving high concentrations of poor children would be permitted to abandon individualized "pull-out" programs criticized by the commission and use ESEA funds to institute schoolwide education reforms. States would also have to expand investment in teacher professional development and target ESEA funds to disadvantaged districts and schools. Finally—and in a point of convergence with many educational liberals in the Democratic Party—the commission recommended that the ESEA implement "opportunity to learn" standards to induce states and localities to reduce financial inequalities between districts and schools so that all children would have greater opportunity to reach high levels of achievement.

Despite its radical approach to reforming the ESEA—and, through the ESEA, restructuring state and local education systems—the report of the Commission on Chapter 1 was extremely well received in the education community and in Congress. A proud Kati Haycock reported to her fellow commissioners that "several members have offered to introduce our bill as written."[48] In part, the report benefited from the prestige and connections of the commission's members, which were widely recognized by policymakers and the press. As one journalist reported, "The panel includes highly regarded compensatory-education experts, representatives from both national teachers' unions and the business community, and widely known reform advocates. Some of the panelists—including Mr. Hornbeck, Marshall S. Smith, the dean of the school of education at Stanford University, and Marc S. Tucker, the president of the National Center on Education and the Economy—also have ties to President-elect Bill Clinton."[49] In a testament to the prestige of the commission's members, Secretary Riley (who, in addition to his other roles in the standards-based reform movement, was a former chairman of the board of CPRE, and thus familiar with Smith's work) tapped Smith to develop the administration's ESEA reauthorization proposal.

Smith subsequently proved "willing to carry water for the Commission" within the Department of Education, according to commissioner William Taylor.[50]

The commission further greased the legislative wheels with a well-planned advocacy campaign. From January to August 1993, it organized numerous briefings with members of Congress and congressional staff; distributed thousands of copies of its report to opinion makers and elected officials; held regional briefings on the report's recommendations throughout the United States; and built support with diverse interest groups within the education community, including teachers, administrators, and groups representing needy populations. These efforts were supplemented with an organized grassroots campaign, in which commissioners passed information about their activities through personal and political networks to grassroots activists and urged them to write members of Congress and the administration in support of the commission's recommendations.[51] At the same time, Marshall Smith helped build support for the commission's proposals within the standards-based reform community by inviting Haycock to speak about the commission's work before his Pew Forum on K–12 Education Reform in October 1992.[52]

Other factors unique to the commission's approach contributed to its influence in the political process. In an unusual step—and in a reflection of the commissioners' deep knowledge of the complex workings of the ESEA—the commission articulated a fully formed legislative proposal, going so far as to develop line-by-line statutory language to guide policymakers during reauthorization efforts. With comprehensive legislative language in hand, the commission possessed considerable legislative advantages over its major competitors—most importantly, educational liberals in the major teachers unions and administrator groups, and educational conservatives and antigovernment activists—which by the end of 1992 had only developed vaguely worded general principles for reform of the ESEA.[53] Because the commission had done much of the difficult legislative work, policymakers were understandably attracted to its plan for reauthorizing the ESEA.

The diverse membership of the Commission on Chapter 1, its cross-cutting political message, and its efforts to reach out to varied audiences—when coupled with the Clinton administration's basic amenability to standards-based reform—paved the way for Clinton's embrace of many of its recommendations. Through the summer of 1993, while Smith was developing the administration's ESEA reauthorization proposal, "there was a steady exchange of drafts and reactions between the Commission and the Department of Education around the Educate America Act (Goals 2000) and the Elementary and Secondary Education Act," according to internal commission records.[54] In a testament to the impact of the commission's recommendations on the administration's proposal and the broader debate about reauthorizing the ESEA, administration officials highlighted to members of Congress "how much common ground exists between the Administration's proposal and the Chapter 1 Commission's recommendations." As Department of Education official Thomas Payzant averred, "There is remarkable consensus both on the major principles and on the specific types of changes needed to reform Chapter 1—high standards for all children, assessments aligned with those standards, a new system of accountability, schoolwide programs and comprehensive schoolwide reform, a dramatically increased emphasis on professional development, strong parental involvement, and substantially greater targeting of resources to where the needs are greatest."[55]

In fact, the administration's proposal, announced in September 1993, endorsed the commission's recommendations in the main, calling for new rules to require states to adopt education standards, aligned tests, and accountability for results in exchange for access to federal ESEA funds. This is not to say that Clinton adopted the commission's recommendations word for word, however. In anticipation of opposition from educational liberals and educational conservatives, the administration sheared off some of the commission's most controversial proposals, bounding the scope of policy change from the start. Fearing complaints from educational liberals about the discriminatory effects of testing (and, more self-interestedly, about the impact of stringent accountability measures on schools and school staff) and concerns from educational conservatives about the untoward expansion of federal authority in education, Clinton's IASA proposal did not detail the testing, reporting, and accountability requirements with the stringency or specificity envisioned by the commission.[56] Moreover, in a bow to educational conservatives and state leaders who viewed "opportunity to learn" standards as an imposition on state and local control of schools and an invitation to tax increases, Clinton dropped this recommendation from his proposal, contending that the authority to finance education resided with states and localities. Thus, as *Education Week* concluded in an August 1993 analysis of a leaked version of the Clinton proposal, "Although it is apparently not as far-reaching, the Administration proposal resembles a plan released last year by the Independent Commission on Chapter 1, a panel of educators, researchers, and child advocates."[57]

Institutional Constraints and the Structure of Goals 2000 and the IASA

While the frustrations of business entrepreneurs and civil rights entrepreneurs with state-level policies led them to look to the federal level for leadership of standards, testing, and accountability, their policy proposals placed considerable responsibility to implement school reforms in the hands of state and local governments. The Goals 2000 proposal worked primarily as a new categorical grant to the states, while the IASA initiative operated through the well-established categorical grant structure of the Elementary and Secondary Education Act of 1965. Under both proposals, then, the federal government set the agenda for standards, tests, and accountability, but states and localities retained the predominant role in planning and implementing many of the most important details, such as the content of standards and assessments. Of equal import, under both measures the federal government possessed relatively modest legal means for holding states and localities to the standards-based reform vision. Because cutting off funding as a penalty for noncompliance was deemed politically inexpedient, Department of Education staff would have to rely on a combination of exhortation and political pressure to encourage states to comply with policy guidelines. Furthermore, while it was believed that the proposed National Education Standards and Assessment Council would play a role in shaping state and local standards through its support of voluntary national standards, it was uncertain how much (or whether) state and local governments would consider its model standards in crafting their own reforms. Given the considerable variation in states' and localities' will and capacity to implement comprehensive standards-based reforms, the structure of Goals 2000 and the IASA invited considerable slippage between the vision touted by business entrepreneurs and civil rights entrepreneurs and the likely outcome of policymaking in states and localities.

Why, then, did business entrepreneurs and civil rights entrepreneurs pursue their preferred reforms through decentralized institutional structures, which seemed to offer questionable prospects of success? First of all, the structure of federal educational commitments channeled the reform impulse toward measures that built on existing programs. As we have seen, existing federal categorical grants—especially the massive commitments embedded in the Elementary and Secondary Education Act—were popular with the myriad education constituencies that benefited from them and with many members of Congress, who enjoyed taking credit for bringing benefits to their districts. Indeed, for many members of Congress, independent of party, the issue of federal education *funding* was much more salient than the substance of federal education *reforms*. In a revealing memorandum to Rhode Island senator Claiborne Pell (a strong congressional advocate of federal standards-based reforms during consideration of the IASA), the senator's staffers contended that "ESEA reauthorization will begin and end with the Chapter I formula" determining the allocation of funds to congressional districts.[58] Business entrepreneurs and civil rights entrepreneurs thus anticipated that new initiatives taking this familiar form (Goals 2000) or, even better, layered atop existing programs (the IASA) would be more attractive—or at least less objectionable—than new measures with novel institutional arrangements and weaker ties to existing interests in Congress and the education community. As John Jennings, a longtime legal counsel to the House Education Committee and close observer of the politics of education reform during the Clinton administration, later explained, "It's harder to get a bill enacted for completely new programs or new ideas than for programmatic changes to old bills."[59] Michael Cohen, who observed the politics of reform from within the Clinton administration, offered a blunter assessment. "You can't get education legislation without the education community," he argued in a personal interview. Trying to build on existing programs offered reformers a way to broaden their base of political support while dampening criticisms. Indeed, Cohen concluded, the IASA could be "more coercive and more specific" in the area of school reform precisely because "it was built on the twenty-five-year foundation of the ESEA."[60] Even the business entrepreneurs associated with the National Alliance of Business's Center for Excellence in Education, accustomed to getting their way on policy matters, recognized the constraints imposed by existing institutional and interest-group pressures. Discussing the ESEA reauthorization in June 1992, the center later reported, "Many members thought that this reauthorization did provide the opportunity to make some major changes in the ESEA programs. However, the ESEA currently authorized identifiable programs with identifiable purposes, and any changes would have to fit within this existing structure."[61]

Beyond the constraints imposed by existing institutions and interests, the harsh budgetary realities of the period left little available slack with which to finance major new investments outside traditional education programs. Federal deficits, which had risen steadily in the Reagan and Bush years, had become a major issue during the 1992 presidential campaign, signaling to reformers and the public that resources for education would be limited. At the start of 1993, White House estimates put the deficit at more than $300 billion for fiscal year 1997, reinforcing Clinton's commitment to deficit reduction as a major priority.[62] This commitment had immediate, and significant, consequences for federal education policy: as one education writer reported, "Compared with such programs in the Health and Human Services and Agriculture departments, [Clinton's 1994] budget is less generous with the Education Department."[63] The expected scarcity of resources also put many of the teacher and administrator organizations on high alert, inducing them to mobilize to protect their pet programs from possible raiding to finance new initiatives. As one Democratic appropriations aide noted in early March 1993, "There will be a real inclination among Democrats to help them along with their school-reform initiative, but they also have their own favorite programs to protect....I don't think [the Clinton administration will] get as much as they want. That program just can't compete with Chapter 1 [of the Elementary and Secondary Education Act]."[64] With resources at a premium, proponents of standards-based reforms undoubtedly recognized the wisdom of eschewing vicious budget battles that would alienate potential allies. Awareness of the hard fiscal constraints on policy expansion thus reinforced the limitations imposed by existing institutions and interests, pushing reformers to propose more-modest institutional reforms.

The final obstacle to a more expansive federal role in promoting standards, testing, and accountability was public opinion. Americans were concerned about the state of the nation's schools and supported efforts at all levels of government to strengthen education. However, business entrepreneurs and civil rights entrepreneurs sensed that the public had little appetite for sweeping expansions of federal authority in education. John Austin, executive director of the Flint Roundtable, a subsidiary of the national Business Roundtable, complained in April 1993 that the public remained "way behind" on the issue of school reform due to "an outdated set of perceptions about the global economy." That same month, David Hornbeck explained that "public-opinion surveys consistently show that Americans may not be satisfied with schools in general, but they tend to think their own schools are doing pretty well. That is viewed as a major barrier to getting systemic reform."[65] Indeed, 47 percent of Americans gave the schools in their community an A or B grade in 1993 (with another 31% giving them a C), and only 9 percent believed that low standards were the biggest problem facing community schools— not exactly a groundswell of support for radical standards-based change.[66] With the public sending mixed signals, supporters of standards-based reforms took a middling course, proposing reforms that significantly increased federal involvement without fundamentally recasting governing authority in schooling.

Together, these considerations encouraged business entrepreneurs, civil rights entrepreneurs, and their allies in the Clinton administration to pursue unorthodox federal standards-based reforms through conventional categorical grant programs. Even if enacted intact, both the Goals 2000 and the IASA initiatives promised what Elisabeth Clemens describes as a "Rube Goldberg-esque" approach to standards-based reform, combining centralized goals with radically decentralized administration and implementation.[67] But passage of the two laws was not assured.

Coalition Building and Enactment of Goals 2000 and the Improving America's Schools Act

In fact, enacting Goals 2000 and the Improving America's Schools Act required negotiating a complex policymaking environment in which multiple groups, with very different interests, were contending for influence. Although the Democrats controlled both the House of Representatives (with 258 members) and the Senate (with 57 votes), many congressional Democrats continued to hew to an educational liberal approach to reforming schools. Focused on maintaining existing categorical programs and raising federal spending on education, these members of Congress expressed considerable skepticism about standards, testing, and accountability reforms that seemed to impose new pressures on disadvantaged students and the teachers, administrators, and schools that served them. As Secretary Riley reported to the president in mid-1993, "[Many congressional Democrats] would prefer not to have this bill [Goals 2000] at all, and instead substantially expand ESEA, with additional programs and funds."[68] When Riley first introduced congressional Democrats to the Goals 2000 proposal in April 1993, Democratic members complained about the bill's inadequate attention to "opportunity to learn" standards, its excessive focus on testing, and its low price tag, leading Republican Bill Goodling, the House Education Committee's ranking minority member, to quip that Riley "got beat up pretty badly by the majority."[69] These sentiments reemerged when the administration's IASA proposal was released in September 1993. Contemplating the standards-based reform ambitions embedded in the administration's proposal, some congressional Democrats must have sympathized with the concerns articulated by Bruce Hunter, a lobbyist for the American Association of School Administrators, an educator group. "It just means what everybody's been saying all along about the standards being voluntary: Bullshit," Hunter moaned. "They're mandatory, and [under the IASA] they're tied to money."[70]

Many congressional Democrats agreed with the educational liberal proposals of the major teacher and administrator organizations, which had banded together to develop an education agenda for the 103rd Congress featuring increased spending and expanded social services. The Reauthorization of Hawkins/Stafford Consortium, a coalition of eighteen major education interest organizations (taking its name from the Hawkins/Stafford Amendments), contended that the key to the achievement of the National Education Goals was a dramatic increase in federal education spending through enhanced targeting of federal funds for disadvantaged groups, an expansion of federal general aid for school modernization and technology, and new categorical programs for health and social services. Another major priority for the consortium was achieving "full funding" for federal education programs, so that all eligible students could make full use of these educational opportunities.[71] The National Coalition of Educational Equity Advocates, comprising dozens of major teacher and school administrator organizations, along with civil rights groups such as the National Urban League, the NAACP, and the National Urban Coalition, took a similar line in its 1993 report,

Educate America: A Call for Equity in School Reform. This group argued for "the need for local, state, and federal governments and agencies to create an integrated system of supports," as well as for "national, state, and local recognition that equity is inseparable from quality in the measure of educational excellence."[72]

The demands of many congressional Democrats and educational liberals for expanded federal investments and more detailed "opportunity to learn" standards, and their skepticism of federal standards-based reforms, departed in important ways from the preferences of business entrepreneurs, civil rights entrepreneurs, and their allies in the Clinton administration. But they also clashed directly with the priorities of most congressional Republicans, educational conservatives, and state leaders. For many congressional Republicans and educational conservatives, the spending demands of congressional Democrats, teacher groups, and some civil rights groups threatened to divert attention from efforts to improve schools. As several top Republicans wrote Riley during consideration of Goals 2000 in April 1993, the bill's discussion of voluntary "opportunity to learn standards" (written into the bill in order to placate congressional Democrats) "is a good example of how this program has tilted away from a focus on increased learning and become preoccupied with a fuzzy notion—which no one seems to be able to clearly define."[73] Rather than increasing federal spending and regulations, Republican congressional leaders such as Richard Armey, Cass Ballenger, John Boehner, and Pete Hoekstra called for decentralizing reforms that channeled funds to states and especially localities, and increased regulatory flexibility for districts and schools.[74] Exhibiting their strong distaste for government regulation, educational conservatives continued to call for private school choice measures to be woven into the Elementary and Secondary Education Act—a proposal that was (as it had been in the debate over America 2000) anathema to educational liberals.

Although congressional Republicans, and their educational conservative supporters, were pleased about the Clinton administration's emphasis on standards and achievement, they worried that the approach favored by business entrepreneurs, civil rights entrepreneurs, and the Clinton administration went too far in extending federal influence in schools, limiting the ability of states and localities to tailor reforms to their unique circumstances. They drew a sharp line between the initiatives of the Bush administration, which they viewed as compatible with state and local control of education, and Clinton's more ambitious approach, which they believed threatened state and local primacy in school matters. According to Chester Finn, Goals 2000 could cause harm by "federalizing" the education problem, "giv[ing] the impression around the country that education is now the federal government's responsibility and lift[ing] it off the shoulders of states and localities."[75] Republican Policy Committee chairman and congressman Henry

Hyde expressed similar fears in response to the IASA, charging that "instead of reinforcing the efforts of parents and teachers to get learning back on track, [the IASA] advances bureaucratic micromanagement of our schools."[76] Clinton's refusal to promote private school choice through Goals 2000 or the IASA was seen by educational conservatives as further evidence of his administration's bureaucratic approach to reforming the nation's schools.

Organizations representing state officials were ostensibly nonpartisan in their affiliations, and thus refrained from the more partisan position-taking of educational liberals and educational conservatives. Similar to their stance on America 2000, state officials were cautiously supportive of the expanded federal involvement and investment in standards-based reform envisioned by the Clinton administration, though, according to the National Governors Association's own internal records, they apparently were not closely consulted in the development of the administration's initiatives.[77] Indeed, according to Raymond Scheppach, executive director of the National Governors Association, state leaders hoped that the federal investment promised by Goals 2000—as long as it did not come with excessive regulatory strings—would promote school improvements and align federal policies with state and local initiatives.[78] Understandably, given their interest in retaining discretion over school reforms, state leaders were more skeptical of the more assertive federal role envisioned in the Improving America's Schools Act. Even so, Gordon Ambach of the Council of Chief State School Officers explained, "states were loath to oppose the IASA in a loud or vigorous way, because doing so would have suggested that state leaders supported a two tier system, in which poor and minority students were held to lower standards" than their more advantaged peers.[79]

If state leaders had questions about Goals 2000 and the IASA, however, they were even more concerned by efforts, spearheaded by congressional Democrats with the backing of educational liberals, to place "opportunity to learn" standards at the top of the agenda. In an August 1993 statement, the National Governors Association Task Force on Education insisted that "states, not the federal government, should assume the responsibility for creating an education delivery system that enables all students to achieve high standards. Each state has the constitutional responsibility to determine its own education delivery system."[80] Further underscoring their position on the issue, they pronounced efforts by congressional Democrats to foster mandatory "opportunity to learn" standards "unacceptable."[81] Maintaining state leaders' support for—or at least acquiescence to—the administration's initiatives was crucial if the proposals were to be enacted into law; the absence of such support would have given many members of Congress, especially on the Republican side, reason to walk away from Goals 2000 and the IASA.

It was evident that neither the petitions of educational liberals for expanded spending and mandatory "opportunity to learn" standards nor the demands of educational conservatives for decentralization and private school choice could readily be enacted into law. Republicans could use the filibuster to block the favored proposals of educational liberals, while Democrats could simply vote down measures recommended by educational conservatives. Yet the stalemate between educational liberals and educational conservatives did not mean that Goals 2000 and the IASA were destined to pass by default. Although there were features of each proposal that were broadly acceptable, each also contained aspects that antagonized one group or another.[82] Supporters of these measures needed to walk a fine line, holding enough Democrats to build the foundation of a legislative majority, without inducing alienated Republicans to support a filibuster in the Senate.

Previous studies have examined the struggles over Goals 2000 and the Improving America's Schools Act in detail. Rather than recount these legislative histories in depth, I focus attention on the means by which Clinton administration officials, business entrepreneurs, and civil rights entrepreneurs worked to build majority coalitions for the standards-based reforms embedded in the two proposals.

In the battle over Goals 2000, Clinton's enthusiastic sponsorship was a key to the bill's enactment. Clinton engaged in a careful process of give and take with both Democrats and Republicans, working with members of both parties to craft a bill that could win the acceptance, if not enthusiasm, of a legislative majority in both chambers. By strongly supporting federal leadership of standards, testing, and accountability, Clinton put pressure on his Democratic colleagues to back away from mandatory "opportunity to learn" standards and expanded federal education spending. Indeed, when House Democrats, led by Jack Reed of Rhode Island, attempted to condition states' access to Goals 2000 funds on their willingness to institute specific corrective actions to ensure "opportunity to learn" for every student—potentially undermining Republican support for the legislation—Clinton denounced the move in a public letter to House Education and Labor Committee chairman William Ford. "Amendments which require states, as a condition of federal support, to commit to specific corrective actions for schools that fail to meet these standards go too far.... The requirements will impede states' efforts to focus accountability on results," Clinton warned. "I urge you not to support amendments that expand the definition or role of opportunity-to-learn standards."[83] Realizing that assent to Clinton's request was necessary to salvage the legislation and avoid embarrassment to their president, the Democrats agreed to water down the "opportunity to learn" provision and include additional language designed to reassure Republicans that the legislation would not lead to expanded federal control over state education finance.[84] Clinton's forceful intervention against "opportunity to learn" standards, however, was accompanied by more solicitous efforts to entice Democrats. The administration made an important concession to educational liberals who feared both the discriminatory effects of testing and the impact of accountability tests on teachers and schools, diluting the testing language in the bill to delay the use of Goals 2000 funds for "high-stakes" assessments for the first five years of the program.[85]

More broadly, the administration sought to convince congressional Democrats that the Goals 2000 program honored hallowed Democratic commitments. Taking up the rhetoric pioneered by civil rights entrepreneurs, Richard Riley, Michael Cohen, and Marshall Smith made the rounds among congressional Democrats to build support for the Goals legislation, averring that "equity and excellence is [sic] the opportunity to learn high standards" and that "common, challenging standards lead to equity/excellence."[86] By addressing Democrats' concern about equality of opportunity and linking it to high standards for all students, Clinton officials reduced the anxiety of their congressional brethren about the likely effects of the legislation on disadvantaged students. Indeed, Democratic representative Thomas Sawyer of Ohio contended, Goals 2000 was "stating clearly our belief that all children can meet high expectations and develop the knowledge, skills and habits of mind that we once expected of only our top students."[87]

Clinton's stand against "opportunity to learn" standards gave Republicans greater confidence in Goals 2000. As a further enticement to Republicans, Clinton accepted provisions that scaled back the federal government's role under Goals 2000 in order to stanch concerns about "excessive" federal intervention in schooling. The final legislation required that national standards be sufficiently general as to preserve state and local authority over curriculum and instruction.[88] Clinton also accepted language highlighting the law's voluntary character, emphasizing that states could not be compelled to take Goals 2000 funds. To soothe fears of a "national school board," the oversight and regulatory powers of the National Education Standards and Assessment Council—now renamed the National Education Standards and *Improvement* Council (NESIC)—were curbed. Most important, states were under no obligation to submit their own standards to NESIC for approval in order to receive Goals 2000 funds, nor were they required to adopt standards that had received NESIC's blessing.[89] At the same time, the Pew Forum on K–12 Education Reform perceptively noted, "while Goals 2000 authorizes the establishment of voluntary national standards, the actual function of those standards and the "how-to's" of their elaboration and certification are still to be determined."[90]

Just as Clinton appealed to Democrats' interest in educational equity, the administration tapped into a core Republican concern by linking Goals 2000 to the nation's economic competitiveness. "If we don't meet the challenges [of today's global economy], then we face, as futurists say, an unacceptable future for many of today's children and many of our communities," Secretary Riley warned in testimony before Congress. "The 'Goals 2000: Educate America Act' is about our first step as a nation to make an acceptable, brighter future for America's children and youth in a very comprehensive, cohesive way."[91] On their own, Riley's arguments may have sounded empty or unconvincing to an increasingly conservative Republican caucus. But the administration's claims were given a major boost by business entrepreneurs, who rallied to support the legislation as it wended its way through Congress. As they had promised administration officials, major business associations executed a comprehensive lobbying blitz—replete with personal visits, letter writing, editorial writing, and so forth—to build support for Goals 2000.[92] According to Susan Traiman of the Business Roundtable, the state business organizations coordinated by the Business Roundtable to promote standards-based reforms also got involved in the act, lobbying members of Congress to back the initiative.[93] Such maneuvers led *Education Week* to conclude in June 1994, after the legislation's enactment, that "the Chamber of Commerce, the N.A.B., and other business groups were key allies in passing the Goals 2000: Educate America Act, the Clinton Administration's education-reform plan."[94]

As should be clear, Goals 2000 was not the first choice of either congressional Democrats or congressional Republicans. However, Clinton's forceful legislative leadership, aided by the efforts of business entrepreneurs to round up votes, helped forge a legislative compromise that fell within the "zone of acceptable outcomes" of enough members of Congress to ensure passage. In the House, the Goals 2000 conference report passed by a 305–121 vote and received 59 Republican votes in addition to those of 246 Democrats. After defeating a filibuster on school prayer by conservative Republican senator Jesse Helms of North Carolina, the Senate ultimately passed Goals 2000 by a vote of 63–22, with 10 crucial Republicans joining 53 Democrats in support of the legislation.[95]

When Congress turned to the Improving America's Schools Act, many of the same concerns that attended debate over Goals 2000 resurfaced, intensified by policymakers' realization that, given states' and localities' dependence on ESEA aid, the administration's bill would effectively force states to adopt standards-based reforms. Enacting the ambitious IASA program thus required a reprise of the cross-partisan coalition building that paved the way for passage of Goals 2000. Clinton again played an important role in mediating between educational liberals, educational conservatives, and state leaders, both by blocking "deal-breaking" proposals and by offering appealing concessions. To placate educational liberals who feared the consequences of test-based accountability for students, teachers, and schools, Clinton's bill eschewed the tough accountability sanctions envisioned by the Commission on Chapter 1. But the president again intervened to block a sweeping "opportunity to learn" proposal, offered by Democratic representative Major Owens of New York, that was supported by much of the House Democratic caucus but reviled by Republicans. The Clinton administration also made positive efforts to reach out to congressional Republicans and their affiliated educational conservative interest groups. In a nod to conservatives' concern about overweening federal involvement, the IASA prohibited the federal government from appraising the content of state policies.[96] Moreover, supporters of federal standards, testing, and accountability reforms had to accept a provision championed by conservative Republican senator Judd Gregg of New Hampshire that forbid the imposition of "unfunded mandates" through the IASA, which gave states a potential weapon for checking federal rules they deemed excessively burdensome.[97]

Astute as they were, Clinton's legislative maneuvers would probably have foundered if not for the parallel efforts of civil rights entrepreneurs. Civil rights appeals helped draw in the top Democratic education policymakers in the Senate, Edward Kennedy of Massachusetts and Claiborne Pell of Rhode Island, who emerged as early sponsors and advocates of the IASA. With enthusiastic support from George Miller of California in the House, civil rights entrepreneurs consolidated a powerful reform coalition. As William Taylor recalls,

> As had been the case with every important civil rights measure, our leader in the Senate was Ted Kennedy, who chaired the education committee at that time. In the House, George Miller, a longtime congressman from San Francisco who had a deep commitment to educational opportunity for poor children, provided intellectual energy and passion. For the most part, we found that we were able to fly under the radar in moving the [Improving America's Schools Act] forward. Most Republicans favored block grants to the states and waivers of requirements, ideas that were antithetical to the principle that school authorities should be held accountable for student progress. But many were also amenable to separate legislation that would make accountability a part of reform.[98]

At the same time, civil rights entrepreneurs sought to educate Democratic members about the merits of the IASA, arguing that higher standards and accountability for results would create more-equitable educational opportunities for poor and minority students. Ultimately, as John Jennings explained, David

Hornbeck, Kati Haycock, and other civil rights–oriented education reformers "influenced liberals by creating a more open attitude that changes should be made to Title I of the Elementary and Secondary Education Act."[99] Although civil rights entrepreneurs failed in their efforts to garner support for "opportunity to learn" standards, they enjoyed greater success in generating Democratic enthusiasm for federal leadership of standards-based reforms. Indeed, the arguments of civil rights entrepreneurs and their allies in the Clinton administration echoed in congressional debate over the IASA. Explaining his support for the legislation, Democratic senator Ben Campbell of Colorado argued that

> when we look at the progress of our schools, however, we discover what our young people have not learned as opposed to what they have learned. All too often the high school diploma is a certificate of attendance instead of a certificate of knowledge. There is an uneven playing field in education. Expectations of students differ not only between socioeconomic classes, but from State to State, and for college-bound students and the forgotten student group that goes to the work force immediately after high school. We need a national framework to funnel our efforts and to reach the 35 percent of our kids who are not ready to participate successfully in school.[100]

The attractiveness of the IASA to members of Congress—especially Republicans—was undoubtedly increased because it enjoyed support from the same business entrepreneurs who were already working hand in hand with Clinton officials on the Goals 2000 legislation. The Commission on Chapter 1's *Making Schools Work for Children in Poverty* fit perfectly with business entrepreneurs' desire to promote standards-based reforms around the nation, leading the NAB's Kolberg (who, of course, served on the commission) to gush that "we're trying to take this largest and most important federal program...and see if through this lever we can achieve the kind of radical reform I think we all see as necessary."[101] Responding to entreaties from Kolberg and other Chapter 1 commissioners, the business community lined up to support the commission's approach, according to Tom Lindsley.[102] In addition to working behind the scenes on behalf of the legislation, business entrepreneurs made a highly visible statement of support during the House's consideration of the IASA conference report. Declaring in a public letter to House Education and Labor Committee chairman William Ford and ranking Republican William Goodling that "ESEA passage will guarantee that for the first time in this nation's history there will be a comprehensive framework and the appropriate federal incentives to support widespread systemic reform efforts," the National Alliance of Business, the U.S. Chamber of Commerce, the

Committee for Economic Development, and the American Business Conference all urged members of Congress to "put partisan differences aside and pass ESEA to help support the long term educational progress and economic security of our nation's future workforce."[103]

In truth, the powerful efforts by the Clinton administration, civil rights entrepreneurs, and business entrepreneurs to promote a standards-based overhaul of the ESEA ultimately induced much of the education community to endorse the IASA. Though the IASA departed from many of the stated objectives of the major teacher and administrator groups, it preserved core ESEA programs and devolved many responsibilities to states and localities (which these groups believed—correctly, as it turned out—would allow them considerable flexibility in implementing reforms within schools). Realizing that IASA reforms protected many important interests, and allowed them discretion in implementing new measures, these groups preferred to see the legislation enacted into law rather than watch it go down to defeat, thereby imperiling essential funding for ongoing education programs for the next fiscal year. According to Jack Jennings, who closely observed the politics surrounding enactment of the IASA from his position on the House Education and Labor Committee staff, "The education community was united and worked hard to secure enactment of the bill.…The national elementary and secondary education organizations pulled together as they had not for many years, and the results showed."[104]

These developments helped carry a major piece of legislation that could easily have fallen victim to battles over standards, testing, "opportunity to learn," school choice, the funding formula, or divisive amendments on social issues such as school prayer, gay rights, and school distribution of condoms (the last three of which were raised by very conservative Republicans in a bid to embarrass Democrats or defeat the bill). Although the vote on the IASA conference report was shaped by partisanship—no doubt due to its proximity to the 1994 congressional elections—the report passed the House 262–132, with 31 Republicans joining 230 Democrats in favor. In the Senate, the breadth of the reform coalition was evinced by the strong vote for cloture of debate on the IASA conference report (75–24, with 19 Republicans supporting) and the final vote on enactment (77–20, with 21 of 41 present Republicans voting in favor).[105]

By October 1994, therefore, Clinton could trumpet an education record exceeding that of every president since Lyndon Johnson. Together, Goals 2000 and the Improving America's Schools Act fundamentally shifted the federal role in education from an emphasis on compensatory education toward a new focus on standards-based reform. As Clinton expected, and as business entrepreneurs and civil rights entrepreneurs hoped, the two acts were to work in tandem to pressure states to adopt coordinated systems of standards, tests, and accountability to hold all children to the same high standards. According to Marshall Smith,

> What Goals 2000 did was give enough money to states, to allow them to put together standards, so it facilitated it, and it provided a structure of sorts. But Title I [of the Improving America's Schools Act] with $8 billion drove it.... Once Congress has said there's going to be a time schedule on this thing, you're going to have standards-based reform in your states.... You lay out this agenda, and people follow agendas like that.[106]

As should be clear, however, Clinton's legislative victories came at the price of compromising some of the more visionary aspects of the federal standards-based reform agenda touted by business entrepreneurs and civil rights entrepreneurs. Federal involvement in promoting standards-based reform was moderated—both during the formulation of the two initiatives and in the debates over their enactment—to secure the approval of educational liberals, educational conservatives, and state leaders, effectively devolving to states and localities some of the most important decisions about how to reform schools, such as the content of standards, assessments, and accountability measures.[107] Ultimately, a Department of Education report later explained, "the standards-based reform framework reflected in both ESEA and Goals 2000 maintains state responsibility and local control of education by supporting states in establishing their own standards for what students should know and be able to do" and recognized that states and localities "carry the main responsibility for elementary and secondary education in this country."[108] Whether this approach would prove successful remained to be seen.

A new federal role in education—albeit one constrained by existing institutional and political realities—was established in 1994 as a result of the enactment of Goals 2000 and the IASA. As this chapter has shown, a framework that considers institutionally bounded entrepreneurship offers important new insights into these developments. First, the leadership of business and civil rights entrepreneurs was essential to the expansion of federal authority in standards, testing, and accountability in education. These entrepreneurs were motivated by the failure of states and localities to manage school reforms on their own and a belief that enhanced federal involvement in education reform would force the issue. Business entrepreneurs and civil rights entrepreneurs generated major policy proposals, engaged in advocacy to get their ideas on the federal agenda, crafted policy frames that appealed to multiple audiences, and built diverse coalitions favoring their proposed reforms. Working closely with the Clinton administration—and sometimes from within the Clinton administration—these figures helped create conditions favorable to the passage of Goals 2000 and the IASA.

In the politically polarized and closely divided 103rd Congress, only legislative initiatives that could secure support from both Democrats and Republicans could be enacted into law. The core constituencies for federal standards, testing, and accountability measures presented their proposals in ways that attracted supporters on both sides of the legislative aisle. This creative synthesis of conservative and liberal themes made federal standards, testing, and accountability reforms attractive to a comparatively broad swath of policymakers and interests and eased their passage into law. Working on a parallel path with the Clinton administration, business entrepreneurs and civil rights entrepreneurs tied appealing rhetoric to a tireless legislative lobbying campaign that helped draw in legislative champions and sway wavering members to support federal standards-based reforms. The broad appeal of the agenda sponsored by business entrepreneurs and civil rights entrepreneurs differed markedly from that of either educational liberals or educational conservatives, accounting for its relative political success.

Even as business and civil rights entrepreneurs worked to shape the trajectory of federal education policymaking, they found that their efforts were significantly bounded by the existing political and institutional landscape. Eager to build on popular existing programs, and hemmed in by limited budgetary resources and ambivalent public support, entrepreneurs relied heavily on federal categorical grants to achieve their objectives, most notably by layering the Improving America's Schools Act atop the venerable structure of the ESEA. Reliance upon the existing structures of federalism was reinforced in the legislative process. As noted above, Clinton administration officials, business entrepreneurs, and civil rights entrepreneurs made pragmatic compromises with skeptics of Goals 2000 and the IASA in order to secure their acquiescence to these initiatives. But these compromises had important programmatic costs. Most important, states and localities were given primary responsibility to implement standards-based reforms. Because states and localities varied considerably in their will and capacity to institute these measures, the two acts invited divergences between what business entrepreneurs and civil rights entrepreneurs envisioned and what many states and localities were positioned to deliver. As political conditions shifted in a more conservative, antigovernment direction following the "Republican Revolution" of 1994, these gaps widened in many states. In this hostile climate, business entrepreneurs and civil rights entrepreneurs faced the daunting task of revitalizing the movement for federal leadership of standards, testing, and accountability.

THE ROAD TO NO CHILD LEFT BEHIND, 1995–2002

The enactment of the No Child Left Behind (NCLB) Act in 2002 was a major moment in the evolution of federal involvement in education. No Child Left Behind intensified the development begun with the Improving America's Schools Act of 1994, in which new conditions of aid were layered atop the Elementary and Secondary Education Act to pressure states to adopt coordinated standards, assessments, and accountability reforms. In an important departure from the IASA, No Child Left Behind imposed relatively detailed demands on states and localities in exchange for access to federal education aid. Under NCLB, states were to test every student in grades 3–8 each year in math, reading, and science; establish a plan for bringing all students to "academic proficiency" by 2014; ensure that each group of students (such as nonwhites, impoverished students, and the disabled) within each school made "adequate yearly progress" toward proficiency every year; implement an escalating series of consequences for schools in which groups of students did not make adequate yearly progress; undertake reforms to ensure that all students were taught by "highly qualified" teachers; and participate every other year in the National Assessment of Educational Progress. The specificity of NCLB's regulations allowed federal policymakers to shape state and local policies to an unprecedented degree. "By requiring specific changes in the basic assessment and accountability systems of states, establishing timelines for improving student achievement, outlining specific sanctions for low-performing school, and commanding many other forms of specific state action," Gail Sunderman and James Kim note, "NCLB...expanded federal power to regulate education."[1]

NCLB also continued and elaborated the shift in the understanding of educational equity begun with enactment of the IASA. By requiring states to adopt the same standards and assessments for all students, the IASA had sought to alter the purpose of the underlying Elementary and Secondary Education Act from a compensatory program that provided additional resources and opportunities for disadvantaged students to a system-wide program that conceptualized "equity" in terms of academic outcomes. No Child Left Behind maintained this approach, insisting on "equality of outcomes" (in the words of political scientist Scott Abernathy) for every child.[2] Under NCLB, however, the enforcement of "equality of outcomes" was to be much more rigorous. Since schools were to be accountable for the achievement of "subgroups" of students, as well as for the "average" student, they could be subject to sanction if even one subgroup failed to make adequate academic progress. Furthermore, the sanctions against schools that did not improve the performance of disadvantaged students were to be much more specific and severe under NCLB, culminating in "restructuring," state takeover, or forced closure. In short, if the IASA aspired to greater equity in terms of academic achievement, NCLB seemed to insist on it, enforcing its demands with the threat of significant sanctions.

Highlighting the impressive scope of NCLB's reforms, some scholars have suggested that the law represented a fundamental break from the past, inaugurating a new era of federal leadership in education.[3] An overemphasis on NCLB's novel features obscures striking continuities with enduring institutional practices, however. In truth, NCLB bore the marks of prior institutional developments. Even as it intensified the regulatory demands of the IASA, NCLB reaffirmed its predecessor's practice of layering standards-based reforms atop that venerable categorical grant, the Elementary and Secondary Education Act. Rather than transform federal education capabilities or fundamentally recast institutional arrangements, therefore, NCLB piled new regulations on old programs. Furthermore, because NCLB piggybacked on the ESEA's system of categorical grants, it delegated considerable policymaking authority to states and localities by default. This fact was likely to have crucial consequences for the implementation of the law over time. Because states and localities varied widely in their political conditions, legal arrangements, and administrative capabilities, the prospects for comprehensive standards, testing, and accountability reforms remained uncertain under the terms of the new law. If NCLB shifted the playing field in favor of more-uniform adherence to the standards-based reform vision, it also invited high-stakes intergovernmental struggles over the scope of the law's implementation.

Why did policymakers enact No Child Left Behind only a few years after adopting two groundbreaking policies in 1994? And why, despite their increased rigor, did the new reforms remain wedded to a set of aging categorical grants that delegated to states and localities many of the most important decisions about how schools were to be reformed? In this chapter I answer these questions, showing that the interplay between institutional constraints and political entrepreneurship explains the bounded character of institutional change between 1994 and 2002. Ironically, the undoing of the Goals 2000 / Improving America's Schools Act regime began almost before the ink on the two pieces of legislation had dried. The Republican Revolution of 1994 crippled implementation of Goals 2000 and the IASA, effectively devolving to state and local governments the initiative to implement standards-based reforms. Left to their own devices, few states by the end of the decade had established the comprehensive reforms touted by business entrepreneurs and civil rights entrepreneurs as the keys to successful school improvement.

While Clinton officials soft-pedaled standards-based reforms to placate Republican opponents of federal involvement in education, business entrepreneurs and civil rights entrepreneurs renewed their crusade for federal leadership of standards, testing, and accountability reforms, arguing that state lapses justified even more-expansive federal rules and requirements to ensure that all children enjoyed access to high-quality schools. Between 1995 and 2000, these figures undertook the painstaking task of rebuilding the legitimacy of federal education leadership with policymakers in Congress and the Clinton administration. Aided by the slow progress of reforms in the states—which undercut states' claim to mastery of standards-based reforms—business entrepreneurs and civil rights entrepreneurs gradually succeeded in winning influential recruits to their cause by the end of the decade. Because they had already laid the groundwork between 1995 and 2000, business entrepreneurs and civil rights entrepreneurs were in a strong position to advocate for a more muscular federal role in education after George W. Bush took office in January 2001. Following his election, Bush provided additional momentum for expanded federal leadership by embracing standards, testing, and accountability reforms and advocating tirelessly for a standards-based overhaul of the ESEA.

In fact, the expansion of federal authority in education was possible because supporters of federal leadership of standards-based reform, now succored by a supportive new president, renewed the bipartisan reform coalition they had assembled in 1994. Whereas educational liberals and educational conservatives again pursued divisive reform strategies, featuring, on the one hand, expanded spending, and on the other, various measures to promote private school choice and regulatory reform, business entrepreneurs and civil rights entrepreneurs attracted both Republicans and Democrats to their cause by crafting appeals that resonated across the partisan divide. Meanwhile, George W. Bush's legislative strategy showed that he had learned from the unhappy experience of his father.

Rather than lead a hopeless crusade for school vouchers, Bush played the role of cross-partisan conciliator, isolating the more extreme members in both parties and building on areas of bipartisan agreement.

NCLB represented a major expansion of federal authority in education, but the law was indubitably shaped by the existing political landscape. Existing policy legacies, an uncertain fiscal environment, and popular misgivings about the expansion of federal authority all encouraged supporters of federal leadership to continue the practice of layering standards-based reforms atop an entrenched program rather than establishing novel arrangements. In practice, this meant that the federal government would set the agenda for standards, testing, and accountability reform to a much greater extent than in the past, but that states and localities would still have primary responsibility—and, hence, considerable discretion—in implementing reforms on the ground. In reality, NCLB represented an untidy compromise, both pushing federal authority to new frontiers and creating numerous new opportunities for state and local challenges to federal power.

I begin this chapter by reviewing how the so-called Republican Revolution affected the progress of standards-based reforms in Congress and the states between 1994 and 2000. Next, I show how these developments shaped the ideas and advocacy of business entrepreneurs, civil rights entrepreneurs, and their allies in Congress. After tracing the various threads that contributed to the reemergence of support for federal leadership of standards-based reform, I examine the politics surrounding enactment of NCLB, both to explain why the legislation passed and understand how it accommodated existing interests and institutions. To conclude, I consider how enactment of NCLB set the stage for subsequent intergovernmental struggles over authority in education—in particular, how it influenced presidential candidate Barack Obama's education agenda in the 2008 election campaign.

The Republican Revolution and the Decline of Goals 2000 and the IASA

On the heels of Clinton's education policy victories, which had seemed to signal a shift toward greater federal involvement in schooling, the policy terrain shifted radically, and in a much more conservative direction. In what was dubbed the "Republican Revolution," the GOP gained fifty-two seats in the House and eight in the Senate in the 1994 midterm elections, seizing unified control of Congress for the first time in forty years. Led by Newt Gingrich of Georgia, who grandiloquently promised voters "the first decisive step back to create a century of freedom for the entire human race," the new Republican majority was stridently conservative and intent on substantially reducing the federal government's role in the economy and society.[4] The GOP's disciplined 1994 campaign featured a "Contract with America," designed by Gingrich, which touted traditional conservative policy proposals such as tax cuts, welfare reform, increased defense spending, a balanced budget amendment, tort reform, and tougher law enforcement. Though education was not a primary focus of the GOP's 1994 campaign, the conservative Republicans' victory had profound implications for the Clinton administration's signature education initiatives. Whereas the Democratic majority had grudgingly supported Goals 2000 and the Improving America's Schools Act, the new Republican majority staunchly opposed federal support for standards-based reforms. Operating under a mandate to "Privatize, Localize, Consolidate, [and] Eliminate," a House Education Task Force set up by the new majority recommended in May 1995 the elimination of the Department of Education and the transformation of the Elementary and Secondary Education Act into a block grant. Republicans also sought to convert Goals 2000 into a block grant, thereby abolishing its standards and testing requirements.[5] Finally, the Republican-dominated House budget committee proposed to balance the federal budget in part by slashing $12.4 billion from the federal education budget, eradicating 150 of the Department of Education's 240 programs. The proposals of Senate Republicans were somewhat less draconian but generally followed the House's emphasis on budget cutting and grant consolidation.

Faced with hostile majorities in both houses of Congress, the Clinton administration was forced to recalibrate its approach to federal education policymaking. The president held the line on the federal education budget, challenging Republicans' plans to balance the budget by slashing federal education spending. Arguing that it was short-sighted and dangerous to make cuts to federal education aid, Clinton proposed to balance the budget by making cuts to other programs.[6] In his 1996 State of the Union address, Clinton vowed to protect education (as well as popular programs such as Medicare and Medicaid) in order to "balance the budget in a way that is fair to all Americans."[7] As Patrick McGuinn argues, Clinton's stand on federal education spending deftly cast Republicans as the enemies of public education, rather than as principled opponents of creeping federal control of schools.

Given that educational entrepreneurs (including educational conservatives associated with the Republican Party) had long claimed that education was an important issue demanding national attention, Republicans' apparent change of heart left the public cold.[8] An April 1996 poll found that Americans favored Clinton over Republicans by a margin of 56 percent to 32 percent when it came to handling education.[9] "It has been very clear and very consistent that there's strong public support for education and strong antipathy for anyone who wants to cut education," explained Mark Mellman, a pollster who helped craft Clinton's strategy. "[Education] is sort of vague at the federal level, but it's a for-it-or-against-it kind of thing. And if you're against it, you're in trouble."[10] Realizing that their radical views on education-spending matters had put them on the wrong side of public opinion, Republicans reversed course, "[giving] up their efforts to cut federal education spending and instead embrac[ing] large increases" of several billion dollars.[11] In the late 1990s, Republicans developed a more nuanced message on education issues, calling for federal programs that provided assistance for education while devolving decision-making to lower levels of government and (in the case of vouchers) to the private sector.

Clinton's apparent victory on the education *spending* front—undoubtedly facilitated by many representatives' (including Republicans') desire to continue channeling federal education funds to their districts—did not mean that federal *standards-based reforms* such as Goals 2000 and the IASA were safe from criticism, however. Realizing that conservative Republicans found the Goals 2000 program odious, Department of Education officials sought to minimize the law's regulatory impact in order to head off further scrutiny. An internal departmental memorandum from November 1995 laid out some priorities to "put into place and implement an effective federal administrative structure for the K–12 federal programs including G[oals] 2000"; at the top of the list were "high quality and *minimal* regulations" and "useful and high quality *non-regulatory* guidance."[12] In the year following enactment of the law, Education officials declined to issue regulatory rules governing use of Goals 2000 funds, allowing states maximum flexibility to use the funds as they saw fit. These efforts failed to satisfy Republican conservatives, however, who won a series of amendments to overhaul Goals 2000 in 1996. The National Education Standards and Improvement Council (NESIC), which was intended to provide some measure of quality control over state and local reforms, was abolished. Republicans also passed amendments to permit states to use Goals 2000 moneys to purchase technology instead of fund the development of standards and assessments, and to allow states to receive Goals 2000 funds without submitting plans detailing how they intended to use the funds. Another amendment released states from the obligation to develop "standards or strategies" to ensure "opportunity to learn."[13] Although Secretary Riley unconvincingly claimed that "there isn't anything [in the amendments] ... that undermines or in any way alters the fundamental goals of the program," these changes obliterated Goals 2000's emphasis on standards-based reforms, effectively transforming the act into a block grant for education-related expenses.[14]

Meanwhile, Clinton was backing away from efforts to hold states, localities, and schools to the requirements of the Improving America's Schools Act. Fearing that rigorous enforcement of the IASA would challenge the norm of allowing states to set their own education agendas, and thereby antagonize conservative Republicans, Secretary Riley circulated a "Dear Senator" letter in July 1995 promising that "we will regulate only when absolutely necessary, and then in the most limited, non-burdensome way possible." Under Riley's new approach, outlined in the letter, the department would issue no regulations for thirty-eight IASA programs and only "limited regulatory guidance" for seven additional programs.[15] Administration officials subsequently granted generous waivers to states and localities seeking relief from federal education regulations, and turned a blind eye when legal deadlines established under the act were not met.[16]

Even the president's impressive victory over Republican challenger Robert Dole in the 1996 presidential election did not bring about a revitalization of the Goals 2000 / IASA regime. Strikingly, Clinton's postelection agenda seemed to borrow a page from the educational liberal playbook, featuring school uniforms, school construction and renovation, class-size reduction, investments in Head Start, and scholarships for college attendance, rather than a systematic standards-based approach.[17] Clinton's 1997 State of the Union address, which featured a "call to action for American education," included only two initiatives related to the standards-based reform agenda: voluntary national tests in reading and math, and expanded federal support for charter schools.[18] In an indication of the administration's hesitance to pursue vigorous federal involvement, the voluntary national tests initiative was extremely modest, proposing short examinations in math and reading in the fourth and eighth grades. Even this modest proposal died with a whimper, however, a victim of cross-partisan political backlash. Educational liberals worried that tests would discriminate against disadvantaged students and make teachers and schools accountable for results, while educational conservatives complained that the tests were the first step toward the nationalization of the curriculum. Banding together in an unusual alliance in 1997 and 1998, educational liberals and educational conservatives dealt Clinton a major defeat by delaying federal involvement in testing until after the 2000 elections.[19]

The shifting political winds placed the initiative for implementing standards-based reforms in the hands of state and local governments. State-level differences began to take their toll on the standards, testing, and accountability agenda almost immediately, illustrating the significant constraints imposed on the standards-based agenda by the institution of federalism. By 1998, according to the letter of the IASA, states were supposed to have enacted both content standards specifying what students were supposed to know and be able to do in reading and math, and performance standards specifying achievement levels in these subjects. While every state adopted content standards in the two subjects, only twenty-two states established performance standards by the deadline (and only twenty-eight had done so by 2001). Since the creation of assessments depended on prior agreement on content and performance standards, state adoption of assessments fell behind schedule. Only eleven states' assessment systems had received full approval from the Department of Education by the 2001 deadline, with twenty others receiving either conditional approval (six states) or a timeline waiver (fourteen states) to finish their examination systems.[20]

Under the IASA, states were responsible for collecting and reporting data on assessment outcomes and devising criteria to hold schools and districts accountable for them, but many struggled to institute meaningful reforms. In 2001 the General Accounting Office reported that many states were "not positioned to hold schools and districts accountable for outcomes of disadvantaged students" due to uneven collection and reporting of student performance data and inconsistent use of exemptions to exclude certain students from accountability tests.[21] The GAO also warned that the formulas used by many states to calculate the progress of schools in raising student achievement were flawed. In some states, the formula grossly exaggerated the number of struggling schools, overwhelming state education agencies and spreading resources too thin. Other states had the opposite problem: by employing lax standards, they made it appear as if virtually no schools were in trouble and thus relieved themselves of the burden of instituting corrective measures.[22]

Over and above these challenges, states struggled to hold all schools to the same high standards. Indeed, rather than hold schools serving concentrations of disadvantaged students to the same standards, states frequently created an inequitable, two-tier system. According to a 2001 Citizens' Commission on Civil Rights report, "about half (28) of the states operate dual systems of accountability in which either: 1) Title 1 and non-Title 1 schools are held accountable using different sets of indicators and/or performance standards or 2) only Title 1 schools are held accountable by the state or district outside of the performance reporting structure."[23] What business entrepreneurs and, especially, civil rights entrepreneurs most feared had apparently come to pass: the IASA had not succeeded in pushing states and localities to adopt high standards for all students.

The Renewal of the Campaign for Federal Leadership of Standards-Based Reforms

Given business entrepreneurs' commitment to federal leadership of the standards-based reform agenda, it is small wonder that these entrepreneurs were disheartened by the impact of the Republican Revolution on Goals 2000 and the IASA.

As Joseph T. Gorman of TRW and the Business Roundtable Education Task Force exclaimed in June 1995, "Everybody understood it was going to be a long, hard journey. I think there is a greater commitment today than five years ago. But there is also a real sense of frustration because we have not been able to move the ball as far down the field as we would have liked."[24]

Conservative Republicans' hostility to federal leadership in education, coupled with the Clinton administration's unwillingness to fight for federal standards-based reforms, convinced business entrepreneurs that they had to increase political pressure on state leaders if they were to make progress. Louis Gerstner, chairman and CEO of IBM and an important figure in Business Coalition for Education Reform and Business Roundtable circles, took the lead in registering business entrepreneurs' disapproval and pressuring state and local leaders to commit to implementing standards-based reforms. Invited by the National Governors Association to address the assembled governors at their 1995 meeting, Gerstner lambasted his audience for failing to provide leadership, criticizing (in the words of one observer) governors' "lack of follow-through on education issues, particularly the need to go from goals to specific standards for what children must learn to be promoted from grade to grade and to graduate from high school."[25] Apparently struck by the sharpness of Gerstner's tone, Tommy Thompson, Republican governor of Wisconsin and chairman of the NGA, responded to the challenge by proposing that business entrepreneurs and governors jointly sponsor a second "Education Summit" to promote standards-based reforms.[26] Business entrepreneurs jumped at the opportunity: individual corporate CEOs, including Gerstner, Robert Allen of AT&T, John Clendenin of BellSouth, George Fisher of Eastman Kodak, John Pepper of Procter & Gamble, and Frank Shrontz of Boeing, played a central role in organizing the proposed summit.

Held March 26–27, 1996, at Gerstner's IBM campus in Palisades, New York, the second Education Summit drew more than forty governors and fifty business leaders, as well as a visit from President Clinton. According to contemporary observers, business leaders took a leading role at the summit, "[sending] a very powerful signal to the governors that education reform was a major priority for corporate America."[27] Gerstner, the event's plenary session speaker, made a vigorous case for immediate action, calling on state leaders to "take risks" and "start to make change happen."[28] In line with Gerstner's exhortations, business attendees at the meeting pressured reluctant governors—many of whom were unenthusiastic about subjecting their states to external scrutiny—into agreeing to create a new "entity," called Achieve, to benchmark state standards and monitor states' progress in raising student achievement.[29]

Even so, the results business entrepreneurs were looking for were slow in coming. A year after the establishment of the new "entity," Achieve could point to few accomplishments.[30] Meanwhile, state and local efforts to institute standards-based reforms dragged on inconclusively. The case can be made, however, that the 1996 summit reinvigorated business entrepreneurs' commitment to the crusade for standards-based reforms. In September 1996, building on conversations stimulated by the activity surrounding the summit, they pledged themselves to the goals of "helping educators and policymakers set tough academic standards, applicable to every student in every school;…assessing student and school-system performance against those standards; [and] using that information to improve schools and create accountability, including rewards for success and consequences for failure."[31]

Frustrated that progress on standards, testing, and accountability reforms remained stalled at the state level—and gaining momentum from growing public antipathy to the Republican Party's strident attack on the federal role in education—business entrepreneurs quickly returned to a full-throated advocacy of federal leadership of standards-based reforms. Susan Traiman, who coordinated education programs with the Business Roundtable, remembered that

> we believed in the idea that the entire nation needed to compete against the world in terms of education. It wasn't sufficient for states to merely compete against one another to see which could produce the highest standards and the best students; as we saw it, that wasn't the right perspective. It was the whole nation that needed to compete. The federal government was in the best position to create clarity about academic expectations and to provide ways for measuring the performance of the nation's students.[32]

Moreover, in light of the disappointing experience of the implementation of the IASA, business leaders resolved to fight much harder for legislative language that would lay out specific testing and accountability requirements. In the words of Sandy Boyd, who worked on education issues with the National Association of Manufacturers in the 1990s, "there was definite interest in building a system in which it was possible to pressure the laggard states to adopt comprehensive reforms."[33]

Business entrepreneurs' renewed commitment to prescriptive federal involvement in education spoke to the power of institutional memory embodied in organizations such as the Business Roundtable's fifty-state reform effort and the National Alliance of Business's Center for Excellence in Education. Providing institutional presence and stability over the course of nearly a decade, business organizations such as these gave business entrepreneurs the ability to remember policy lessons and learn from past reform efforts. This learning capacity was further enhanced by the hundreds of affiliated state and local business coalitions working on education issues in virtually every state, which regularly reported on their (lack of) progress in implementing standards based reforms.[34] The memory of the failures engendered by relatively soft regulatory policies stimulated among business leaders an appetite for more-vigorous efforts by the federal government. "Having been thwarted by lax federal implementation and a lack of progress in the states," explained Milton Goldberg, a prominent figure in the National Alliance of Business during the 1990s, "business leaders felt like the 'tunnel' of education reform was growing too long. By the late 1990s, they were looking for light at the end of the tunnel, in terms of requirements for proficiency, progress, and accountability."[35]

Thus, in a series of high-level meetings between 1997 and 1999, the leaders of the Business Coalition for Education Reform (BCER) drew on input from the Business Roundtable, the U.S. Chamber of Commerce, the National Alliance of Business, the National Association of Manufacturers, and other major business organizations to forge consensus on major principles for the reauthorization of the ESEA. According to contemporaneous documents, they also "sought advice from our collective memberships and from a network of over 500 state and local business-led coalitions across the country working directly on these education priorities."[36] The product of years of formal and informal conversations, the Business Coalition's statement of principles called on policymakers to further intensify the federal commitment to standards, testing, and accountability reforms embedded in the IASA.[37] Ed Rust, chairman of State Farm Insurance and a major player in education circles within the business community, summarized the BCER's position in June 1999 congressional testimony:

> States should set clear expectations for academic content with substantial depth and breadth. Federal aid should be used to encourage continuous improvements in state academic standards and assessments, and the creation of sound accountability systems. Accountability should be measured by student performance results, not by administrative compliance, and those results should be disclosed publicly. Parents and the community at large should know how well their schools are doing and how they compare with schools elsewhere.[38]

Recognizing that the IASA had neglected the importance of teacher reform to broader standards-based reform, the BCER also insisted that the new ESEA reauthorization set standards for teachers, to ensure that "at a minimum, teachers…have expertise in the content areas they teach."

This approach diverged sharply from the paths being pursued by most Democrats and Republicans. Much to the enthusiastic approval of educational liberals, especially in the major teachers unions, many congressional Democrats made expanding federal *spending* on schooling their top priority in the late 1990s.

"Democrats believe that every public school must be a school where children are mastering the basics; where classrooms are not overcrowded; where the environment is safe, disciplined, and drug-free; where there are adequate textbooks and equipment; where teachers are well-qualified and dedicated; and where facilities are up-to-date and in good repair," House Democrats declared in 1999.[39] Between 1997 and 1999, most Democrats focused on expanding federal commitments to programs such as Even Start and Head Start and extending federal support to new teacher hiring, class-size reduction, and school rehabilitation and modernization initiatives.[40] Suggesting educational liberals' continuing focus on school resources, the House Democratic Policy Committee declared in March 1999 that "class size reduction is *our number-one education priority* in this session of Congress, and…Democrats intend to fulfill this important commitment to America's public schools."[41] This approach was popular, politically, but it also appealed directly to teachers' and administrators' interest in channeling additional funds to schools and strengthening their own economic and political position. Consequently, however, these proposals held little appeal with congressional Republicans, and made little headway.

If educational conservatives were retreating from the over-the-top rhetoric that had characterized the early Republican Revolution, they remained committed to their traditional agenda of private school vouchers, block grants, and consolidation. In July 1998, House Republicans unveiled a major report, "Education at a Crossroads," which maintained that "successful schools and school systems were not the product of federal funding and programs" but were characterized by "parents involved in the education of their children; local control; emphasis on basic academics; dollars spent on the classroom, not bureaucracy and ineffective programs."[42] Major Republican initiatives from the period reflected these conservative convictions. In September 1998, House Republicans pushed the "Dollars to the Classroom" bill, which combined thirty-one programs into a $2.74 billion block grant, through that chamber.[43] Another Republican bill, the "Teacher Empowerment Act" of 1998, consolidated several existing teacher improvement grants into a larger block grant to promote the improvement of teacher quality, the hiring of special-education teachers, and the reduction of class sizes. In June of the following year, Republicans announced the "Academic Achievement for All Act" (also known as "Straight A's" or "Super Ed-Flex"), which would have created a fifteen-state pilot program allowing participating states to transform fourteen federal education programs into block grants in exchange for a promise to the federal government to improve student achievement over a five-year period.[44] Mainstream Republican offerings thus echoed earlier educational conservative proposals—with their relatively limited political appeal—rather than novel recommendations that spoke to a broader audience.

In sum, neither congressional Democrats nor congressional Republicans seemed to be particularly receptive to entrepreneurial efforts to promote standards, testing, and accountability reforms in the mid- to late 1990s. In this unfavorable environment, business entrepreneurs engaged in what political scientists would call "softening up"—that is, sustaining a position with a view to shaping the agenda when political conditions improved.[45] But business entrepreneurs were not content merely to wait for more favorable conditions to emerge. All the while, they were working closely with rising Republican star and eventual Republican presidential nominee George W. Bush of Texas on an approach to further integrate standards, testing, and accountability reforms into federal education programs. In truth, the collaboration between business entrepreneurs and the Texas governor had deep roots. Led by Texas Chamber of Commerce chairman Glenn Biggs and chamber president Larry Milner, business leaders had founded the Texas Business and Education Coalition (TBEC) in 1989 to lobby in favor of standards-based reforms.[46] Closely affiliated with the Business Roundtable, TBEC played a central role in constructing Texas's education accountability regime: indeed, a TBEC founder chaired the commission that designed the state's system.[47] When Bush ran for governor of Texas in 1994, he realized that he needed to consolidate ties with the state's business community in order to achieve his educational objectives. Bush called on Sandy Kress, a TBEC board member and paid lobbyist for its government relations arm, to shape his education policy positions.[48] In the ensuing years, Kress served as the governor's unofficial education adviser and chief liaison to the Governor's Business Council, an advisory council of Texas CEOs.[49]

With the support of the state's business leaders, Bush refined Texas's standards and accountability system—then one of the most stringent in the nation—ending the practice of "social promotion," expanding testing, and increasing support for charter schools. Bush's steady administration of the state's standards and accountability regime earned plaudits from the business community: TBEC executive director John Stevens gushed in a 1999 editorial in the *Dallas Morning News* that "a fair analysis can lead to only one conclusion: George W. Bush has been good for education in Texas."[50] However, in a preview of future tensions between Bush and the increasingly conservative rank and file within the national Republican Party, the governor's emphasis on centralized standards and accountability for results made many of the state's conservative Republicans squeamish: like conservatives elsewhere, Texas conservatives would have preferred measures devolving control to local governments and opening schools to market competition.[51] Indeed, in 1998, *Texas Monthly* reported that a conservative "five-member faction on the [Texas State Board of Education]...since 1995 has formed a permanent and intractable opposition to Bush, to his education reforms, to his appointed education commissioner, Mike Moses, to the Texas Education Agency, which Moses heads, and to any colleague who doesn't fit their notions of what a conservative ought to be."[52]

Drawing on the lessons he had learned in Texas politics, Bush decided to make education reform a central pillar of his 2000 presidential campaign.[53] Bush's position reflected the pragmatic blend of accountability and opportunity that had served him so well as governor. The issue was pitched perfectly to illustrate the presidential candidate's "compassionate conservatism," soften the Republican Party's harsh "anti-government" image, and thereby win over moderate voters to the GOP banner.[54] Bush undoubtedly focused on education in significant part because the issue was riding high in the polls; indeed, in discussing education, he drew on many of the popular warrants for action that had been pioneered by proponents of "excellence in education" and standards-based reform since the 1980s.

Notably, however, Bush's approach remained closely informed by the standards, testing, and accountability reforms advocated by Texas's business community. These ties were based not only in shared ideology, but also in personnel: of considerable import, Bush hired erstwhile TBEC lobbyist Sandy Kress to serve as his chief education adviser. Reflecting business entrepreneurs' belief that the federal government needed to take a more central role in the standards-based reform movement, Kress urged the Republican presidential candidate to embrace a muscular approach to federal education policymaking that would use federal funds as a lever for promoting rigorous standards-based reforms in schools throughout the land. "Unhappily, after spending billions and billions of dollars on education, the federal government has made virtually no meaningful difference in helping educate our children," Kress wrote in a summer 1999 memorandum to Bush. "As a result of this cynical, shameful, and wasteful behavior, other politicians have decided that there should be no federal role in education at all."[55] Kress counseled that Bush should eschew the behavior of these "other politicians"—a barely veiled reference to conservative Republicans—and instead endorse an effort to build on the IASA by pressuring states and localities to adopt coordinated standards-based reforms.[56] Bush embraced Kress's (and TBEC's) counsel. As Kress later explained Bush's education strategy,

> A few states, notably Texas, North Carolina, and Massachusetts, developed comprehensive systems of standards, assessments, and accountability, and these states saw phenomenal gains in student achievement. But most other states were moving the ball forward only very slowly. No Child Left Behind was designed to further the standards based reform movement, to take it to every state in the nation. It was designed to take the wisdom from Texas, North Carolina, and Massachusetts, and extend it to all states.[57]

Compared with the attention given to the ideas of business entrepreneurs, Bush's engagement with the ideas of educational conservatives was modest at best. Though he took counsel from prominent educational conservatives, Bush downplayed vouchers and grant consolidation—the two issues closest to the hearts of these conservatives—focusing instead on the themes of annual testing and accountability for results.[58] In an indication of the gulf between the presidential candidate and the educational conservatives in the GOP caucus, Bush personally intervened to block an effort to make the abolition of the Department of Education a plank of the 2000 Republican Party platform.[59] According to Margaret Spellings, a close Bush education advisor who later became Bush's second secretary of education, "The standard shtick [among Republicans prior to 2000] had been 'abolish the Department of Education,' 'no federal intervention'—that sort of thing. And that changed with Bush."[60]

Bush won a hard-fought presidential contest against Democratic contender and vice president Al Gore, who had trumpeted his own package of education reforms during the campaign.[61] In the ensuing weeks, the president-elect wasted no time in drawing business entrepreneurs into his education councils. Indeed, according to Susan Traiman of the Business Roundtable, "Bush really reached out to the Business Roundtable and asked for our support. He asked us to work with him, arguing that additional federal involvement really could make a difference."[62] Predictably, the president's January 2001 "No Child Left Behind" blueprint, while paying lip service to school vouchers and grant consolidation, featured requirements to make ESEA funding conditional on state adoption of a highly specific array of standards, testing, and accountability reforms. Under the blueprint, states would have to establish content standards in reading, math, science, and history; institute annual assessments for every child in grades 3–8; report the progress of all students, disaggregated by race, gender, English language proficiency, disability, and socioeconomic status; expect yearly academic progress for each student; and institute a series of sanctions against low-performing schools, including offering public school choice, private school choice, and supplemental services.[63] Thrilled with the proposal, the Business Coalition for Excellence in Education—a larger successor organization to the Business Coalition for Education Reform—promised to lobby intensively for its enactment.[64]

To students of education policy, the linkages between the business community and Bush's education proposals may be familiar. The contributions of civil rights entrepreneurs to federal standards, testing, and accountability reforms are less well known, but no less important. Beneath the radar, civil rights entrepreneurs such as Kati Haycock, Phyllis McClure, David Hornbeck, William Taylor, and Dianne Piché spent the years following the Republican Revolution trying to revive support for federal leadership of standards-based reforms with members of Congress. These labors were undergirded by civil rights entrepreneurs' efforts to sustain and expand their organizations and networks. Perhaps most notable in this regard was the emergence of the Education Trust—founded by Haycock—as a major player on the education policy scene. The Education Trust's "only motivation [was] to improve achievement among poor and minority kids."[65] Securing stable funding from philanthropies such as the Ford Foundation, the Carnegie Corporation, and the Hewlett Foundation, the Education Trust played a central role in shaping the education debate in the late 1990s, according to contemporary accounts, in no small part due to its ability to generate timely information about the educational achievement of disadvantaged students.[66] Importantly, the Education Trust's ideas and analyses garnered it a strong reputation even beyond its traditional base with Democrats such as Edward Kennedy and George Miller. As Krista Kafer, who was with the Heritage Foundation in the late 1990s, explained, many educational conservatives "thought the Education Trust was great" due to its unwavering emphasis on accountability for results.[67]

In the mid-to-late 1990s, civil rights entrepreneurs sponsored a series of major research projects geared to shifting the debate on federal education policymaking. Some of these reports took direct aim at the behavior of federal policymakers, charging that their unwillingness to support federal standards-based reforms was directly responsible for the low achievement of disadvantaged students. Dianne Piché of the Citizens' Commission on Civil Rights (and a former member of the Commission on Chapter 1) issued a study in the fall of 1998, *Title I in Midstream,* which concluded that "the shortcomings of [Title I of the IASA] flow in large measure from the failure of federal, state and local officials to heed the call of the new law to renovate and reform the educational system." "There is wide variance in the degree to which states have complied with the requirements of the new Title I," Piché argued. "The federal government's failure to take the actions needed to implement and enforce the new Title I has also retarded educational progress."[68] The Center for Law and Education, an organization codirected by Paul Weckstein (another Commission on Chapter 1 member), released a similarly worded tract in the summer of 1999. Examining the implementation of the IASA in Wisconsin and Illinois, the center concluded that the two states "ignored the requirements that states ensure schools are moving toward an end-date by which time all students will meet standards, and that schools not doing so are identified as in need of improvement."[69] Echoing the Citizens' Commission on Civil Rights, the Center for Law and Education concluded that these developments undermined educational progress, especially for disadvantaged students.

To bolster the case for renewed federal leadership, civil rights entrepreneurs set out to provide concrete evidence that coordinated standards-based reforms raised student achievement, especially among poor and minority students. In perhaps the most ambitious such effort, the Education Trust administered a survey of twelve hundred high-performing schools serving concentrations of poor students in the fall of 1998 to identify the factors contributing to their effectiveness. Analyzing the data, Education Trust concluded that "the findings [of our analysis] seem to validate the policies" promoted by the Improving America's Schools Act.[70] Similar research efforts by leading civil rights entrepreneurs such as the Citizens' Commission on Civil Rights, Center for Law and Education, and Education Trust helped solidify support for the strengthening of federal standards-based reforms within the civil rights movement. Citing research by the Citizens' Commission on Civil Rights as a justification for its position, the Leadership Conference on Civil Rights, an umbrella coalition of civil rights organizations, declared in April 2000 that "the Leadership Conference on Civil Rights and many other civil rights organizations, parents and educators support measures to strengthen accountability so that all students, including poor and minority students, benefit from standards-based reform, as well as to provide parents the means to make their children's schools more responsive."[71]

As Charles Barone, then a chief legislative assistant for Democratic representative George Miller, recalls, the reports of organizations such as the Citizens' Commission on Civil Rights, the Education Trust, and the Center for Law and Education also helped revive enthusiasm for expanded federal leadership in school reform in Congress by "showing that states were using bad tests and weren't disaggregating their test score trends by race, poverty, and other characteristics."[72] With states struggling to implement standards-based reforms and test scores showing little sign of improvement, the claim that states and localities could reform schools on their own lost some of its luster, and it became easier to win members of Congress back to the idea that reinvigorated federal involvement was needed if schools were really going to improve. "Going state-by-state on standards and accountability was a very slow strategy," Kati Haycock explained. "It was becoming apparent to a lot of people in Congress and the education community that a much more efficient strategy was to get the feds to make them do it."[73]

As evidence mounted that states and localities had failed to make much educational progress, civil rights entrepreneurs found members of Congress increasingly ready to listen to their proposals. As the schedule for reauthorizing the IASA approached, civil rights entrepreneurs began to collaborate with influential Democrats on reform proposals.[74] As Haycock recalls, "Between 1998 and 2000 we were working with [George] Miller's and [Edward] Kennedy's staffs on the reauthorization. They were bonkers about what had happened to the IASA. They were ticked with the administration for its failure to enforce the IASA and with the states for failing to implement standards based reforms and get accountability for results."[75] Civil rights entrepreneurs and their Democratic allies agreed that the major lesson of the previous few years was that a mere return to the IASA status quo would not be sufficient to strengthen schools. What was needed was *intensified* federal involvement to promote standards, testing, and accountability reforms. The Education Trust insisted that "the accountability provisions established in the 1994 reauthorization of Title I provide a solid framework, but lessons learned since then point to shortcomings of the '94 amendments. Congress must use those lessons to *strengthen and improve* the law."[76]

Thus, in 1999, with the support of civil rights activists, Miller championed a Title I reform proposal, the "Student Results Act," which anticipated No Child Left Behind by mandating that states be held accountable for closing the achievement gap, bringing all students to proficiency within ten years, and assuring that all teachers were well qualified.[77] Perhaps surprisingly, given Republicans' continued dominance of the House, the Student Results Act proved popular, passing the House in a bipartisan vote. As the Student Results Act wended its way through the House, civil rights groups—led by the Center for Law and Education—teamed up with Democratic senator Jeff Bingaman of New Mexico to develop extremely specific interventions for schools that repeatedly failed to raise the achievement of disadvantaged students. As education policy scholar Elizabeth DeBray Pelot explains, these "policy proposals would survive into the 107th Congress and become the foundation for the accountability provisions in No Child Left Behind."[78]

The ideas championed by civil rights entrepreneurs even influenced the "Public Education Reinvestment, Reinvention, and Responsibility Act" of 1999 (often dubbed the "Three R's bill"), a proposal offered by Senate New Democrats that is widely viewed by scholars as a precursor of NCLB.[79] Three R's, which proposed to increase the flexibility of federal regulations in exchange for tougher accountability for academic achievement, is usually interpreted as an election-year gambit by New Democrats to seize the initiative on the increasingly salient issue of education. Yet, in developing the Three R's program, Progressive Policy Institute analyst Andrew Rotherham drew on the ideas that civil rights entrepreneurs had promoted throughout the 1990s. Rotherham assumed that the federal government would, in his words, "stay the course" on standards-based reform embedded in the IASA while adding new performance incentives, funding, and regulatory relief.[80] Perhaps more telling, Rotherham's memorandum outlining Three R's relied heavily on the recommendations in the Citizens' Commission on Civil Rights' 1999 missive, *Title I in Midstream: The Fight to*

Improve Schools for Poor Kids, to justify its approach.[81] The Three R's bill also apparently borrowed its accountability and adequate yearly progress language from the accountability proposal developed by civil rights entrepreneurs and Senator Bingaman.[82]

In short, and to a degree heretofore unappreciated, civil rights entrepreneurs made a large mark on the major preelection standards, testing, and accountability proposals. To be sure, in the midst of the 2000 presidential election campaign, each of the proposals described above failed to be enacted into law. Nonetheless, even Bush's close adviser Sandy Kress has called civil rights entrepreneurs the "intellectual fathers of NCLB" for their advocacy of policy provisions—notable for their stringent focus on the achievement of disadvantaged students—requiring states to report the assessment scores of subgroups of students and hold schools accountable for subgroup performance.[83] Indeed, Kress has suggested, "…The accountability provisions [of NCLB] were built on the foundation of the 1994 Improving America's Schools Act [which had, in turn, borrowed heavily from the Commission on Chapter 1's *Making Schools Work for Children in Poverty* framework]. The goal was to build muscle where there was little or none…Education Trust was deeply involved, as were key members of Congress from both sides of the aisle."[84] In fact, the proposals advocated by civil rights entrepreneurs and their congressional allies went *further* than Bush's No Child Left Behind blueprint by insisting that all students reach "academic proficiency" within ten years and by requiring all teachers to be "highly qualified" by 2005.[85] "Miller and Kennedy were already headed in the direction favored by Bush" by 2000, explains National Governors Association executive director Raymond Scheppach, creating the potential for cooperation and compromise between top congressional Democrats and the Republican standard-bearer following the election.[86]

The fact was that it was the shared understandings surrounding standards-based reforms forged by business entrepreneurs and civil rights entrepreneurs over the previous decade that formed the basis for an alliance with the Bush administration on education issues. Civil rights entrepreneurs admired Bush's education leadership in Texas: Amy Wilkins of the Education Trust went so far as to assert that the Texas model "is one of the best hopes for introducing *equity* into American education," while Anne Lewis of the Edna McConnell Clark Foundation insisted that "poor children [in Texas] are getting what they never had before: a common expectation and a common curriculum….Until that floor was there, you didn't know what teachers were teaching and children were learning."[87] At the same time, however, civil rights entrepreneurs correctly perceived that, in the words of the Citizens' Commission on Civil Rights, "many of the proposals [in George W. Bush's NCLB plan] for standards, assessments, and accountability build upon or duplicate the 1994 reforms [that is, the IASA]. We note that these reforms were broadly supported by civil rights and advocacy organizations, parents and educators, the previous Administration, and, significantly, a bipartisan agreement of the Congress."[88] Whatever their qualms about Bush's proposals in other policy areas, then, civil rights entrepreneurs were thus willing to enter into a tactical alliance with the president in order to secure standards-based reforms.

Layering Standards-Based Reforms on the ESEA—Again

Business entrepreneurs, civil rights entrepreneurs, and their allies contemplated significant changes to the ESEA. But both the No Child Left Behind blueprint and the various proposals recommended by congressional Democrats also presumed important continuities with past practices. Most obviously, all the major recommendations reviewed thus far proposed to reform schools by layering new conditions atop old ESEA funding streams. Indeed—and perhaps in spite of the contrary experience presented by the IASA—the No Child Left Behind blueprint and the various Democratic initiatives assumed that, in the words of William Taylor, "the standards based reforms that were adopted by Congress in 1994 [with the Improving America's Schools Act] can be made to work."[89] To put this in broader institutional perspective, these proposals assumed that the "Rube Goldberg-esque" (to use Elisabeth Clemens's term again) arrangement, in which the federal government would set standards and then delegate to states and localities the implementation of reforms, would continue into the indefinite future.

Why did proponents of standards-based reform persist in attempting to reform schools by layering new conditions atop the ESEA, despite the fact that the experience of the IASA suggested that this approach had considerable limitations? To answer this question, it is necessary to understand how familiar political and institutional constraints established boundaries on the kinds of changes that were possible. First of all, the system of institutions and interests that had grown up around the existing federal role in education discouraged reformers from pursuing a more aggressive course of action. The backlash against Goals 2000 and the IASA in the wake of the Republican Revolution drove home the lesson to business entrepreneurs, civil rights entrepreneurs, and their allies that many powerful interests on the left and the right still questioned the legitimacy of federal involvement in standards, testing, and accountability reform.[90] Though resistance to federal involvement in education was gradually softening, business entrepreneurs, civil rights entrepreneurs, and their allies realized that this did not mean that expanding federal leadership of standards, testing, and accountability reforms would be easy. As Sandy Kress recalls,

> The Improving America's Schools Act was pretty weak, in terms of its regulatory requirements. But taking standards based reforms "national" was a very hard thing. States resisted reforms under [Education Secretary Richard] Riley: they didn't want to have standards; they didn't want to have tests; they didn't want to disaggregate their test score data so they could be held accountable for the performance of all students. They resisted like crazy. So we knew there would be a lot of pushback against No Child Left Behind.[91]

Anticipating substantial opposition to renewed federal leadership, business entrepreneurs, civil rights entrepreneurs, and their allies again calculated that layering reforms on the ESEA offered the most politically tractable means to accomplish a standards-based overhaul of the education system. Just as it had in 1994, the ESEA's embeddedness in the politics of education made it an inviting vehicle for federal standards-based reforms: in effect, supporters of standards-based reforms strategized they could piggyback their favored policies on the popularity of the underlying programs. The Citizens' Commission on Civil Rights bluntly acknowledged this strategy when it noted in 1999 that "as the federal government's role in education continues to be debated, Title I is likely to be front and center in the debate. This will be true, if for no other reason, because of the sheer size of the appropriation and the reach of the program into every congressional district."[92] Following its own advice, the Citizens' Commission proposed to reform, and tighten implementation of, the IASA as the chief means for improving education for disadvantaged children. Looking back on enactment of NCLB, Kress expressed much the same sentiment, albeit in terms of minimizing opposition among educational liberals, educational conservatives, and state leaders: "I think NCLB was as muscular as it could be politically and still pass. The feds are a '7 percent investor' after all, and the states and districts are at 93 percent. Many states vigorously resisted what was done, and I believe they would have stopped any bill that was more aggressive."[93]

In previous years, a poor fiscal situation had limited the sights of proponents of federal leadership of standards, testing, and accountability reforms. The situation was somewhat different at the start of Bush's presidency: in fact, the federal government ran surpluses over the last few years of Clinton's term in office, alleviating some of the pressure created by deficits. However, to honor a campaign pledge and shore up the support of conservative Republicans, Bush had devoted much of the surplus to tax cuts. Realizing that increased appropriations could soothe opposition to federal standards-based reforms, business entrepreneurs, civil rights entrepreneurs, and their allies proposed to use remaining funds to secure a major increase in federal education spending. Rotherham's Three R's plan suggested coupling "Democratic demands for greater federal investment in elementary and secondary education with Republican demands for greater local decision-making, all within a new rubric of accountability based on student performance," while Miller's "Student Results Act" promised "Significant New Resources in Exchange for Tough Accountability."[94] Even newly elected President Bush dangled the promise of an additional $25 billion for education programs.[95] As Kati Haycock later suggested, this reflected a conscious political strategy to increase support, or at least to moderate opposition, to federal standards, testing, and accountability reforms. "Some of the anxiety [among standards-based reform skeptics] was resolved by the high reauthorization levels" supported by business entrepreneurs, civil rights entrepreneurs, and their allies, she explained.[96] Rather than deficits, then, competing demands for funds (and the political imperative to pay off potential critics in order to secure their acquiescence) eliminated fiscal slack that might have financed more-sweeping departures from existing policy practices.

Finally, public ambivalence about an *expansion of prescriptive federal authority* (as opposed to maintenance of existing federal involvement) discouraged proponents from a more expansive approach. By the end of the 1990s, many Americans were voicing increasing opposition to conservative Republicans' efforts to roll back the federal role in education; but that did not mean they were enthusiastic about a dramatic expansion of federal involvement. In January 2000, a Gallup / CNN / *USA Today* poll found that 65 percent of the public would have liked the federal role in elementary and secondary education to remain the same or decline, while 31 percent wanted it to increase.[97] Later that year, polls found that 49 percent of Americans believed that the federal government had "too much say in the decisions that affect the local public schools" (only 16 percent believed it had too little), and 61 percent professed that they would like to see federal influence decline.[98] As in past years, public opinion polls did not evince widespread enthusiasm for more-vigorous federal leadership. Public ambivalence about expanded federal involvement in education imposed real limits on what business entrepreneurs, civil rights entrepreneurs, and their allies could safely propose, encouraging them to chart a moderate course building on existing policies that delegated core educational decisions to state and local governments.

From the start, then, business entrepreneurs, civil rights entrepreneurs, and their political allies proposed to build on, rather than radically reconstruct, existing federal commitments in education. To get their way, however, these reformers would have to revive the bipartisan coalition that had given life to Goals 2000 and the Improving America's Schools Act.

Coalition Building and the Enactment of No Child Left Behind

Ascending to the presidency in part on the strength of his education proposals, and enjoying unified control of the federal government (until Vermont senator James Jefford's defection handed the Senate to the Democrats in May 2001), President Bush seemed on his way to securing a significant legislative achievement in education. But the politics of enacting No Child Left Behind were actually more delicate than they appear in retrospect.

From the start, Bush (along with business entrepreneurs and civil rights entrepreneurs) faced considerable difficulties from within the Republican Party. Republicans had never previously enjoyed unified control of government during a reauthorization of the Elementary and Secondary Education Act, and many hoped to exploit the opportunity to put a strong educational conservative stamp on the law. Echoing past educational conservative proposals, Chester Finn, Diane Ravitch, and Bruno Manno recommended that the ESEA be reformed to feature Straight A's block grants and "portable" funds (in essence, school vouchers) that could be used by students at either public or private schools.[99] Their proposals received the imprimatur of many mainstream educational conservative organizations, such as the American Enterprise Institute and Finn's Thomas B. Fordham Foundation (the successor to the Educational Excellence Network). A number of staunchly conservative groups, including the Eagle Forum, Focus on the Family, and the Family Research Council, went even further, declaring that they would withhold support from the final legislation unless it contained measures to promote private school choice.

Bush's own instincts were more moderate, hewing closely to the standards-based reform approach long touted by business entrepreneurs. Even if Bush had wanted to hinge the reauthorization debate on vouchers, grant consolidation, and deregulation, however, it is unlikely that he would have made much progress. Educational liberals inside and outside Congress had strongly opposed such measures during the 2000 presidential campaign, claiming that they would undermine public schools and discriminate against historically disadvantaged students.[100] Of course, educational liberals also had a significant material stake in ensuring that these measures did not become a major part of the reauthorization, because they posed a threat to the funding streams educational liberals prized, as well as to the bargaining position of teachers unions in negotiations with school districts. Though Democrats controlled neither the House nor the Senate (until Jeffords's defection), their strength in the Senate meant that they could block legislation that veered too far toward educational conservatism. With educational liberal groups, led by the teachers unions, already skeptical about the standards-based reform paradigm, it would not take much for many Democrats to walk away from the No Child Left Behind proposal and thereby deny Bush the early policy victory he so desired. This reality profoundly influenced Bush's legislative strategy: several years later, in response to an interviewer's question about why the Bush administration "capitulated" to Democrats on vouchers during congressional debate over No Child Left Behind (discussed at greater length below), Margaret Spellings bluntly retorted, "We couldn't pass it. Duh, right?"[101]

Prospects were further complicated by the fact that many state leaders were extremely ambivalent about the expansion of prescriptive federal rules related to standards, testing, and accountability reform. As the states' response to the IASA clearly indicated, state leaders preferred to retain as much discretion as possible for themselves in implementing federal education programs. Going into the debate surrounding the reauthorization of the IASA, organizations representing state interests trumpeted a variety of measures featuring grant consolidation and regulatory flexibility. The National Governors Association touted "performance partnerships," which would have given states and localities much more flexibility under federal education programs to use funds for standards, testing, teacher recruitment, class-size reduction, and other reforms as they saw fit.[102] Viewing it as a formula for greater state autonomy, state legislators endorsed educational conservatives' Straight A's proposal. Speaking before Congress about Straight A's, Kansas state representative and National Conference of State Legislatures delegate Ralph Tanner exclaimed that "[Straight A's] is a bargain we could all live with!"[103]

Proponents of federal standards, testing, and accountability reforms thus faced a task parallel to that confronted by reformers in 1994: assembling a coalition large and diverse enough to pass legislation into law, while preserving the central elements of their program. In the debate over NCLB, the president, business entrepreneurs, and civil rights entrepreneurs each played an important role in building such an alliance. Much as Clinton had in 1993–94, Bush played the role of cross-partisan conciliator, offering concessions to attract support while blocking "deal-breaking" proposals that threatened to fracture his coalition. Bush was especially solicitous of congressional Democrats, realizing that Democratic support was the key to passing legislation in the closely divided Senate. Prior to his inauguration, the president-elect invited a bipartisan delegation of congressional education leaders—including educational conservatives such as John Boehner and Judd Gregg, New Democrats such as Evan Bayh and Tim Roemer, and civil rights ally George Miller—to confer on education issues. Although Kennedy was not included, the gathering sent the signal that Bush would seek a bipartisan bill, especially after it was leaked that the president had admitted he was willing to trade away school vouchers to accomplish other policy objectives.[104] Just after taking office, Bush reinforced the cause of a bipartisan bill by meeting privately with Senator Kennedy and securing his agreement to work together on reform legislation.[105] Bush's courtship of Kennedy was a boon to the cause of federal leadership of standards-based reform: in an important sense, Kennedy was the "bridge" between civil rights entrepreneurs and educational liberals in the Senate, who viewed Kennedy as their leader. The Massachusetts "liberal lion" was also widely regarded as a skillful legislative tactician and "dealmaker."[106] The prospects of bipartisan legislation were further brightened by the fact that Bush was committed to a significant expansion of federal education aid, which appealed to educational liberals anxious to extend the ESEA and other federal programs.

Although some aspects of Bush's approach—especially mandatory testing and government accountability—still concerned many Democrats, Bush's overtures helped keep Democrats from defecting en masse. Bush held to his pledge to work for a bipartisan bill, deferring to Democrats on matters they viewed as "deal breaking." During the negotiations over No Child Left Behind in April to May 2001, administration officials acquiesced to the removal of voucher provisions from the House and Senate bills.[107] In subsequent statements to the press, Sandy Kress "made it clear [Bush] would declare victory even if the House bill stays as it is," according to *CQ Weekly*.[108] When educational conservatives attempted to revive school voucher proposals on the floor in the House and the Senate, these floor amendments were defeated, with some Republicans joining Democrats in opposition in order to protect the bipartisan compromise. The president also proved willing to compromise on grant consolidations and regulatory reform. During Senate negotiations on the legislation in April and May 2001, Kennedy had backed a Straight A's pilot as an olive branch to conservatives.[109] However, on the House side, Congressman Miller declared that "Straight A's is a deal-killer" and threatened to pull Democratic support from the bill.[110] Desirous to avoid a fight that might topple other NCLB reforms, Bush agreed drop the amendment.[111] In a compromise that ultimately satisfied Democrats, school districts (rather than states) were permitted to transfer funds among various categorical programs, giving them additional flexibility to address specific school needs within existing categorical arrangements.

Whereas Bush's compromises helped keep Democrats at the negotiating table, civil rights entrepreneurs consolidated Democratic support with an energetic lobbying and educational campaign. As Andrew Rotherham explains, civil rights entrepreneurs possessed considerable "moral authority" with educational liberals in the Democratic Party because of their steadfast advocacy on behalf of disadvantaged groups. Consequently, when civil rights entrepreneurs came out in strong support of the NCLB framework—despite its sponsorship by a Republican president—it made a large impression on congressional Democrats, signaling that the legislation was something they should support.[112] The fact that civil rights entrepreneurs' proposals to strengthen the IASA through greater emphasis on testing, accountability, and teacher quality also enjoyed the imprimatur of broader civil rights coalitions such as the Leadership Conference on Civil Rights—as evinced by the LCCR's own public statements—gave these recommendations further weight with congressional Democrats.[113] Civil rights entrepreneurs also sought to influence congressional Democrats' opinions by providing them with data they believed vindicated standards-based reforms. For example, Education Trust analyst Craig Jerald published a laudatory analysis of Texas's education reforms, *Real Results, Remaining Challenges*, which suggested that Texas-style reforms would help improve schools throughout the nation.[114] According to David Shreve of the National Conference of State Legislatures, civil rights entrepreneurs may also have persuaded some Democrats that standards-based reforms—especially tests that disaggregated performance reports by race, ethnicity, and poverty level—would reveal enduring inequities in state and local education finance regimes, providing parents and students with leverage to sue in court for additional resources.[115]

As a result of the Bush charm offensive and lobbying by civil rights entrepreneurs, many Democrats proved willing to vote with the president on potentially divisive issues, such as mandatory annual testing. As it had in previous years, the testing proposal stirred fears among some educational liberals that assessments were unfair to disadvantaged students and threatened to impose stringent accountability sanctions on teachers and schools, while also raising red flags among educational conservatives about federal "control" of education. On the House floor, an unusual liberal-conservative coalition led by Democrat Barney Frank and Republican Peter Hoekstra championed a provision to strike the mandatory testing provisions from the bill.[116] A similar left-right coalition in the Senate attempted to make the testing provisions voluntary.[117] In both instances, significant numbers of Democrats joined with Republicans to vote down these measures, preserving what Bush administration officials viewed as the "heart" of the president's proposal.

As Bush forged compromises with congressional Democrats, Republicans began to grow restive.[118] Speaking for many Republicans, conservative representative Jim DeMint of South Carolina complained that Bush's campaign promise to "leave no child behind" had morphed into "leave no Democrat behind."[119]

Of particular concern to educational conservatives, the No Child Left Behind Act that was taking shape featured many more new (and specific) federal regulations than they would have preferred and neglected priorities such as school vouchers and grant consolidation. In truth, by pursuing bipartisan legislation from the start, Bush had seriously narrowed educational conservatives' room for maneuver on the issues that concerned them most. Just as Clinton's embrace of federal standards, testing, and accountability initiatives tended to push congressional Democrats to adopt the broad contours of his approach, however, so did Bush's legislative leadership pressure Republicans to accept much of his NCLB initiative. With Bush staking his political capital on standards, testing, and accountability reform, Republican members of Congress realized they could not desert NCLB without inflicting political damage on their president. As conservative Republican congressman Mark Souder of Indiana explained, Bush "had a very narrow win [in the 2000 presidential election], and we don't want to do anything to jeopardize his No. 1 initiative....But that doesn't mean we like it."[120] It is also likely that the president gained some leeway with conservatives on No Child Left Behind because of his impressive conservative record on other issues, such as taxes, energy, and the environment.[121] According to Michael Petrilli, a former Bush education adviser and analyst with the Thomas B. Fordham Foundation, "Education is just not as salient with most conservatives as issues like taxes, defense, regulation, and so forth"; having been largely satisfied on these other issues, conservatives were willing to go along on one of Bush's top priorities even as it departed in significant respects from their preferred position.[122]

Congressional Republicans' lurch toward federal standards, testing, and accountability reforms was reinforced by a vigorous lobbying campaign by business entrepreneurs. Meeting regularly with White House officials, especially Kress, to plot strategy, the Business Coalition for Excellence in Education executed a comprehensive legislative blitz on behalf of NCLB between January and December 2001. According to the organization's own internal documents, the Business Coalition testified before congressional committees on 3 occasions, transmitted more than 31 letters to congressional committees, members, and congressional leadership, and arranged over 180 visits with congressional staff during deliberation of NCLB. Business Coalition members also placed op-eds favoring the legislation in major newspapers such as the *New York Times*, the *Washington Post*, the *Baltimore Sun*, and *USA Today*.[123] Meanwhile, state Business Roundtable representatives—primarily local business leaders— were urged to "writ[e] letters and mak[e] calls to share lessons learned at the state level and to urge the 107th Congress to pass bipartisan education reform legislation that significantly improves public education in this country," according to Business Roundtable documents.[124] This massive lobbying blitz, which

Tom Lindsley describes as giving Republican lawmakers a "reality check" on federal education policymaking, was joined to a rhetorical campaign appealing to Republicans' concern for the economic bottom line.[125] In language geared to appeal to GOP members, business entrepreneurs in the Business Coalition for Excellence in Education explained that they supported federal standards, testing, and accountability reforms because "in a world of global competition and rapid technological advances, U.S. schools must prepare all students for the challenges of the 21st century."[126] Looking back on business entrepreneurs' lobbying on behalf of the legislation, Margaret Spellings concluded that "The business community [was] a huge ally in the development, implementation, and support for No Child Left Behind."[127]

These political strategies were joined to a conscious effort to shield fragile negotiations from the purview of interest groups (from both ends of the political spectrum) believed to be hostile to the legislation. Throughout the legislative debate over NCLB, but especially during conference committee negotiations between the House and Senate, supporters of federal leadership worked assiduously to limit the access of educational liberal and educational conservative interest groups to the proceedings.[128] The top negotiators limited their own interaction with lobbyists, and directed their staffs not to discuss the details of the legislation with interest-group representatives.[129] Legislators' tight control over the NCLB negotiations restricted the ability of interest groups representing educational liberals or educational conservatives to influence the content of the law. In the end, the "Unions' Positions [were] Unheeded on ESEA," *Education Week* reported, but many educational conservatives were also unhappy with the final product.[130] "It's a modest improvement over current law.... Nothing to celebrate," declared Chester Finn in December 2001.[131] The influence of state leaders—who were expected to oppose many of the new federal mandates—was also sharply curtailed. "We were never a big player in discussions surrounding No Child Left Behind," Raymond Scheppach of the National Governors Association later acknowledged. "Bush didn't really consult with us much at all."[132]

This process of coalition building, compromise, and lobbying resulted in broad cross-partisan support for NCLB. The House passed its version of the legislation in late May 2001 on a 384–45 vote, while the Senate bill passed in June by a 91–8 margin. Although conference negotiations were arduous, neither intensified lobbying by educational liberals and educational conservatives nor the terrorist attacks of September 11, 2001, derailed the proceedings. Indeed, by galvanizing lawmakers to demonstrate the responsiveness of the federal government in the wake of a national tragedy, the September 11 attacks arguably helped move the conference proceedings to their conclusion. The votes to approve the conference report of NCLB were overwhelming in both the House, which passed the legislation by a 381–41 vote, and the Senate, which voted for enactment 87–10.

Though the president and the "Big Four" (Miller, Kennedy, Gregg, and Boehner) received much of the public credit for the legislation, the convergence of business entrepreneurs and civil rights entrepreneurs around intensified federal leadership paved the way for enactment of NCLB. According to Patricia Sullivan of the American Federation of Teachers,

> The reason for the huge shift to accountability for results was the growing impatience of three groups with the states and with the state of education: the business community, led by the Business Roundtable; the civil rights groups, led by Kati Haycock and the Education Trust; and members of Congress and President Bush. Business leaders were angry that students lacked fundamental skills, and resented that they had to spend so much money on retraining their workers. Civil rights groups were so tired of disadvantaged students getting pushed aside on matters of high standards and accountability for results. Members of Congress and President Bush saw a political opportunity to profit from this convergence of interests, and they took it.[133]

Indeed, NCLB embodied the strong standards, testing, and accountability reforms that business entrepreneurs and civil rights entrepreneurs had been advocating for more than a decade. The law significantly expanded federal authority in education, while providing new resources and some additional regulatory flexibility. Under the law, states were to adopt academic standards and establish assessments that evaluated students' progress toward the standards. They were to test virtually all students in grades 3–8 each year, as well as once in high school, in reading and mathematics by the 2005–6 school year. By 2007–8 they were also to implement science assessments once during each of the three major grade levels: elementary, middle, and high school. Results of the tests—disaggregated for racial and ethnic groups, income levels, students with disabilities, students with limited English proficiency, and migrant students—had to be made available to parents and the public. To ensure that "no child was left behind," states were required to develop plans for bringing all students to academic "proficiency" by 2014, and to monitor the annual progress of schools in moving all students toward the proficiency objectives. As a check on the quality of state standards and assessments, the law obliged states to participate every other year in the National Assessment of Educational Progress.

No Child Left Behind required states to take an escalating series of steps against schools that failed to make annual progress toward state-developed academic goals. If a school failed to make adequate progress for two consecutive years, the state was to provide technical assistance to the school and permit the school's students to transfer to other public schools within the district. The school district was obligated to cover the costs of transportation for students exercising the school choice option. A third consecutive year of inadequate improvement required the state to allow the school's students to use their share of ESEA Title I funds to purchase "supplemental educational services," such as after-school tutoring, from public or private sources. States were supposed to deal with schools that failed to make adequate yearly progress for four or five consecutive years by implementing major changes to staffing, curriculum, and governance. If a school failed to make adequate progress for four consecutive years, the state was to implement "corrective actions" such as replacing school staff or requiring the school to introduce a new curriculum and materials. Schools failing to make adequate progress for five consecutive years faced "reconstitution," which could mean reopening as a charter school or turning operation of the school over to the state.

Unlike previous reauthorizations of the ESEA, NCLB dealt with "teacher quality" in detail. Under NCLB, states were required to have a "highly qualified teacher"—defined as a teacher with full certification or licensure, a college degree, and demonstrated competence in subject matter and pedagogy—in every classroom by the 2005–6 school year. Additionally, all new teachers hired with ESEA Title I funds were required to be "highly qualified," while "paraprofessionals" hired with Title I money were to have completed at least two years of college, attained an associate's or higher degree, or met a quality standard established at the local level. To help enforce this provision, parents were given the right to demand information about teacher qualifications from their schools.

These new regulatory requirements were accompanied by a significant expansion of federal education aid. In the 2002 fiscal year, the Department of Education's budget was to rise by $6.7 billion, to almost $49 billion (more than $4.4 billion above Bush's original request).[134] The law also authorized a new, $900 million "Reading First" program to help states and districts establish "scientific, research-based" reading programs for children in grades K–3, as well as a $450 million "Mathematics and Science Partnerships" program to encourage state and local stakeholders to forge partnerships to promote student achievement in these subjects. An additional $300 million was allocated to promote charter schools. States were also given new flexibility in their use of ESEA funds. States and school districts were allowed to transfer up to 50 percent of the funding received for teacher-quality programs, educational technology, school innovations, and safe and drug-free schools among these programs, or to Title I of the ESEA. NCLB also authorized new demonstration projects permitting up to 7 states and 150 school districts to consolidate a broader range of federal education program funds under special five-year performance agreements negotiated with the secretary of education.

As the foregoing suggests, NCLB heralded significant changes in the structure of authority in education, especially by imposing new, and more rigorous, standards-based reform conditions on ESEA aid. As in the past, however, states retained the authority to design their own standards, assessments, and teacher-quality provisions. The law explicitly declared that nothing within its pages could be construed to authorize any federal official or agency to "mandate, direct, or control a State, local educational agency, or school's specific instructional content, academic achievement standards and assessments, curriculum, or program of instruction."[135] This meant that while NCLB could pressure states to adopt standards-based reforms, the rigor of these measures were likely to vary significantly across states. While the National Assessment of Educational Progress was to provide an external check on the quality of state standards and assessments, NCLB prohibited penalties from being assessed based on NAEP performance. Indeed, nothing in the final law required *states* (as opposed to schools or school districts) to demonstrate improvement in the performance of their students.[136]

These important limits on federal involvement are attributable to the demands of legislative compromise. In order to secure the acquiescence of skeptical members of Congress, proponents of federal standards, testing, and accountability reforms were forced to accept proposals that left much of the implementing authority in the hands of states and localities.[137] The pursuit of legislative agreement also led to the proliferation of ambiguous legislative provisions, which offered significant opportunities for state and local officials to exercise discretion in implementing the law.[138] For example, while NCLB required states to develop strategies for bringing all students to academic "proficiency" by 2014, each state was allowed to determine its own year-by-year trajectory toward the 100 percent proficiency target. This meant that states could, if they chose, chart extremely implausible courses toward "proficiency," in effect betting that this aspect of the law would be amended or repealed prior to the 2014 deadline. On the accountability front, the apparently ironclad system of sanctions contained an escape hatch for states leery of imposing stringent accountability measures on struggling schools: a provision enabling states to use "any other restructuring" as a method of reform. Since "any other restructuring" was not defined by the law, states were left with discretion to determine how they would deal with failing schools.[139] Similarly, the "highly qualified teacher" provisions, though seemingly straightforward, contained language that allowed states and localities considerable freedom in the course of implementation.[140] Most important, states were permitted to deem in-service teachers as "highly qualified" under the flexible High Objective Uniform State Standard of Evaluation (HOUSSE) procedure, which allowed states to award teachers credit for their years of active service, as well as for activities such as attending meetings or giving presentations. This meant that in-service teachers might not have to demonstrate subject-matter competency or knowledge of pedagogical techniques in order to be deemed "highly qualified."[141]

No Child Left Behind represented an episode of bounded institutional change in the development of federal education policy. The law significantly expanded federal authority in education by instituting rigorous new standards-based reform conditions on receipt of federal education aid under the ESEA. Henceforth, states seeking ESEA aid would have to conform to a relatively specific standards-based reform template revolving around coordinated standards, assessments, and accountability measures. But NCLB's reliance on the ESEA as its source of leverage inevitably bounded the scope of change sought by the law's main proponents. As a traditional categorical grant program, the ESEA delegated to states and localities many of the design details and implementation decisions. NCLB followed this institutional path, providing states and localities with considerable flexibility to design their own standards and assessments and implement accountability and teacher-quality reforms. Additionally, a review of some of the law's details suggests that NCLB skeptics won important concessions that granted them discretion in implementing the law's provisions.

The bounded change represented by NCLB is attributable to the interplay of political entrepreneurship with political and institutional constraints. Frustrated by the slow progress of standards-based reforms and the uneven implementation of the IASA after the Republican Revolution of 1994, business entrepreneurs and civil rights entrepreneurs mobilized to rejuvenate federal education leadership. Between 1995 and 2000, these figures worked closely with certain members of Congress, and with leading presidential candidate George W. Bush, to develop strategies for strengthening federal leadership of standards-based reforms. The unsteady progress of standards-based reforms at the state level, coupled with the lackluster growth of student achievement, allowed business entrepreneurs and civil rights entrepreneurs to win important converts to their cause by the end of the decade. Before the 2000 election, in fact, these figures had recruited many allies willing to promote policies that anticipated the No Child Left Behind Act. Following Bush's election in 2000, business entrepreneurs, civil rights entrepreneurs, and the Bush administration used a variety of strategies to consolidate a bipartisan coalition in support of federal leadership of standards, testing, and accountability reform. While the president played the role of bipartisan "deal-maker," business entrepreneurs and civil rights entrepreneurs undertook vigorous lobbying and educational campaigns to shore up support among Republicans and Democrats, respectively. The result was a politics that deflected many of the demands of educational conservatives and educational liberals and focused the ESEA reauthorization around standards, testing, and accountability.

Nonetheless, the impact of NCLB's standards, testing, and accountability reforms was tempered by existing institutions and enduring political constraints. Eager to head off the political opposition, supporters of federal leadership of standards-based reforms agreed to piggyback their proposals on the popular ESEA program, which had the consequence of devolving much of the responsibility and discretion to implement reforms to state and local governments. These supporters were also forced to sacrifice some measures (such as holding states accountable for academic performance) and dilute others (such as accountability sanctions) in order to hold together their legislative coalition. State and local governments thus retained a central role in implementing the law's numerous, and frequently ambiguous, provisions. In the end, the NCLB regime simultaneously extended federal authority and invited vigorous struggles between the federal government, the states, and various education constituencies over the terms of that authority.

As the next chapter shows, such struggles erupted almost immediately after NCLB was signed into law, ushering in a prolonged period of conflict over implementation of the act. By 2007, the politics surrounding NCLB had become toxic, undermining efforts to reauthorize the law at the scheduled time. In the meantime, the NCLB regime had evolved. Under pressure from multiple quarters, the Bush administration loosened some NCLB regulations, allowing states and localities more flexibility to chart their own reforms. Many states and localities also exploited silences and ambiguities within the statute to avoid implementing some of the more ambitious reforms envisioned by NCLB's chief advocates. Entering into office in the midst of the nation's most severe economic crisis since the Great Depression, Barack Obama faced a less auspicious environment for federal standards-based reform in 2009 than George W. Bush had eight years earlier. As we shall see, however, Obama has in many ways continued on the path set by his predecessor, embracing vigorous federal efforts to promote high standards, regular assessments, and accountability for results.

"YES WE CAN" IMPROVE AMERICA'S SCHOOLS?

From No Child Left Behind to President Obama's Education Initiatives, 2003–2011

Democratic candidate Barack Obama's historic 2008 campaign for the presidency featured two memorable themes: "Yes We Can" and "Change We Can Believe In." The first suggested Obama's conviction that vigorous government action, when closely tied to public values, could accomplish great things in foreign and domestic policy. The second theme signaled that Obama intended to offer an alternative to the political and ideological commitments of the George W. Bush administration, which had been discredited by the war in Iraq and the financial collapse of 2008. In speeches before enthusiastic crowds, candidate Obama joined these themes in order to present a political vision that contrasted starkly with that offered by Bush and, by association, with Obama's opponent in the presidential contest, Republican senator John McCain. "For eight long years," Obama exclaimed in typical lament, "our President sacrificed investments in health care, and education, and energy, and infrastructure on the altar of tax breaks for big corporations and wealthy CEOs—trillions of dollars in giveaways that proved neither compassionate nor conservative." Turning to a description of the agenda for his presidency, Obama declared that

> instead of spending twelve billion dollars a month to rebuild Iraq, I think it's time we invested in our roads and schools and bridges and started to rebuild America. Instead of handing out giveaways to corporations that don't need them and didn't ask for them, it's time we started giving a hand-up to families who are trying pay their medical bills and

send their children to college. We can't afford four more years of skewed priorities that give us nothing but record debt—we need change that works for the American people.[1]

According to a *Washington Post* report on Obama's acceptance address at the 2008 Democratic National Convention, "Obama described the great challenges of the next presidency as restoring the values Bush has abandoned, fixing the things Bush has broken, and fundamentally changing the errant course Bush has set for our nation." "Obama," the *Post* concluded, was "the Anti-Bush."[2] To many observers, Obama's historic election victory seemed to herald a profound shift in foreign and domestic policymaking, perhaps even a new era in American politics. As the *New York Times* proclaimed on November 5, 2008, the morning after Obama's victory, "The election of Mr. Obama amounted to a national catharsis—a repudiation of a historically unpopular Republican president and his economic and foreign policies, and an embrace of Mr. Obama's call for a change in the direction and the tone of the country."[3]

In truth, however, the "Anti-Bush" appellation that Obama had embraced in the campaign was more apparent in some areas of policy than in others. Whereas the Democratic standard-bearer sought to distinguish himself from the president on the issues of paramount importance in the campaign—management of the economy, the war in Iraq, and health care—Obama took a more ambiguous tack when it came to education. Indeed, when speaking about Bush's signature education reform, No Child Left Behind, the Democratic candidate mixed praise with his criticism. As Obama declared in an important address on education in May 2008,

> I believe that the goals of [No Child Left Behind] were the right ones. Making a promise to educate every child with an excellent teacher is right. Closing the achievement gap that exists in too many cities and rural areas is right. More accountability is right. Higher standards are right. But I'll tell you what's wrong with No Child Left Behind. Forcing our teachers, our principals and our schools to accomplish all of this without the resources they need is wrong. Promising high-quality teachers in every classroom and then leaving the support and the pay for those teachers behind is wrong. Labeling a school and its students as failures one day and then throwing your hands up and walking away from them the next is wrong. We must fix the failures of No Child Left Behind.[4]

Obama "certainly isn't saying: 'Let's Get Rid of [No Child Left Behind]'" *Education Week* concluded in July 2008; rather, he "sounds as if he wants to get NCLB right."[5]

Since his election as president, Obama's views on federal education policy have come into sharper focus. Far from pursuing "Change We Can Believe In," President Obama has endorsed many of the policies of his predecessor. Arne Duncan, Obama's secretary of education and a longtime proponent of standards-based reforms, has underscored the administration's commitment to standards, testing, and accountability, declaring that "we can never let up on holding everyone accountable for student success. That is what we are striving for."[6] The president's signature Race to the Top initiative attempted, with some apparent success, to use federal economic stimulus funding as leverage to pressure states to raise education standards, expand charter schools, tie teacher evaluations to student test scores, and turn around chronically struggling schools. Likewise, Obama's proposal to reauthorize No Child Left Behind reaffirmed the federal government's strategy of using ESEA assistance to promote standards-based reforms. While this approach drew plaudits from business entrepreneurs, civil rights entrepreneurs, and former Bush officials, it surprised and disappointed many educational liberals, who viewed Obama's education policies as "Bush III."[7] Yet, at the same time, Obama's policies exasperated educational conservatives and many state leaders, who resented what they viewed as a "command and control" approach to reforming the nation's schools.

Obama's presidency is still young, precluding a comprehensive account of his education initiatives. In the coming years, the 2010 midterm election results, in which Republicans recaptured the House of Representatives and picked up six seats in the Senate, will undoubtedly complicate the president's efforts to make further headway on education issues. Nonetheless, we can learn a great deal by situating the policies Obama has pursued thus far within the context of longer-term trends of institutionally bounded change in federal education policy. Obama's education agenda has its origins in the political struggle surrounding implementation of No Child Left Behind. Federal efforts to implement that act fostered widespread dissatisfaction among educational liberals, educational conservatives, state leaders, and the public at large. Faced with growing backlash against the law, Bush administration officials mirrored Clinton's earlier actions in response to the Republican Revolution of 1994, granting states and localities flexibility in implementing some of NCLB's most stringent provisions. At the same time, state and local governments exploited ambiguities within the law to bound the scope of the educational changes favored by business entrepreneurs, civil rights entrepreneurs, and their allies in the Bush administration. Fed by the Democrats' recapture of Congress in 2006, the controversy over implementation of NCLB intensified over time, obstructing efforts to reauthorize the act prior to the 2008 presidential election.

In a reprise of their actions following the Republican Revolution of 1994, business entrepreneurs and civil rights entrepreneurs once again mobilized to defend and strengthen the federal role in education. Pointing to apparent weaknesses in state and local reforms, business entrepreneurs and civil rights entrepreneurs contended that *even more vigorous* federal commitments were needed to shore up the nation's schools. Though they failed in their quest to reauthorize NCLB prior to the presidential election, these figures appear to have succeeded in laying the groundwork for the Obama administration's education policies. Many of the features of Obama's Race to the Top initiative and NCLB reauthorization proposal bear a striking resemblance to proposals recommended by business and civil rights entrepreneurs during the debate over NCLB's reauthorization in the later years of Bush's presidency. Led by Duncan, Obama's Department of Education has sought to sustain the course charted by the Bush administration, despite the challenges posed by the ongoing economic crisis and the sharp disagreement over the federal role in education.

But federal involvement in the standards-based reform movement remains on unsteady ground. Though innovative, the Race to the Top initiative was part of the American Recovery and Reinvestment Act, meaning that it may not receive federal appropriations in the future. Perhaps more important, the administration made the strategic choice to push off reauthorization of NCLB until after the 2010 elections in order to focus on higher priorities, such as health care reform and financial regulation. Huge Republican gains in both houses of Congress in those elections—made possible in part by public fears of overweening government in a time of stagnant economic growth and spiraling deficits—subsequently undermined prospects for a reauthorization prior to the 2012 presidential election. Thus, while Obama made impressive strides in shaping the education agenda during the first two years of his term, it is an open question whether he can sustain a vigorous federal role in the standards-based reform movement over the long term without a timely reauthorization of NCLB. Indeed, since the 2010 elections, Obama has begun to relent to pressure from educational conservatives, educational liberals, and state officials by granting states, localities, and schools a reprieve from NCLB's requirements.

I begin this chapter by describing the political backlash against NCLB, showing how it worked to limit the scope of reforms favored by business entrepreneurs, civil rights entrepreneurs, and their allies. Analyzing the agendas of business entrepreneurs, civil rights entrepreneurs, educational liberals, educational conservatives, and state leaders during the failed reauthorization of 2007–8, I argue that the proposals of business entrepreneurs and civil rights entrepreneurs anticipated many of the initiatives of the Obama administration. Next, I discuss the Obama administration's Race to the Top initiative, illustrating how it extends the logic and principles of No Child Left Behind in an effort to shore up standards-based reforms at the state and local levels. The final part of the chapter speculates on education policy in the Obama administration in light of the 2010 elections.

The Bounded Implementation of the No Child Left Behind Act

Following passage of NCLB in January 2002, attention turned to the implementation of the law's many complex and controversial provisions. From the start, the Bush administration proclaimed its commitment to enforcing both the letter and the spirit of the law. Meeting with state education officials at Mount Vernon soon after the law's enactment, Secretary of Education Rod Paige declared that "No Child Left Behind is now the law of the land. I took an oath to enforce the law, and I intend to do that. I will help states and districts and schools comply— in fact I will do everything in my power to help—but I will not let deadlines slip or see requirements forgotten."[8] Whereas previous administrations had given states considerable latitude in implementing ESEA provisions, Bush's Department of Education was noted for repeatedly denying state waiver requests.[9] In a testament to the administration's determination to implement the letter of the law, in the summer of 2003 the Department of Education withheld nearly $800,000 in ESEA funds from the state of Georgia, which had failed to complete its work on assessments required by the act. This was the first time in the entire history of the ESEA that a state had been penalized for failing to comply with federal rules.[10]

In short, when it came to enforcement of NCLB's requirements during the early years of implementation, the administration's overarching strategy was to try to "hold the line, hold the line, hold the line," according to Eugene Hickok, who served as the Department of Education's deputy secretary and undersecretary under Paige.[11] It would be wrong, however, to present the Bush administration as completely inflexible on the matter of implementation of NCLB; in fact, Bush's Department of Education allowed states some flexibility on technical, but important, issues, accepting state requests to use more-forgiving measures to calculate adequate yearly progress and high school graduation rates.[12] Even so, as states and localities began to implement the law's requirements—especially the controversial testing, adequate yearly progress, and sanctions initiatives— frustration with the Bush administration's implementation of NCLB mounted. In part this was because implementation of the law's many complex requirements may have imposed considerable fiscal and administrative burdens on state and local governments.[13] But the backlash against NCLB was also fed by the fact that the law had an immediate and profound impact on state and local education *politics.* NCLB's standards and accountability provisions affected schools in communities throughout the nation: as the adequate yearly progress and accountability provisions entered into force, a growing proportion of schools (including some suburban schools viewed as successful by parents, students, and teachers) were labeled "in need of improvement" and subject to sanction under the law. Although high-poverty, high-minority, and large urban schools were most likely to be identified for improvement, 15 percent of all schools were so identified in 2006–7, according to a comprehensive 2010 study by the Department of Education; in some states, however, the proportion of identified schools reached 30, 40, and even 50 percent. Some schools remained mired in improvement status for several consecutive years and thus faced the prospects of increasingly intensive government intervention.[14]

These developments were not received with equanimity by state officials, who complained that the law—and the Bush administration's implementation strategy—imposed excessive burdens on state and local governments. According to Joan Wodiska of the National Governors Association, "We thought that [NCLB] was all right, but the regulations and rules really started to tie the hands of the states. The implementation of the law was really bad; there were just too many rules, and the oversight was too tight."[15] At the NGA's winter conference in March 2004, *Education Week* reported, "Many of the nation's governors…called for changes to the No Child Left Behind Act or its regulations, even as the Bush administration continued to defend its level of cooperation with states under the law."[16] The governors' complaints about NCLB echoed in statehouses throughout the land, giving rise to what was frequently described as a state "rebellion" against the law. By the middle of 2004, in fact, more than half the nation's states had introduced resolutions challenging the No Child Left Behind Act; Colorado, Illinois, Maine, Utah, and Virginia actually passed laws preempting NCLB or permitting local districts to ignore the law's provisions.[17]

Many educational liberals joined in denouncing the act for imposing unworkable demands on states, districts, and schools, and for failing to provide adequate funding for implementation.[18] As Bruce Hunter of the American Association of School Administrators recalls, "Our members couldn't believe what [No Child Left Behind] entailed for education. When I tried to explain the Act to them, they didn't believe it was possible. When they finally understood what the law was, they were extremely angry, and their anger only grew over time.…We drove home our concerns to every member of Congress. We drove it home again, and again, and again."[19] Most ominously for the administration, the powerful National Education Association—which had remained quiescent during the debate over enactment of NCLB—initiated what NEA president Reg Weaver described as a "full-court, legislative press to fix and fund" the law in 2003.[20] "I think any pretense of support [for No Child Left Behind] has been swept away," declared NEA chief counsel Robert Chanin.[21] In addition to its vigorous legislative campaign—backed by a well-funded drive to increase the organization's membership—the NEA initiated a lawsuit to enjoin implementation of NCLB on the grounds that the law imposed "unfunded mandates" on the states.[22] The American Federation of Teachers' public criticism of NCLB was more muted. Behind the scenes, however, the AFT lobbied heavily to protect teacher interests; for example, it engaged in an aggressive (and ultimately successful) lobbying campaign against regulations proposed by the Department of Education that would have restricted collective bargaining rights for contracts under NCLB.[23] At the same time, some civil rights organizations, led by the NAACP, began to express concerns about implementation of NCLB. Explaining that his organization did not oppose the law, NAACP chairman Julian Bond nonetheless cautioned that NCLB seemed to lack adequate funding and "fostered a kind of drill-and-kill curriculum" that encouraged teaching to the test.[24]

Educational conservatives, especially conservative congressional Republicans, expressed ambivalence about NCLB. As the previous chapter showed, these figures were not overly enthusiastic about the ambitious federal involvement anticipated by NCLB; at the same time, though, they were loath to criticize their popular president, especially after the September 11 attacks. However, as the law's provisions went into effect—and as they began to hear from angry constituents—conservative Republicans began to express concerns about NCLB. By late 2004, members of the conservative House Republican Study Committee were warning Bush that he would "have a more difficult time convincing conservative members to vote for more government." According to Indiana congressman Mike Pence, conservative Republicans were planning to work to "undo" No Child Left Behind and provide much more flexibility to states and localities in implementing federal education laws.[25] Other educational conservatives took a less confrontational line, while remaining convinced that the law needed to be reformed to reduce federal involvement in education. Certainly, educational conservatives were skeptical about Bush's proposal to incorporate secondary schools within NCLB's accountability regime. "Conservative Republicans worried about federal control may not cotton to the Bush idea of extending No Child Left Behind to the high school level," Chester Finn predicted.[26]

Meanwhile, public opinion polls offered mixed support for NCLB. According to a 2004 Education Testing Service Poll, Americans were evenly split between those who felt favorable about the law (39 percent) and those who felt unfavorable (38 percent), with 20 percent saying they did not know enough about the law to form an opinion.[27] The 2004 *Phi Delta Kappa / Gallup Poll of the Public's Attitudes toward the Public Schools* found that 24 percent were favorable toward NCLB and 20 percent opposed, but that a stunning 55 percent did not know enough about the law to say.[28] Furthermore, according to a January 2004 survey, Americans did not view providing funding for implementation of NCLB as a high priority; indeed, while 10 percent would have used additional federal funds to implement the law, 52 percent would have preferred that additional funds go to reducing class sizes, while 12 percent would have opted to restore or expand arts learning programs.[29]

As partisan divisions over social policy, taxes, and the war on terrorism sharpened antagonisms in Washington, Democratic criticism of NCLB intensified. During the 2004 presidential campaign, many Democrats—including every one of the contenders for the Democratic presidential nomination—derided the Bush administration for bungling implementation of the law and for failing to provide adequate funding for reforms.[30] John Kerry, the eventual presidential nominee, declared during the campaign that "this president committed to resources and reforms in No Child Left Behind, but he has fallen $27 billion short and implemented the law with a top-down, Washington-knows-best attitude that hurts students." Kerry promised to "put new resources into our schools and make reform work by fully funding No Child Left Behind, creating a new bargain with America's teachers, and beginning a national campaign to raise high school graduation rates."[31] Even George Miller and Edward Kennedy, Bush's staunchest allies during the debate over enactment of No Child Left Behind, proposed "corrective legislation" (in the words of a Kennedy aide) in 2004 that would have significantly expanded regulatory flexibility and increased federal education funding to states and localities.[32]

Brushing aside criticisms of the law, Bush campaigned hard on NCLB during the 2004 campaign, touting the law as his chief domestic policy accomplishment. "We're not backing down," Bush promised on the campaign trail. "I don't care how much pressure they try to put on the process. I'm not changing my mind about high standards and the need for accountability."[33] At the same time, however, Bush administration officials were quietly implementing a series of reforms that granted increased discretion to state and local governments, much as Clinton had done after the Republican Revolution of 1994. The Department of Education announced a series of new policies that affected how students with disabilities, limited English proficiency, or a history of "significant medical emergency" were counted for accountability purposes, and changed how states could calculate participation rates in state and local tests.[34] These changes, which granted states greater flexibility to exclude from testing student populations disproportionately likely to score poorly on assessments, seemed to make it somewhat easier for districts and schools to make adequate yearly progress and thereby avoid falling under NCLB's sanctions regime.[35] After his victory in the 2004 election, Bush made further policy adjustments that seemed designed to placate critics of NCLB. He sacked Education Secretary Rod Paige, who was unpopular with many in Congress and the education community, replacing him with his close adviser Margaret Spellings. In April 2005 Spellings announced "a new common sense approach" to NCLB, which would grant states and localities additional flexibility under the law as long as they adhered to what Spellings dubbed the law's "bright lines"—assessments in grades 3–8, disaggregation of student achievement data, proficiency for all students by 2014, highly qualified teachers, and school choice.[36] Some of these technical changes attempted to make NCLB conform to evolving standards of best practices, and were supported by business entrepreneurs, civil rights entrepreneurs, educational liberals, educational conservatives, and state leaders alike. For example, Spellings supported state efforts to institute "growth models" of student achievement—which measured the progress of individual students from one year to the next—rather than the "status model" required under NCLB, which compared the achievement of one cohort of students against that of the previous year's cohort. Recognizing that NCLB's stringent accountability system failed to differentiate between schools with severe difficulties and those with more minor challenges, Spellings offered a pilot program that allowed participating states to create a more nuanced accountability system distinguishing "between schools and districts in need of intensive intervention and those that are closer to meeting their goals."[37]

Other changes were more controversial, however. For example, in response to an administration decision to grant states flexibility in establishing the minimum size a student group must reach in order to be counted for accountability purposes, the Democrats for Education Reform, a pro-standards-based reform group, charged that the reform was a political ploy designed to allow schools to hide the poor performance of disadvantaged students:

> Schools have even been allowed to monkey around with disaggregating their AYP [adequate yearly progress] data by race and ethnicity. States have allowed schools to omit significant numbers of low-performing students by setting large minimum sizes—known as N-sizes—for calculating a subgroup's test scores.... The games being played here are outrageous. Ohio set an N-size of 45 for kids with disabilities. California's N-size is 100. These are telling shenanigans for a law meant to Leave *No Child Behind*, and the Bush education department has abided them.[38]

While the Bush administration introduced new flexibility under NCLB, state and local governments were exploiting the discretion they enjoyed under the law to bend the policy to their own purposes. To be fair, between 2002 and 2008, states made remarkable progress in adopting standards, testing, accountability, and teacher-quality reforms required under NCLB.[39] While states adhered to the letter of the law, however, some seemed not to be honoring its spirit. Rather than institute rigorous standards, challenging tests, and vigorous accountability policies, some states appeared to be using their discretion under the law to make it relatively easy for schools to meet performance expectations. Indeed, a 2010 U.S. Department of Education evaluation of states' and localities' implementation of standards and testing reforms concluded that "states used the flexibility provided by NCLB to establish accountability systems that varied in terms of the rigor of their academic standards, the level at which they set proficiency, the type of assessments they use, and the manner in which they calculated AYP and set their annual proficiency targets."[40] The story about implementation of NCLB's "highly qualified teacher" provisions, which required states to take steps to ensure that teachers possessed adequate pedagogical and subject-matter knowledge, was much the same. While states made considerable progress in implementing the letter of the law, the Department of Education determined in 2010, "Variation in state policies concerning highly qualified teachers continues to raise questions about whether some states have set sufficiently high standards for considering teachers to be highly qualified."[41]

Failed Reauthorization, Blueprint for Future Policy?

As the scheduled reauthorization of NCLB approached, two facts were clear. First, while NCLB raised federal involvement in education to new heights, pushback from educational liberals, educational conservatives, and state leaders moderated its influence. Arguably, NCLB played a major role in inducing states throughout the nation to adopt comprehensive standards-based reforms. But this ostensible success masked more subtle limitations on federal influence: standards, testing, and accountability regimes varied considerably in their scope and rigor. In short, as had occurred following enactment of the IASA in 1994, the implementation of NCLB revealed the serious institutional constraints on federal involvement in education.

Second, it was obvious that the law was becoming increasingly unpopular, despite efforts by the Bush administration to recalibrate NCLB to make it more appealing to the public. In June 2007, 40 percent of Americans viewed NCLB unfavorably, while only 31 percent held a favorable opinion. Some 26 percent of Americans believed the law was helping schools, but 27 percent believed it was hurting them, while 41 percent thought NCLB was making no difference.[42] Hopes for reauthorizing the law in 2007, as scheduled, were further dimmed by growing partisan conflict over taxes, the war in Iraq, and other issues, which only deepened after Democrats' recapture of Congress in the 2006 midterm elections. With Bush's fortunes in decline and the 2008 presidential campaign looming, there was little incentive for the new majority party to work with the president on his signature domestic initiative. As Representative George Miller (now House Education and Labor Committee chairman) bluntly concluded in July 2007, after the Democratic takeover of Congress, "I can tell you that there are no votes in the U.S. House of Representatives for continuing the No Child Left Behind Act without making serious changes to it."[43]

Unfortunately for Miller, the major groups invested in the reauthorization of NCLB each held very different beliefs about the kinds of "serious changes" that were needed. As in previous debates over how to reform the federal role in education, the major conflict was between, on one hand, business entrepreneurs and civil rights entrepreneurs, who favored refining and expanding federal standards-based reforms, and, on the other, educational liberals, educational conservatives, and state leaders, who (for different reasons) sought dramatic changes to existing policies. Just as they had following the 1994 Republican Revolution, business entrepreneurs and civil rights entrepreneurs sought to deflect criticism of federal standards-based reforms and prepare the way for more ambitious federal involvement. Led by the Business Coalition for Student Achievement (the most recent incarnation of the Business Coalition for Excellence in Education), the National Center for Educational Accountability, the Education Trust, the Citizens' Commission on Civil Rights, the National Council of La Raza, and the Links, Incorporated (a professional association for women of color), these groups banded together in 2005 in a new organization, NCLB Works!, to strengthen federal leadership of standards-based reform, "refute misinformation about [NCLB] and...report data on 'turnaround' schools," according to Susan Traiman of the Business Roundtable.[44] In a remarkable display of their support for the continuation and expansion of NCLB, John Castellani of the Business Roundtable and William Taylor of the Citizens' Commission on Civil Rights both joined Secretary of Education Margaret Spellings at a January 2008 National Press Club roundtable on the Act, where they were recognized by Spellings as "trailblazers" and "fellow warriors" on behalf of federal standards, tests, and accountability policies.[45]

Of particular note, business entrepreneurs and civil rights entrepreneurs proposed to reinforce NCLB in order to remedy what they viewed as the limitations of existing state and local policies. First, because "some states have chosen to dumb down their academic standards in order to achieve proficiency," as U.S. Chamber of Commerce president Thomas Donohue put it in a December 2007 address, business entrepreneurs and civil rights entrepreneurs proposed to require states to establish standards aligned with *college and workplace* expectations.[46] Second, because they believed that NCLB's "highly qualified teacher" provisions had failed to motivate states to raise the quality of their teaching forces, business and civil rights entrepreneurs argued that Congress should require states to evaluate teachers based on whether they were successful in raising students' achievement.[47] As Kati Haycock explained in a September 2006 statement, "We need to move from measuring teacher *qualities* to teacher *effectiveness*. Teachers who cannot demonstrate that they can boost student learning should get assistance, but then should not continue teaching if they do not improve."[48] Third, in order to accomplish this teacher training objective, the federal government should "provide resources to develop statewide data systems that offer timely and accurate collection, analysis, and use of high quality longitudinal data" on student achievement and teacher effectiveness, according to the Business Coalition for Student Achievement.[49] Similarly, Amy Wilkins of the Education Trust maintained in a March 2007 statement that "Congress should provide dedicated funds to each state for the development and operation of education information management systems and set minimal requirements for such systems. One such requirement should be that the systems have the ability to match individual teacher records to individual student records and calculate growth in student achievement over time."[50]

The priorities of many educational liberals could not have been more different. Whereas business entrepreneurs and civil rights entrepreneurs proposed to refine and extend NCLB, educational liberals called for a fundamental overhaul of the law. According to Monty Neill of FairTest, an organization known for its criticisms of standards and accountability policies,

> NCLB's central strategy—pressuring schools to continually raise students' test scores or be subjected to escalating sanctions—is fundamentally defective. This strategy assumes that schools already have the capacity, i.e. resources, knowledge and skills, to effectively educate all children at challenging levels or to make the necessary changes to do so, but that they are simply not trying hard enough. In reality, many schools currently lack such capacity, regardless of the amount of pressure exerted on them.[51]

Many of the major educational organizations (including the National Education Association, the American Federation of Teachers, and the educational administrator groups) joined with important unions such as the AFL-CIO and the American Federation of State, County, and Municipal Employees and civil rights organizations such as the NAACP and the American Civil Liberties Union in a new organization called the Forum on Educational Accountability in order to shape the reauthorization debate. This group, which was closely affiliated with educational liberals within the Democratic Party, contended that "rather than making accountability the central component of ESEA, the law must make capacity-building central."[52] Thus, it proposed to scrap major provisions of the law, such as the 100 percent proficiency goal, the adequate yearly progress requirement, the annual testing requirement, and the sanctions regime. In their place, the forum proposed a new system that devolved much more authority to local governments, teachers, and parents; dramatically reduced the use of standardized testing; and reorganized accountability to emphasize assistance, rather than sanctions, in addressing problems in schools. Echoing the traditional educational liberal argument that inadequate resources undermined schools' efforts to raise student achievement, the forum called for expanded federal funding to build capacity in struggling schools, reduce class sizes, promote individualized instruction, and enhance teacher professional development and training.[53]

Educational conservatives associated with think tanks and advocacy organizations such as the Heritage Foundation, the American Enterprise Institute, the Hoover Institution, and the Cato Institute advocated yet another agenda for reforming NCLB, focused on increasing flexibility for states and localities in implementing standards, testing, and accountability reforms. At the extreme, advocates at the Cato Institute proposed to "End [NCLB], Don't Mend It," on the grounds that NCLB only encouraged states to lower their standards in order to avoid implementing accountability policies.[54] Other educational conservatives, such as Dan Lips of the Heritage Foundation, called on policymakers to allow states to "opt out" of NCLB so that they could enter into individualized educational "performance agreements" with the Department of Education.[55] Still other educational conservatives, led by figures such as Chester Finn, Rick Hess, and John Chubb, and working through a task force affiliated with the Hoover Institution, were more sympathetic to NCLB's goals and recommended tightening NCLB in some ways, while making it more flexible in others. For example, these figures argued that states should be required to work to establish *common*, "college and career ready" standards, and to hold schools accountable for preparing students to meet them. These educational conservatives also recommended that NCLB be amended to require states to adopt comprehensive education information systems that could measure student achievement growth and link it to the performance of teachers and administrators. However, to provide more flexibility to states and more fairness to schools, these educational conservatives called for a more nuanced accountability system that differentiated between schools that barely missed "adequately yearly progress" and those with endemic difficulties.[56]

State leaders argued that while the intentions of NCLB were laudable, the law imposed excessive regulatory burdens without providing adequate funding for implementation. Building on the momentum of the "rebellion" of 2003–6, state leaders hoped to carve out new areas of flexibility in implementing NCLB. In 2005 the National Conference of State Legislatures (NCSL) demanded that the federal government "give states broader authority to define student-achievement goals and more latitude to devise the strategies to help students reach those goals," according to *Education Week*.[57] Going into ESEA reauthorization talks, the NCSL recommended "fixing the law and at the very least, adequately funding the process and requirements before considering additional federal requirements for states, districts, and schools."[58] Joining with the Council of Chief State School Officers and the National Association of State Boards of Education, the National Governors Association took a similar position, calling for more flexibility in the measurement of student achievement, the implementation of accountability measures, and the recognition of new teachers as "highly qualified."[59]

These conflicting agendas set the stage for a clash over the NCLB reauthorization. In August 2007 George Miller released a four-hundred-page "discussion draft" designed to draw the major players into a grand coalition for reauthorizing the law. Miller's draft was an obvious effort to chart a middle way, incorporating some provisions that would please the critics of NCLB, as well as others that would appeal to the law's defenders.[60] To address the criticisms that the law's provisions were too stringent and inflexible, Miller's proposal introduced new features that delegated important decisions to state and local governments. Among other things, the draft encouraged the use of growth models, as opposed to status models, to gauge student achievement; permitted states and localities to use multiple measures (such as written work and student "portfolios," as well as graduation rates and the number of students completing Advanced Placement classes), rather than merely test scores, to evaluate student performance; allowed states to use local tests for accountability purposes, rather than relying solely on state examinations; instituted differentiated accountability for struggling schools, with the intensity of sanctions varying depending on the degree of distress; and promised a dramatic increase in education spending. But the "discussion draft" also contained provisions designed to appeal to the business entrepreneurs and civil rights entrepreneurs who had been NCLB's staunchest defenders. In an acknowledgment that NCLB encouraged state and local governments to set low standards so that schools could more readily meet expectations, Miller's plan offered incentives to states to develop "college and career ready" standards and tests. To address the concern that states used misleading measures to plump their graduation rates, Miller proposed to establish a uniform standard for calculating graduation rates. Additionally, the draft called for performance pay for teachers and principals and new measures for turning around low-performing middle and high schools.[61]

In sum, the "discussion draft" seemed to offer something for everyone. Despite Miller's best efforts, however, the draft ended up pleasing no one; interested parties treated the framework "like a piñata," Miller later recalled.[62] Business entrepreneurs and civil rights entrepreneurs charged that Miller had capitulated to critics of NCLB. The Business Coalition for Student Achievement expressed "deep concern" about "provisions included in the draft that we believe would undermine the current accountability for all students to reach proficiency and would provide a path by which many states would create accountability systems so complex as to be rendered meaningless."[63] Similarly, Amy Wilkins of the Education Trust snapped that "it's hard from a policy point of view to make sense of the accountability provisions in [Miller's] draft, but their political meaning is quite clear. The efforts to dumb-down the definitions of progress and success by well-financed and ill-informed defenders of the status quo are gaining traction."[64]

Meanwhile, educational liberals, educational conservatives, and state leaders complained that Miller's draft failed to address their respective concerns. According to the Forum on Educational Accountability, "The modest changes in the House Education Committee's discussion draft…will not solve the problems [of NCLB]. Minor tinkering won't fix the law's reliance on high-stakes testing, unrealistic achievement targets, and punitive mandates."[65] For their part, state organizations such as the National Governors Association fumed that "the discussion draft does not recognize the leading role of governors in education reform" and failed to extend the regulatory flexibility they had sought.[66] Educational conservatives expressed dismay that Miller's draft expanded federal authority and imposed new administrative burdens on states and localities.[67] In early 2007, conservative Republican Peter Hoekstra of Michigan introduced legislation that would dismantle NCLB and give states wide latitude in spending ESEA funds.[68]

Though negotiations continued behind the scenes, the conflagration over Miller's draft marked the end of serious efforts to reauthorize NCLB prior to the presidential election. Both Democrats and Republicans preferred to wait out the results of the 2008 election in the hope that the outcome would produce conditions more favorable to the enactment of their education priorities. In an indication of the polarization of the debate over the law, the most important piece of NCLB legislation introduced in 2008, cosponsored by conservative Republican Sam Graves of Missouri and liberal Democrat Tim Walz of Minnesota, would have suspended NCLB's accountability measures until the law was reauthorized. The "NCLB Recess until Reauthorization Act," backed by an unusual alliance of educational conservatives and educational liberals—and loudly supported by the National Education Association—was only withdrawn after the Education Trust, the Citizens' Commission on Civil Rights, and the Leadership Conference on Civil Rights lodged public protests with George Miller and House Appropriations chairman David Obey.[69] In their letter explaining their opposition to the NCLB Recess until Reauthorization Act and support for No Child Left Behind,

Wade Henderson and Nancy Zirkin, the president and vice president of the Leadership Conference on Civil Rights, averred that "[the Leadership Conference on Civil Rights] *believes that NCLB is a civil rights law, and that some of the requirements of NCLB constitute, in essence, the rights of children to obtain a quality education.*"[70]

Because education was not a particularly salient issue in the 2008 campaign, it was unclear how federal education policy would be affected by the election. "Neither presidential candidate has talked much about education on the campaign trail," *Education Week* reported in late October 2008. Assuming that Obama would win the election, the journal expressed confusion about his approach to education policymaking. As reporter Alyson Klein wondered aloud, "Would Education Be a Priority in an Obama Administration?"[71]

The Obama Administration, Race to the Top, and the Expansion of Federal Involvement in Standards-Based Reform

Perhaps surprisingly, given the severity of the recession and the contentiousness of the fight over health care reform, Klein's question can be answered in the affirmative. The Obama administration *has* made education a priority, using federal funding in the economic stimulus legislation as leverage to impel states to adopt new standards, testing, and accountability reforms.

Though some view these reforms as sui generis to Obama, the truth is that there is a striking affinity between the Obama administration's education agenda and the initiatives touted by business entrepreneurs and civil rights entrepreneurs (and, to a lesser degree, educational conservatives like Chester Finn and John Chubb) during the NCLB reauthorization battle of 2007–8. This affinity begins with Obama's secretary of education, Arne Duncan, who in many ways embodies the tactical alliance between business entrepreneurs and civil rights entrepreneurs described throughout this book. Duncan acquired as a young man a strong personal interest in the education of the disadvantaged; during his teenage years, he worked at a Chicago youth center, run by his mother, which provided tutoring and mentoring to disadvantaged South Side youngsters.[72] Duncan's formal involvement in school reform began in 1992, when he joined Ariel Investments, a private Chicago-based money management firm founded by prominent African American entrepreneur (and close Obama adviser and fund-raiser) John W. Rogers Jr., to manage its Ariel Education Initiative.[73] The Ariel Education Initiative managed tutoring and mentoring programs for disadvantaged students and helped start a school, the Ariel

Community Academy, on the South Side. Subsequently, in 1999, Duncan went to work for the Chicago Public School District under the direction of staunch standards-based reform advocate Paul Vallas. Two years later Duncan succeeded Vallas as CEO, becoming chief of one of the nation's largest, and most troubled, school districts. During his eight-year tenure, Duncan advocated numerous reforms—including basing teacher pay in part on performance, closing chronically struggling schools, and expanding charter schools and privately managed schools—which were lauded by the Chicago Commercial Club and the Bill and Melinda Gates Foundation and reviled by some teacher advocates and community activists.[74]

As Duncan moved to the federal Department of Education, he knew he would enjoy the support of business entrepreneurs in his efforts to promote standards-based reforms; indeed, the *Chicago Tribune* reported that he was "counting on business leaders to help push through school reforms."[75] But it would be incorrect to view Duncan simply as an advocate of business interests. Duncan also received firm backing from the civil rights community; writing in support of his nomination for secretary of education, the Leadership Conference on Civil Rights averred that

> during Mr. Duncan's seven years leading [Chicago Public Schools], the system made steady and sustainable improvements by most academic measures, including both test scores and graduation rates, while also laying the foundation for continuing growth. It is clear from a review of his record and the wide variety of programs implemented in Chicago, Mr. Duncan's approach to improving schools was not driven by ideology, but rather by results. With the magnitude of the task awaiting the new Secretary of Education, no other approach is likely to succeed.[76]

"[Education reform] is the civil rights issue of our generation and it is the one sure path to a more equal, fair and just society," Duncan declared in his inaugural address as Obama's secretary of education, echoing claims that had long been made by civil rights entrepreneurs.[77] Equally telling, Duncan titled his first major statement on the Elementary and Secondary Education Act "Reauthorization of ESEA: Why We Can't Wait," in a deliberate echo of the famous Martin Luther King Jr. address, declaring that "we cannot wait any longer" to institute education reforms for disadvantaged children. Citing evidence of high dropout rates and low student achievement among disadvantaged students, Duncan proclaimed that "we need to bring a greater sense of urgency to this task—built around our collective understanding that there is no more important work in society than educating children and nothing should stand in our way—not adult dysfunction, not politics, and not fear of change."[78]

Given Duncan's close ties to business entrepreneurs and civil rights entrepreneurs, it is no surprise that the administration's Race to the Top (RTT) initiative, the most ambitious effort of Obama's first eighteen months, embraced many of the priorities of these groups. In contrast, "none of the reforms was a typical Democratic crowd-pleaser," the *Washington Post* reported in September 2009; but neither did they warm the hearts of educational conservatives, who viewed the Obama administration's reforms as a further expansion of federal influence in education.[79] RTT used $4.35 billion from the American Recovery and Reinvestment Act (widely known as the "economic stimulus") as leverage to induce states to adopt college- and career-ready standards and assessments; build data systems that measure student growth and success and link student achievement to teachers and administrators; recruit and reward effective school personnel; and turn around struggling schools.[80] Unlike NCLB, which provided funding to every accepting state by formula, Race to the Top was a competitive grant: states had to apply for RTT funding and were either granted or denied funds based on their ability to demonstrate to department officials and peer reviewers that they had comprehensive plans for instituting reforms. Additionally, applying states could not have any legal, statutory, or regulatory barriers to linking data on student achievement to teachers and principals for the purposes of evaluation. While groups as diverse as the National Conference of State Legislatures, the National Governors Association, the National Education Association, and the American Federation of Teachers pleaded for flexibility under the program, the Race to the Top application was quite prescriptive (and, at over one hundred pages, quite lengthy), testifying to the administration's ambition to use the funds to "spur its vision of reform nationwide," as the *Los Angeles Times* reported in August 2010.[81]

It was apparent that Obama's gambit was to dangle federal funds before cash-strapped states to "strong-arm" policymakers to accept his standards, testing, and accountability agenda, as the *Washington Post* reported in July 2009.[82] Traveling the country in an effort to drum up support for the initiative, Duncan repeatedly named states that he viewed as poor candidates for Race to the Top funds—due to legislative caps on charter schools or bans on the linking of student test scores with teacher data—in an effort to pressure them to change course.[83] Duncan's efforts seem to have had an effect: by August 2010, at least thirty-one states had altered laws or administrative policies in order to enhance their chances of securing a Race to the Top grant.[84] For example, Michigan passed a law that will require teacher and administrator evaluations to be tied to student performance; California removed a data firewall that prevented student achievement data from being linked to teachers; and Delaware, Illinois, Louisiana, and Tennessee all lifted caps on the number of charter schools that could be incorporated within their borders. By the end of 2009, forty-eight states had also joined the Common Core State Standards project organized by the National Governors Association and the Council of Chief State School Officers—which is attempting to devise a common set of academic standards—in order to boost their chances of being awarded an RTT grant.[85]

Despite Duncan's tough talk, some commentators expected that the Department of Education would be lenient in its administration of Race to the Top, disbursing federal funds to virtually every applicant (this would have been consistent with the manner in which federal education funds were usually allocated). In a major surprise, Duncan awarded grants to only two states— Delaware and Tennessee—out of the forty-one that applied for the first "round" of funding announced in April 2010.[86] In late August 2010 the administration announced the winners of the second round of its Race to the Top competition. Ten (Florida, Georgia, Hawaii, Maryland, Massachusetts, New York, North Carolina, Ohio, Rhode Island, and Washington, D.C.) of the thirty-seven applicants were awarded grants, nearly exhausting the more than $4 billion initial allocation.[87] Following each round, there were complaints in some quarters that the administration's award decisions lacked transparency and consistency. Even so, *Education Week* concluded in September 2010, "With the conclusion of the second round of the federal Race to the Top competition, states across the country—winners and losers alike—are vowing to move forward with ambitious plans to reshape teacher-evaluation systems, fix struggling schools, revamp antiquated data systems, and make other changes aimed at raising student achievement."[88]

To be clear, it is too soon to judge RTT's long-term consequences for schooling. Only the passage of time will allow us to evaluate whether RTT had any positive impact on student achievement. However, the program did generate considerable interest in federal standards-based reforms, inducing states to change their policies and commit to far-reaching new initiatives.[89]

The Obama administration's strong emphasis on standards, testing, and accountability reforms elicited praise from business entrepreneurs and civil rights entrepreneurs. Craig Barrett of Intel, William Green of Accenture, and Ed Rust of State Farm Insurance—the cochairmen of the Business Coalition for Student Achievement—declared in April 2010 that "we applaud Secretary Duncan for the strong execution of Phase I of the Race to the Top competition," contending that "the reform agenda focused on collaborative approaches to maximizing student achievement."[90] Later that year, the Education Trust gushed that "the great promise of this competitive grant program [Race to the Top] is its ability to drive meaningful, powerful improvements to boost student learning. Catalyzing sweeping policy changes from Connecticut to California, Race to the Top has led state after state to commit to the hard work necessary to ensure that all children get the kind of world-class education they need and deserve."[91]

Yet the administration's tough approach also sparked controversy, including among groups otherwise intensely loyal to the president. In early July 2010 the House, led by the chamber's Democrats, voted to cut $800 million from Race to the Top and other Obama education initiatives in order to finance a massive $10 billion spending bill designed to help states keep teachers on the job (funding was eventually restored after Obama threatened to veto the bill).[92] A few days later the National Education Association voted to take a position of "no confidence" in the Race to the Top program.[93] Even some civil rights groups, including the NAACP, the National Urban League, the Lawyers' Committee for Civil Rights Under Law, and Jesse Jackson's Rainbow PUSH Coalition, complained that RTT's emphasis on competition was at variance with the principle of opportunity for all they viewed as central to the civil rights movement.[94]

Sensing that educational liberals were growing restless about RTT, Obama traveled to the National Urban League's centennial convention to defend his program. In his address before the convention, the president vigorously reasserted his commitment to standards, testing, and accountability reforms, declaring that "the single most important thing we've done is to launch an initiative called Race to the Top." The president also made the argument—frequently articulated by civil rights entrepreneurs—that standards-based reforms were civil rights measures that advanced opportunities for historically disadvantaged groups. "I know there's a concern that Race to the Top doesn't do enough for minority kids, because the argument is, well, if there's a competition, then somehow some states or some school districts will get more help than others," Obama said. "Let me tell you, what's not working for black kids and Hispanic kids and Native American kids across this country is the status quo. That's what's not working."[95] "Forcefully defending his signature initiative," in the words of *Education Week*, Obama appeared to mollify the gathered conventioneers, who repeatedly interrupted his speech with applause.[96]

The Failed NCLB Reauthorization, the 2010 Elections, and the Future of Federal Education Policy

For good or for ill, Race to the Top induced states to commit to significant education reforms, while providing funding to states with especially ambitious reform proposals that conformed to the administration's priorities.[97] But the program faces important political and institutional headwinds, suggesting that its long-term impact is uncertain. Facing severe budget deficits as a result of continuing slow economic growth, many state governments have been slashing spending on elementary and secondary education. In this unfavorable context, it is unclear whether states will be able to sustain energy to implement standards, testing, accountability, and teacher-quality reforms—especially if they did not win RTT grants.[98] In fact, there are reports that even some of the states that *won* RTT grants are already scaling back their reform ambitions due to inadequate funds or lack of capacity, leading the Obama administration to approve state requests to extend deadlines for implementing reforms.[99] In any case, RTT is ultimately "a short-term effort," as education analyst Chad Alderman has noted, rather than an ongoing program with a regular appropriation.[100] Although the Obama administration secured $700 million for a one-year extension of Race to the Top in a budget deal to fund the federal government through September 2011, it is unclear whether funds will be available under the program in subsequent years, especially in an era of record deficits and tight budgets.[101]

In the past, business entrepreneurs, civil rights entrepreneurs, and their political allies sought to institutionalize standards, testing, and accountability reforms by integrating them into the Elementary and Secondary Education Act. While this strategy has obvious limitations, as noted throughout this book, it has also allowed controversial reforms to piggyback on the popularity of a broadly supported grant program, and thereby influence state and local government policies in ways that would otherwise be impossible. Like Bill Clinton and George W. Bush, Obama proposed to use the ESEA as a vehicle to advance standards-based reforms. Obama's "blueprint" for reauthorizing NCLB, announced in March 2010, sought to build on that act by transforming RTT themes into new conditions of receipt of federal aid under the ESEA. Indeed, as Duncan explained in testimony before the House Committee on Education and Labor,

> This blueprint builds on the significant reforms already made in response to the American Recovery and Reinvestment Act of 2009 around four areas: (1) Improving teacher and principal effectiveness to ensure that every classroom has a great teacher and every school has a great leader; (2) Providing information to families to help them evaluate and improve their children's schools, and to educators to help them improve their students' learning; (3) Implementing college- and career-ready standards and developing improved assessments aligned with those standards; and (4) Improving student learning and achievement in America's lowest-performing schools by providing intensive support and effective interventions.[102]

In the administration's proposal, many of NCLB's standards, testing, and accountability requirements would remain in place, albeit with changes that elaborated on initiatives begun during Bush's administration, such as the use of growth models and differentiated accountability (in a significant departure from NCLB, however, Obama would jettison the 2014 deadline for 100 percent "proficiency," which is viewed as unrealistic). But states would have to adopt more-rigorous, "college and career ready" standards and assessments, either on their own or by participating in multistate consortia, such as that organized by the National Governors Association and the Council of Chief State School Officers. They would also have to develop data systems "to gather information that is critical to determining how schools and districts are progressing in preparing students to graduate from high school college- and career-ready." To deal with persistently struggling schools, states would be required to implement one of the four turnaround "models" specified in RTT; and states would ultimately have to take control of how federal funds are spent in schools with chronic and severe achievement gaps. Consistent with RTT, states would have to develop new measures of teacher and principal "effectiveness"—ultimately replacing NCLB's "highly qualified teacher" regime—based in significant part on the actual academic performance of students.[103]

In short, Obama's approach to reauthorizing ESEA suggested considerable continuity with initiatives long touted by business entrepreneurs and civil rights entrepreneurs and institutionalized by Clinton and Bush in the IASA and NCLB, respectively. Unlike his predecessors, however, Obama failed to take swift action to see that his proposals were enacted in a timely fashion. His blueprint for reforming NCLB did not materialize until well into his second year in office (Clinton, who was criticized at the time for tardiness, submitted a proposal in September of his first year, while Bush's blueprint emerged during his first week in office). To make matters worse, the administration did not make a vigorous effort to focus congressional attention on the reauthorization. Given the scale of the economic crisis in 2009 and the unexpected intensity of the debate over health care reform during Obama's first year in office, the delay was understandable. But as policymakers and education analysts realized, the late start meant that it would be virtually impossible to complete the reauthorization prior to the 2010 midterm elections.[104] As the president's approval ratings deteriorated through the summer and fall of 2010, and members of Congress prepared to face an angry electorate in the midst of ongoing economic instability, the effort to reauthorize NCLB slowed to a crawl.

The 2010 midterm elections, which delivered the House of Representatives to the Republican Party and increased the GOP's Senate presence by six seats, make a delay of the reauthorization of NCLB until after the 2012 presidential election almost inevitable. Though Secretary Duncan gamely declared that "we're looking forward to reauthorizing and hopefully moving pretty quickly," Republican leaders embraced a sharply conservative line on educational matters.[105] On election night, Republican John Boehner, who became Speaker of the House at the start of the new Congress, promised that Republicans would "take a new approach [to education policymaking] that hasn't been tried before in Washington—by either party." "It starts with cutting spending instead of increasing it," Boehner explained. "Reducing the size of government instead of expanding it."[106] Meanwhile, facing a challenging postelection political environment, Obama seemed to be making efforts to defuse criticisms of his approach to education, much as Clinton had after the Republican Revolution of 1994 and Bush had after the 2006 elections. Indeed, by early 2011, the Obama administration was bowing to pressure from conservative Republicans and from state leaders to provide even more flexibility in implementing provisions of No Child Left Behind.[107] As *Education Week* reported in April 2011, the Obama administration was in the process of issuing a record number of waivers from NCLB regulations:

> With Secretary Arne Duncan at the helm, the U.S. Department of Education is gradually—and sometimes quietly—chipping away at key parts of the No Child Left Behind Act as states and districts demand more relief from the elusive goal that all students be what the law terms "proficient" in reading and math by 2014. The pressure on Mr. Duncan to waive substantial parts of the 9-year-old federal school-accountability law is only growing as Congress continues to drag its feet on reauthorizing the Elementary and Secondary Education Act, of which NCLB is the latest version.[108]

In August 2011, the administration announced a revised waiver plan that would allow states to apply for relief from some NCLB requirements as long as they agreed to adopt other education reforms such as raising standards, helping teachers and principals improve, and intervening in the lowest performing schools.[109]

Not surprisingly, the Obama administration's move toward increased flexibility under NCLB has raised serious concerns among civil rights entrepreneurs and business entrepreneurs, who have argued that these steps could undermine educational opportunities for disadvantaged students. Testifying to their concern—in particular, the concern that regulatory flexibility will encourage states to develop policies that allow schools to avoid accountability for the performance of disadvantaged students—in April 2011 the Congressional Black, Hispanic, and Asian Pacific American Caucuses sent a letter to administration officials and top lawmakers on the House and Senate education committees, emphasizing "the federal responsibility to require strong accountability through performance goals for all schools and students." A similarly worded letter was sent by an "Education Reform Coalition" including, among others, civil rights groups such as the Children's Defense Fund, the Education Trust, the League of United Latin American Citizens, and the National Council of La Raza, and business entrepreneur groups such as the Business Roundtable and the U.S. Chamber of Commerce, urging Obama to continue to support federally led standards, testing, and accountability reforms.[110] As the letter emphasized, "We believe strongly that the new ESEA must continue to require, in exchange for federal funding, state and local accountability for the academic achievement of *all* children, including and *especially* for racial and ethnic minorities, English language learners, children with disabilities, and children from low-income families."[111] "There's a lot of uncertainty [about the Obama administration's intentions]," said Raul González, the director of legislative affairs for the National Council of La Raza. "It's important for the administration to clarify what they mean" on the matter of accountability for poor and minority students.[112]

Of course, the changes of political fortune detailed in previous chapters suggest that it would be premature to conclude that Obama's blueprint, and NCLB, are doomed. However, the developments of the past year are suggestive of the formidable political and institutional constraints on entrepreneurship in federal education policymaking. Beginning his presidency with an innovative education initiative that shaped the education debate during the first two years of his administration, Obama suffered a sudden reversal that left the scope of his reforms in doubt. The coming years will reveal whether this episode merely marks another period of reaction against federal standards, testing, and accountability reforms—to be followed by yet another era of renewed federal involvement—or whether it is the first phase in a new pattern of political development in education policymaking.

INSTITUTIONALLY BOUNDED ENTREPRENEURSHIP AND THE FUTURE OF AMERICAN EDUCATION POLICYMAKING

In this book I have traced the development of education policymaking in the United States over a period of several decades. Through many twists and turns, this development has been characterized by two central tendencies. First, through laws, regulations, and grants-in-aid, the federal government has gradually come to play a much more central role in the governance of education in the United States. While the federal government historically refrained from intervening in curricular and pedagogical matters, today it plays an important leadership role in stimulating the spread of coordinated standards, testing, and accountability reforms. Most notably, contemporary standards-based reforms train a spotlight on the achievement of historically disadvantaged students and impose pressure on states and localities to take steps to improve these students' performance. Nevertheless, the expansion of federal authority in education does not mean that responsibility for core educational decisions is now centralized within the federal government. A major irony of political development in federal education policy is the persistence of long-standing, decentralizing institutional commitments in spite of important centralizing policy changes. Indeed, the second central theme of this book is that the new federal role has been largely grafted onto the traditional, decentralizing mechanism of federal involvement in education: the system of categorical grants (most notably, the Elementary and Secondary Education Act) that provides federal aid to state and local governments to institute education programs. The result has been that, despite the ostensible expansion of federal authority during this period, many pivotal educational decisions have been devolved to state and local governments, leading to considerable variation in the scope and rigor of standards, testing, and accountability reforms. Over time, an increasingly complex intergovernmental system of regulations, rules, and policies related to standards-based reforms has developed, enmeshing the federal, state, and local governments in a dense policymaking network in which all vie for responsibility and control.

While America's contemporary standards, testing, and accountability regime is byzantine in organization, it is also ambiguous in its educational consequences. Arguably, the palpable evidence of educational inequalities generated by standards-based assessments, as well as data demonstrating that students in some schools can make impressive gains in the face of formidable obstacles to achievement, creates strong political pressure to address educational inequities. Perhaps more than at any previous point in the history of American education policymaking, the academic achievement of historically disadvantaged groups is now at the forefront of the debate over school improvement. As political scientist Scott Abernathy explained in a 2007 description of the No Child Left Behind Act,

> NCLB holds the promise of being one of the great liberal reforms in the history of U.S. education.... The reason lies in the goals. Desegregation and the Americans with Disabilities Act were both about equality of opportunity; No Child Left Behind aims to provide equality of outcomes. This is a very radical and ambitious goal. No longer content to provide access to education for traditionally excluded populations, we are now demanding that these students receive equally good educations. In other words, we are now demanding equality of quality.[1]

Although equality of quality may still be very far off, there is some evidence that standards, testing, and accountability reforms can produce modest-to-moderate gains in student achievement, especially in mathematics. According to a recent review by prominent policy analysts Helen Ladd and Douglas Lauen, the general conclusion of much recent research on standards, testing, and accountability policies is that "the introduction of a school-based accountability program generally raises achievement when achievement is measured by the high-stakes test used in the accountability system. Studies also report small positive achievement effects when achievement is measured by a low-stakes test, such as the National Assessment of Education Progress (NAEP)."[2] In a recent evaluation of the effects of NCLB on student achievement, Thomas Dee and Brian Jacob provide important evidence that the law has sparked modest to moderate achievement gains, at least in mathematics, in states that had not previously adopted comprehensive standards-based reforms.[3]

However, as has been well documented, NCLB-style reforms are not without their limitations. If standards, testing, and accountability reforms have the potential to enhance student achievement on average, there is considerable ongoing debate about how achievement gains are distributed among students of different races and achievement levels; some studies find that the benefits of accountability are distributed broadly, while others caution that gains may be concentrated among students of certain racial groups, or among those nearest the "proficiency" cutoff point.[4] Standards, testing, and accountability reforms may have undesirable spillover consequences for the ways schools operate, as well. To meet achievement expectations, schools may narrow their curricula, engage in more teacher-directed forms of learning, and focus on preparation for exams; in the extreme, they may resort to undesirable "gaming" strategies to artificially boost test scores.[5] In any case, overall student achievement gains in recent years as measured by the National Assessment of Educational Progress are far from overwhelming. More worrisomely, while African American and Hispanic students, especially younger students, have exhibited modest gains in achievement over the past decade, the achievement gaps between these students and their white peers remain large.[6] If standards, testing, and accountability reforms have accomplished more than their detractors claim, then they also have achieved less than their supporters have hoped.

Given that the politics surrounding contemporary education policymaking have often been acrimonious, and that the results of standards, testing, and accountability policies have thus far been ambiguous, it would be appealing to present the politics of federal education policymaking as a kind of morality tale, in which good intentions were crushed by the machinations of evildoers. In fact, that is what some scholars on both sides of the political aisle have done, though the identities of the heroes and villains differ depending on who is telling the story. For some conservative writers, the story of standards, testing, and accountability reforms is a tale of good policies defeated by the "special interests." Leading a host of conservative critics of the National Education Association and the American Federation of Teachers, Terry Moe recently suggested that teachers unions are to blame for the alleged failure of recent school reforms. As Moe argues,

> For the last quarter century, the United States has struggled to meet this challenge [of reforming the nation's schools]. And it has failed. The teachers unions are not solely responsible for that failure. But as the single most powerful group in American education by many orders of magnitude, they have played an integral role in it. Through their bottom-up power in collective bargaining, they have burdened the schools with perverse organizations that are literally not designed for effective

education. Through their top-down power in the political process, they have blocked or weakened sensible reforms that attempt to bring change and improvement.[7]

Not to be outdone, some liberal scholars have presented standards, testing, and accountability reforms as a conservative plot to discipline students, teachers, and schools, dovetailing with a broader reactionary objective of subordinating social justice to the dictates of market capitalism. From this perspective, standards-based reforms—of dubious educational value in themselves—have also crowded out more egalitarian social policies seeking to fight poverty and political inequality. According to Michael Apple,

> a "new" set of compromises, a new alliance, and new power bloc have been formed that have increasing influence in education and all things social. This power bloc combines multiple fractions of capital who are committed to neoliberal marketized solutions to educational problems, neoconservative intellectuals who want a "return" to higher standards and a "common culture," authoritarian populist religious fundamentalists who are deeply worried about secularity and the preservation of their own traditions, and particular fractions of the professionally oriented new middle class who are committed to the ideology and techniques of accountability, measurement, and "management." Although clear tensions and conflicts exist within this alliance, in general its overall aims are to provide the educational conditions believed necessary both for increasing international competitiveness, profit, and discipline and for returning us to a romanticized past of the "ideal" home, family, and school.…
>
> *The objectives in education are the same as those that guide its economic and social welfare goals.* They include the dramatic expansion of…the free market; the drastic reduction of government responsibility for social needs; the reinforcement of intensely competitive structures of mobility both inside and outside the school; the lowering of people's expectations for economic security; the "disciplining" of culture and the body; and the popularization of what is clearly a form of Social Darwinist thinking.[8]

Though coming from sharply different political perspectives, the two sets of claims share the common theme that the tortuous institutions and ambiguous (if not perverse) outcomes that characterize contemporary education policymaking in the United States can be ascribed to the self-interested malevolence of one set of social forces or another.

I believe that these stock tales simplify—indeed, caricature—a much more complicated, and theoretically interesting, pattern of political development. In this book, I have presented an argument that, although perhaps less satisfying to more ideologically inclined readers, I believe is closer to the truth. I have traced the development of contemporary education policymaking in the United States—with all its possibilities and limitations—through the lens of institutionally bounded entrepreneurship. As I have shown, political entrepreneurs, driven by the desire to improve education and achieve other policy goals, have provided much of the impetus for the expansion of federal involvement in standards, testing, and accountability over time. Notably, the most consistent educational entrepreneurs spanned the ideological gamut: on one hand, business entrepreneurs sought standards-based reforms so that schools would be positioned to produce employees with the skills needed to meet the challenges of global economic competition; on the other, civil rights entrepreneurs believed standards, testing, and accountability reforms were needed to ensure that schools provided more-equitable opportunities for historically disadvantaged groups. Again and again, these figures spurred the expansion of federal authority by identifying problems within the status quo, developing policy solutions, courting allies, and consolidating cross-partisan coalitions to support their initiatives.

Yet these entrepreneurs were repeatedly constrained by existing institutions and interests, encouraging a halting, uneven pattern of political development. Anticipating resistance from the defenders of the existing system of categorical grants—especially among teachers and school administrators—political entrepreneurs repeatedly elected to layer their proposed reforms atop existing programs rather than manufacture new institutions from whole cloth. Recognizing the fiscal constraints imposed by budget deficits and the imperative to consolidate political support, political entrepreneurs declined to seriously challenge existing budgetary commitments. Wary of antagonizing conservative policymakers distrustful of federal "control" of education, political entrepreneurs accepted that states and localities would retain preeminence in designing standards and tests and implementing accountability policies. In their turn, both liberal and conservative forces sought to bend standards, testing, and accountability reforms to their own purposes. Moreover, once each new federal law was enacted, many states and localities exploited legal ambiguities and took advantage of shifting political currents to moderate the effects of the rigorous standards-based reforms favored by business entrepreneurs and civil rights entrepreneurs. Finally, public support for school reforms—especially when new measures were perceived as interfering with local schools—was often fleeting. Far from embracing ambitious, though potentially disruptive, attempts to address school problems, many citizens preferred to keep schools as they were, even if existing school institutions suffered from limitations.

As we have seen, each reaction against federal encroachment has stirred business entrepreneurs and civil rights entrepreneurs to shore up sagging federal authority through more-intensive conditions on grants-in-aid and more-vigorous oversight of state and local policymaking. These reformers have repeatedly found allies among policymakers, on both sides of the legislative aisle, exasperated by the slow and uneven pace of school improvement. Yet this has also meant that these figures have persisted in strategies that, given prevailing political dynamics, were likely to yield ambiguous results. Over time, the result of this political pattern has been greater federal involvement, more-complex policymaking, and greater intergovernmental and interinstitutional conflict between the proponents and opponents of standards, testing, and accountability. Meanwhile, dramatic improvement in academic achievement remains ephemeral.

Moving beyond the case of federal education policy, my analysis suggests several broader lessons, identifying directions for future research on the politics of institutional change. My analysis of the activities of business entrepreneurs and civil rights entrepreneurs makes contributions to our understanding of the politics of political entrepreneurship in the contemporary American political system. First, it points to the crucial role played by policy expertise and political longevity in shaping the opportunities for entrepreneurship. Business entrepreneurs associated with the National Alliance of Business, such as William Kolberg, or with the Business Roundtable, such as Louis Gerstner and Ed Rust, and civil rights entrepreneurs such as William Taylor of the Citizens' Commission on Civil Rights and Kati Haycock of the Education Trust, were widely perceived as possessing considerable authority on education issues, as well as political standing with their respective audiences. The respect they enjoyed stemmed in significant part from their reputations as experts with long experience in education policymaking, intimate knowledge of policymaking details, and ability to generate helpful data and proposals for use by policymakers. Furthermore, and of equal importance, these figures possessed longevity: engaged in the politics of education policymaking for decades, they were savvy insiders who knew all the important players in the education policymaking system. Consequently, they could readily secure foundation funding to support their initiatives, maintain close relationships with policymakers and bureaucrats, and forge alliances with multiple constituencies. These figures were also ideally positioned to observe policy dynamics over long spans of time and thereby draw valuable lessons about more and less promising means for achieving their objectives.

A second major theme of my study of these political entrepreneurs is that their relative influence in the policymaking process was due to their ability to appeal to diverse political audiences. In the sharply partisan post-1980 policymaking environment, in which the Democrats and Republicans were also relatively closely matched, neither traditional liberal policymaking approaches nor conventional conservative initiatives could secure the large majorities needed to ensure enactment, especially in the Senate. In contrast—and much as Daniel Carpenter's bureaucratic entrepreneurs achieved influence by building diverse coalitions of esteem—business entrepreneurs and civil rights entrepreneurs experienced relative success because (especially in tandem) they were able to present their proposals in ways that appealed both to Democrats and to Republicans.[9] More to the point, the standards, testing, and accountability agenda these groups advocated partook of ideas and themes from both conservatism and liberalism, without simply splitting the difference between them. For conservatives, there was the prospect of securing accountability for public institutions, thereby ensuring that taxpayer funds were well spent. For liberals, standards-based reform seemed to offer a new way—especially attractive in light of the modest accomplishments of the original ESEA—of advancing the cause of equality of educational opportunity for disadvantaged groups. To be sure, standards, testing, and accountability reforms were not always the first choice of either Republicans or Democrats. However, in a political environment in which first choices were usually unobtainable, standards, testing, and accountability reforms fell within the "zone of acceptable outcomes" of each. Because business entrepreneurs and civil rights entrepreneurs were able to attract both Democrats and Republicans to their cause, they were able to prevail over groups whose narrower ideological agendas lacked sufficient backing to be enacted into law.

This does not mean that enactment of federal standards, testing, and accountability reforms was inevitable, however. These policies should not be seen as "split the difference" initiatives enacted simply because more-preferred outcomes could not be secured. Such a characterization takes for granted the creative, and historically grounded, process undergirding the rise of these policy ideas to prominence. A major theme of my institutionally bounded entrepreneurship approach is that the elaboration and refinement of standards, testing, and accountability reforms was a drawn-out process, entailing major analytical refinements over the course of several decades (which, as the previous chapter suggests, are still very much under way). It bears remembering that these figures' initial agenda, revolving around the idea of excellence in education, suffered from considerable programmatic blind spots, which hindered its realization in practice. Subsequent iterations of standards-based reform have responded to additional perceived limitations, which only became apparent over the course of time as policies embodying these ideas were instituted in practice.

Indeed, the course of this ideational development was profoundly influenced by policymaking developments on the ground in states and localities around the country, which required observation, analysis, and interpretation. The increasing specificity and stringency of the standards, testing, and accountability initiatives proposed by business entrepreneurs and civil rights entrepreneurs was a direct reaction to the uneven implementation of previous reforms. Finally, standards, testing, and accountability initiatives would likely have remained obscure and esoteric ideas had they not been aggressively marketed by their proponents over the course of several decades. However "natural" it may seem for standards, testing, and accountability to have come to the fore in the wake of the political and electoral challenges to the Great Society and educational equity in the 1980s, this book shows conclusively that these policies only gained prominence due to extensive and prolonged effort by their proponents and that they continue to face vigorous opposition to this day.

In the introduction to this book I posed several puzzling questions: How do we explain the expansion of federal involvement and investment in education in an era of ostensible conservative ascendance and partisan polarization? Why do federal standards, testing, and accountability reforms focus such attention on the achievement of historically disadvantaged students? Why do federal standards-based reforms operate through such complex, confusing institutional channels? This book contends that political entrepreneurship characterized by advocacy by diverse forces, development of broadly appealing policy themes, and application of policy expertise and policy learning go a long way in providing answers. Federal education policymaking enjoyed continued—indeed, even expanded—robustness during the 1980s, 1990s, and 2000s because business entrepreneurs and civil rights entrepreneurs forged an agenda that could thrive in the contemporary political environment.

Yet, in appreciating the important changes in education policymaking that have occurred over the past several decades, it is essential not to lose track of the equally important limits on full-scale transformation. In truth, business entrepreneurs and civil rights entrepreneurs were always confronted with considerable opposition to their initiatives, from various sources, and this opposition set the boundaries on the kinds of changes that were possible. A major theme of institutionally bounded entrepreneurship in federal education policy is the striking persistence of long-standing institutions, interests, and ideas during a period of policy change often described as "transformational" in the literature.[10] Indeed, despite three decades of foment over education policymaking, the overall structure of the system, in which the federal government seeks to induce desired reforms through a "Rube Goldberg-esque" array of grants and inducements, remains largely in place, while many long-standing policies (such as the ESEA) continue to operate, albeit in altered form. Some of this persistence is explainable in terms of "path dependence," in which constituencies nurtured by earlier policies (most notably, the teacher and administrator groups) retained considerable capacity to limit the scope of new policy changes. Business entre-preneurs and civil rights entrepreneurs developed new ideas and organizations capable of rivaling, and sometimes besting, those of educational liberals, but they did not destroy educational liberals' capacity to develop their own ideas or their ability to mobilize in the political arena. Consequently, business entrepreneurs and civil rights entrepreneurs could never dictate policy outcomes; they always had to bargain with entrenched, and often hostile, interests over the content of education policy.

Continuity can also be ascribed to the United States' federal system, in which states and localities jealously guarded their prerogatives against federal encroachment. State and local officials not only possessed considerable political power and legal authority of their own; many of them also enjoyed an alliance, grounded in shared opposition to overweening federal involvement, with the Republican Party. Lacking the ability to eject these forces from the political scene, business entrepreneurs and civil rights entrepreneurs ultimately had to concede that standards, testing, and accountability reforms would operate through tradi-tional state and local channels. Subsequently, states and localities implemented standards-based reforms in ways that conformed to local interests, cultures, and administrative capacities, sometimes reinforcing entrepreneurs' intentions, and sometimes departing from them.

While path dependence and federalism play important parts in explaining the continuity of traditional educational institutional forms, the stickiness of public attitudes about education deserves more attention than is usually granted. In spite of their professed concern about the quality of the nation's schools, many Americans have expressed considerable ambivalence about reforms that presume to alter established decentralized governing arrange-ments in education. Though business entrepreneurs and civil rights entrepre-neurs seem to have convinced many Americans that alterations to schools were needed, they have not been able to further convince them that changes that reduced local autonomy and discretion were desirable.[11] Citizens' mixed views have directly contributed to the churning style of education reform described in this book: demanding change from their elected officials, citizens have sub-sequently rebelled against the changes these officials have wrought; then, dissat-isfied with the slow pace of education reform, they have yet again empowered officials to enact even more stringent reforms. This pattern has repeated several times over the course of recent development in education policymaking, and is likely to continue into the future.

In sum, my analysis of institutionally bounded entrepreneurship in education provides a model of institutional change that neither exaggerates the autonomy and creativity of political entrepreneurs nor insists on a form of institutional determinism in which established policy paths are impervious to change. What is most important in explaining institutional change is neither political entrepreneurship nor institutional constraints, per se, but the dynamic interaction between them. This interaction unfolds over time, making institutional change an inexorably historical process. My approach suggests an ongoing, grinding pattern of political change, in which political entrepreneurs and institutional constraints continually readjust in response to previous moves in the political game. It also suggests that political development is likely to be an unsteady march, subject to reversals, wrong turns, and contingent events, even if the overarching pattern of change seems clear.

What, if anything, does my analysis of institutionally bounded entrepreneurship in education policymaking suggest about the future of political development in education? The saga of Obama's Race to the Top and NCLB "blueprint" initiatives, recounted in the previous chapter, provides strong evidence that the dynamics structuring earlier bouts of change in education policymaking remain in force. Even as the stakes of school reform rise, the old battles between proponents and opponents of standards, testing, and accountability continue to resonate, producing patterns of reform and reaction that echo previous configurations. Meanwhile, in schools throughout the nation, academic achievement inches forward—probably in part due to standards-based reforms—but not nearly quickly enough, especially for the nation's most disadvantaged students.

Some scholars, led by Stephen Skowronek, have proposed that our political era is characterized by "institutional thickening," in which political forces are so dense and so evenly matched that significant departures from the status quo are no longer possible.[12] Writing in a similar vein, Christopher Howard has described social policymaking as exhibiting "change, but little progress" over the past several decades.[13] In my view, institutionally bounded entrepreneurship in education implies a more complex lesson than that suggested by Skowronek or Howard. Arguably, some of the changes produced by institutionally bounded entrepreneurship in education have been welcome—in particular, the insistence that political institutions take responsibility for the achievement of historically disadvantaged students. However, other changes, reflected in evidence that standards-based reforms may induce rote, teacher-directed education and more narrow curricula, are unwelcome. The real question, then, is not whether the political dynamics recounted in this book will continue, but whether an alternative political pattern—and one with superior prospects for schooling—can be forged in the contemporary political environment.

In any case, the fundamental tension explored throughout this book—between Americans' aspirations for better and more equitable schools throughout the nation and their insistence that schools remain responsive to local interests and ideas—is unlikely to be resolved in the foreseeable future. The political struggles between business entrepreneurs, civil rights entrepreneurs, educational liberals, educational conservatives, and state leaders were ultimately both about how best to improve the nation's schools, and about who should have the authority to determine how to improve them. They were also about who had the right to speak for the interests of historically disadvantaged groups, and about how these interests should be balanced against the interests of the broader community. Fittingly, given education's central place in American political and social life, these struggles reflect core conflicts between equality and democracy—as well as conflicts about different visions of equality and democracy—that have animated our nation's politics since the founding. Thus, we can only expect that they will inform the debates that will carry the politics of school reform into the future.

Abbreviations

AS	Papers of Albert Shanker, Walter P. Reuther Library, Wayne State University, Detroit, Michigan
BR	Papers of Bella Rosenberg, Walter P. Reuther Library, Wayne State University, Detroit, Michigan (At the time the records from this collection were accessed, this collection was still being processed, so box and folder numbers may be subject to change.)
CEF	Papers of Chester E. Finn Jr., Hoover Institution on War, Revolution, and Peace, Stanford University, Palo Alto, California
CP	Papers of Senator Claiborne Pell, University Library Special Collections and Archives Unit, University of Rhode Island, Kingston, Rhode Island
GHWB	Papers of President George H. W. Bush, George H. W. Bush Presidential Library, College Station, Texas
GMA	Papers of Gordon M. Ambach, Education Policy Papers, B1829, New York State Archives, Cultural Education Center, Albany, New York
NGA	National Governors Association Historical Files, National Governors Association, Washington, DC
OASE: KC	Office of the Assistant Secretary of Education: Records of Kay Casstevens, National Archives and Records Administration, College Park, Maryland (At the time the records from this collection were accessed, this collection was still being processed, so box and folder numbers may be subject to change.)
OUSE: MS	Office of the Undersecretary of Education: Papers of Marshall S. Smith, National Archives and Records Administration, College Park, Maryland (At the time the records from this collection were accessed, this collection was still being processed, so box and folder numbers may be subject to change.)
PM	Papers of Hawaii Representative Patsy Mink, Manuscript Division, United States Library of Congress, Washington, DC
RA	Papers of Texas Representative Richard Armey, Carl Albert Center, University of Oklahoma, Norman, Oklahoma
WJC	Papers of President William J. Clinton, William J. Clinton Presidential Library, Little Rock, Arkansas

Notes

INTRODUCTION

1. Alyson Klein, "Obama Cites Schools in Inaugural Address," *Education Week*, January 20, 2009.

2. Michele McNeil, "Duncan Carves Deep Mark on Policy in First Year," *Education Week*, January 19, 2010.

3. Paul Manna, *Competitive Grant-Making and Education Reform: Assessing Race to the Top's Current Impact and Future Prospects*. American Enterprise Institute Working Paper, October 2010.

4. Quoted in "GOP Gains Could Prompt Funding, Policy Shifts," *Education Week*, November 4, 2010.

5. Sam Dillon, "Obama Returns Some Powers of Education Back to the States," *New York Times*, September 23, 2011.

6. Paul Manna, *Collision Course: Federal Education Policy Meets State and Local Realities* (Washington, DC: CQ Press, 2010), 3.

7. National Center for Education Statistics, *Digest of Education Statistics* (Washington, DC: U.S. Department of Education, 2011), table 186; U.S. Department of Defense, "Defense Department Budget FY '09" (Washington, DC: Government Printing Office, 2009).

8. National Center for Education Statistics, *Condition of Education* (Washington, DC: U.S. Department of Education, 2011), Indicator 38, "Education Indicators by Country," http://nces.ed.gov/programs/coe/pdf/coe_ifn.pdf.

9. National Center for Education Statistics, *Digest of Education Statistics 2010* (Washington, DC: U.S. Department of Education, 2009), table 180, "Revenues for Public Elementary and Secondary Schools, by Source of Funds: Selected Years, 1919–20 through 2007–08." http://nces.ed.gov/programs/digest/d10/tables/dt10_180.asp?referrer=list.

10. National Center for Education Statistics, *The Condition of Education* (Washington, DC: U.S. Department of Education, 2008), 52.

11. See, for example, Organization for Economic Cooperation and Development, *Education at a Glance 2009* (Organization for Economic Cooperation and Development, 2009), Indicators A6, A7, and A9.

12. For a recent discussion see Eric A. Hanushek and Ludger Woessmann, "The Role of Cognitive Skills in Economic Development," *Journal of Economic Literature* 46 (2008): 607–68.

13. Torben Iversen and John Stephens, "Partisan Politics, the Welfare State, and Three Worlds of Human Capital Formation," *Comparative Political Studies* 20 (5) (2008): 3.

14. See, for example, William Reese, "Public Schools and the Elusive Search for the Common Good," in *Reconstructing the Common Good in Education: Coping with Intractable American Dilemmas*, ed. Larry Cuban and Dorothy Shipps (Stanford: Stanford University Press, 2000).

15. Jennifer Hochschild and Nathan Scovronick, *The American Dream and the Public Schools* (Oxford: Oxford University Press, 2004), 124. Emphasis added.

16. Kaiser Health Tracking Poll conducted by the Henry J. Kaiser Family Foundation, June 9–14, 2011. Available at the Roper Center for Public Opinion Research, University of Connecticut, Storrs, CT.

17. Nicholas Kristof, "Education's Ground Zero," *New York Times*, March 21, 2009.

18. Iversen and Stephens, "Partisan Politics," 3.

19. Classics in American political development focusing on Temporary Assistance for Needy Families, Social Security, Medicare and Medicaid, unemployment, health insurance, subsidies, and tax expenditures include Theda Skocpol, *Protecting Soldiers and Mothers: The Political Origins of Social Policy in the United States* (Cambridge, MA: Harvard University Press, 1992); Paul Pierson, *Dismantling the Welfare State? Reagan, Thatcher, and the Politics of Retrenchment* (Cambridge: Cambridge University Press, 1994); Edwin Amenta, *Bold Relief: Institutional Politics and the Origins of Modern American Social Policy* (Princeton, NJ: Princeton University Press, 1998); Suzanne Mettler, *Dividing Citizens: Gender and Federalism in New Deal Public Policy* (Ithaca, NY: Cornell University Press, 1998); Robert Lieberman, *Shifting the Color Line: Race and the American Welfare State* (Cambridge, MA: Harvard University Press, 1998); Christopher Howard, *The Hidden Welfare State: Tax Expenditures and Social Policy in the United States* (Princeton, NJ: Princeton University Press, 1997); and Jacob Hacker, *The Divided Welfare State: The Battle over Public and Private Social Benefits in the United States* (Cambridge: Cambridge University Press, 2002). An important exception to the trend is the edited volume *Conservatism and American Political Development*, which contains historical case studies of conservatives' responses to the development of federal education policy. See Brian J. Glenn and Steven M. Teles, eds., *Conservatism and American Political Development* (Princeton, NJ: Princeton University Press, 2008).

20. Suzanne Mettler, *Soldiers to Citizens: The G.I. Bill and the Making of the Greatest Generation* (New York: Oxford University Press, 2005).

21. On the complex lineages of Obama's social policy reforms see Suzanne Mettler, "Reconstituting the Submerged State: The Challenges of Social Policy Reform in the Obama Era," *Perspectives on Politics* 8 (3) (2010): 803–24.

22. Lawrence M. Mead, *The New Paternalism: Supervisory Approaches to Poverty* (Washington, DC: Brookings Institution Press, 1997); Vesla M. Weaver, "Frontlash: Race and the Development of Punitive Crime Policy," *Studies in American Political Development* 21 (2007): 230–65; Eva C. Bertram, "The Institutional Origins of 'Workfarist' Social Policy," *Studies in American Political Development* 21 (2007): 203–29; Sanford F. Schram, Richard C. Fording, and Joe Soss, "Neo-Liberal Poverty Governance: Race, Place, and the Punitive Turn in US Welfare Policy," *Cambridge Journal of Regions, Economy, and Society* 1 (2008): 17–36; Loic Wacquant, *Punishing the Poor: The Neoliberal Government of Social Insecurity* (Durham, NC: Duke University Press, 2009); Jonathan Simon, *Governing through Crime: How the War on Crime Transformed American Democracy and Created a Culture of Fear* (Oxford: Oxford University Press, 2007)

23. Joe Soss, Sanford Schram, Linda Houser, and Richard Fording, "The Third Level of U.S. Welfare Reform: Governmentality under Neoliberal Paternalism," *Citizenship Studies* 14(6) (2010): 739–54.

24. See, for example, Michael W. Apple, *Educating the "Right" Way: Markets, Standards, God, and Inequality*, 2nd ed. (New York: RoutledgeFalmer, 2006); David Hursh, "Assessing No Child Left Behind and the Rise of Neoliberal Education Policies," *American Educational Research Journal* 44 (3) (2007): 493–518; and Hursh, "Exacerbating Inequality: The Failed Promise of the No Child Left Behind Act," *Race, Ethnicity, and Education* 10 (3) (2007): 295–308; William Lyons and Julie Drew, *Punishing Schools: Fear and Citizenship in American Public Education* (Ann Arbor: University of Michigan Press, 2006).

25. Pauline Lipman, "Education Accountability and the Repression of Democracy Post-9/11," *Journal of Critical Education Policy Studies* 2:1 (2004), http://www.jceps.com/index.php?pageID=article&articleID=23.

26. Donald Critchlow, *The Conservative Ascendancy: How the GOP Right Made Political History* (Cambridge, MA: Harvard University Press, 2007); Mark Smith, *The Right*

Talk: How Conservatives Transformed the Great Society into the Economic Society (Princeton, NJ: Princeton University Press, 2007); Andrea Campbell, "Parties, Electoral Participation, and Shifting Voting Blocs," in *The Transformation of American Politics: Activist Government and the Rise of Conservatism*, ed. Paul Pierson and Theda Skocpol (Princeton, NJ: Princeton University Press, 2007).

27. For the argument that polarization leads to gridlock that blocks the updating of social policies, see, for example, Nolan McCarty, "The Policy Effects of Political Polarization," in Pierson and Skocpol, *Transformation of American Politics*.

28. See Elisabeth Clemens, "Lineages of the Rube Goldberg State: Building and Blurring Public Programs, 1900–1940," in *Rethinking Political Institutions: The Art of the State*, ed. Ian Shapiro, Stephen Skowronek, and Daniel Galvin (New York: NYU Press, 2006).

29. A recent rigorous evaluation of NCLB's impact on student achievement is Thomas Dee and Brian Jacob, "The Impact of No Child Left Behind on Students, Teachers, and Schools," *Brooking Papers on Economic Activity*, (Fall 2010): 149–94.

30. This theme is explored at length in Manna, *Collision Course*.

31. Thus, political scientist Lawrence Jacobs has recently called for "more theory and research that analyze *both* the enduring nature of institutions and social relations *and* the dynamics of change." Lawrence R. Jacobs, "Democracy and Capitalism: Structure, Agency, and Organized Combat," *Politics & Society* 38 (3) (2010), 251. Emphasis added.

32. Of course, the study of political entrepreneurship has a long history in political science. For classic work on political entrepreneurship and policy change see John Kingdon, *Agendas, Alternatives, and Public Policies*, 2nd ed. (New York: HarperCollins, 1995); Frank R. Baumgartner and Bryan Jones, *Agendas and Instability in American Politics* (Chicago: University of Chicago Press, 1993); Nelson Polsby, *Political Innovation in America: The Politics of Policy Initiation* (New Haven: Yale University Press, 1984); Deborah Stone, *Policy Paradox and Political Reason*, 2nd ed. (New York: HarperCollins, 2002). For an important recent overview of the literature see Adam Sheingate, "Political Entrepreneurship, Institutional Change, and American Political Development," *Studies in American Political Development* 17 (2003): 185–203.

33. Sheingate, "Political Entrepreneurship," 185.

34. Weaver, "Frontlash," 236.

35. William Riker notes how political entrepreneurs can selectively introduce issues and dimensions to upset the status quo and force attention to new problems. See Riker, *The Art of Political Manipulation* (New Haven: Yale University Press, 1986).

36. This point is nicely made in Daniel Carpenter and Gisela Sin, "Policy Tragedy and the Emergence of Regulation: The Food, Drug, and Cosmetic Act of 1938," *Studies in American Political Development* 21 (2007): 149–80.

37. For an excellent discussion of the role of ideas in undermining the status quo and providing a blueprint for reform see Mark Blyth, *Great Transformations: Economic Ideas and Institutional Change in the Twentieth Century* (Cambridge: Cambridge University Press, 2002), chap. 2.

38. Carpenter and Sin, "Policy Tragedy," 151.

39. Stephen Skowronek, "The Reassociation of Ideas and Purposes: Racism, Liberalism, and the American Political Tradition," *American Political Science Review* 100 (3) (2006): 388.

40. Sheingate, "Political Entrepreneurship," 193; see also Eric Schickler, *Disjointed Pluralism: Institutional Innovation and the Development of the U.S. Congress* (Princeton, NJ: Princeton University Press, 2001), chap. 1.

41. Schickler, *Disjointed Pluralism*, chap. 1.

42. See Andrew Polsky, "When Business Speaks: Political Entrepreneurship, Discourse and Mobilization in American Partisan Regimes," *Journal of Theoretical Politics* 12 (4) (2000): 455–76.

43. Justin Crowe, "The Forging of Judicial Autonomy: Political Entrepreneurship and the Reforms of William Howard Taft," *Journal of Politics* 69 (1) (2007): 76.

44. John Gilmour, *Strategic Disagreement: Stalemate in American Politics* (Pittsburgh: University of Pittsburgh Press, 1995), chap. 2.

45. Robert Kagan, *Adversarial Legalism: The American Way of Law* (Cambridge, MA: Harvard University Press, 2001).

46. This is not to say that elected officials cannot be entrepreneurial. Indeed, several scholars, including Eric Schickler and Randall Strahan, have traced the entrepreneurial activity of members of Congress. Rather my point is that, when it comes to matters of policy, unelected figures, who are not constrained by the electoral imperative, are more likely to be able to develop novel policy ideas (and supporting evidence and arguments) than are elected officials, who must inevitably focus their energies on the next campaign. See Schickler, *Disjointed Pluralism;* Strahan, *Leading Representatives: The Agency of Leaders in the Politics of the U.S. House* (Baltimore: Johns Hopkins University Press, 2004).

47. See Daniel Carpenter, The Forging of Bureaucratic Autonomy: Reputations, Networks, and Policy Innovation in Executive agencies, 1862–1928 (Princeton, NJ: Princeton University Press, 2001).

48. Walter Power and Jeannette Colyvas, "Microfoundations of Institutional Theory," *Sage Handbook of Organizational Institutionalism,* ed. Kerstin Sahlin-Andersson, Roysten Greenwood, Christine Oliver, and Roy Suddaby (London: Sage Publications, 2008), chap. 10.

49. See, for example, James Mahoney and Kathleen Thelen, "A Theory of Gradual Institutional Change" in *Explaining Institutional Change: Ambiguity, Agency, and Power,* ed. James Mahoney and Kathleen Thelen (Cambridge, UK: Cambridge University Press, 2010); Jacob Hacker, "Policy Drift: The Hidden Politics of US Welfare State Retrenchment," in *Beyond Continuity: Institutional Change in Advanced Political Economies,* ed. Wolfgang Streeck and Kathleen Thelen (Oxford: Oxford University Press, 2005).

50. Weaver, "Frontlash," 236.

51. This is a central insight from the research on "path dependence" made famous in political science by Paul Pierson. See, e.g., Paul Pierson, "Increasing Returns, Path Dependence, and the Study of Politics," *American Political Science Review* 94 (2) (2000): 251–67.

52. Schickler, *Disjointed Pluralism,* 13. See also Stuart Chinn, "After Victory: Institutional Recalibration and Political Change," delivered at the 2007 Annual Meeting of the American Political Science Association, August 30–September 2, 2007.

53. A classic work on the importance of veto points is George Tsebelis, *Veto Players: How Political Institutions Work* (Princeton, NJ: Princeton University Press, 2002).

54. Lieberman, "Ideas, Institutions, and Political Order," 702.

55. Mahoney and Thelen, "Theory of Gradual Institutional Change," 10–14.

56. Margaret Weir, "States, Race, and the Decline of New Deal Liberalism," *Studies in American Political Development* 19 (2005): 158; Desmond King and Robert Lieberman, "American State Building: The Theoretical Challenge," in *The Unsustainable American State,* ed. Lawrence Jacobs and Desmond King (Oxford: Oxford University Press, 2010), 308.

57. Jacob Hacker and Paul Pierson, "Tax Politics and the Struggle over Activist Government," in Pierson and Skocpol, *Transformation of American Politics.*

58. See, for example, Paul Pierson, "The Deficit and the Politics of Domestic Reform," in *The Social Divide: Political Parties and the Future of Activist Government,* ed. Margaret Weir (Washington, DC: Brookings Institution, 1998); Eric Patashnik, "Ideas, Inheritances, and the Dynamics of Budgetary Change," *Governance* 12 (2) (1999): 147–74.

59. For recent discussions of literature on the impact of public opinion on policy outcomes, see, for example, Paul Burstein, "Public Opinion, Public Policy, and Democracy: Old

Expectations and New," *Handbook of Politics*, ed. Kevin Leicht and Craig Jenkins (New York: Springer, 2008). Burstein's earlier work also investigated the conditions under which public opinion was most likely to influence policymaking, e.g. "Why Estimates of the Impact of Public Opinion on Public Policy Are Too High: Empirical and Theoretical Implications," *Social Forces* 84 (4) (June 2006): 2274–89; and "The Impact of Public Opinion on Public Policy: A Review and An Agenda," *Political Research Quarterly* 56 (1) (2003): 29–40.

60. Lawrence Jacobs and Robert Shapiro describe intense, and intensifying, conflicts among rival groups of political elites to influence public opinion in their book *Politicians Don't Pander: Political Manipulation and the Loss of Democratic Responsiveness* (Chicago: University of Chicago Press, 2000). They update their argument in "Simulating Representation: Elite Mobilization and Political Power in Health Care Reform," *The Forum* 8 (1) (2010), Article 4, http://www.bepress.com/cgi/viewcontent.cgi?context=forum&article=1 360&date=&mt=MTMxNDAzMzI5MA==&access_ok_form=Continue.

61. For similar critiques, see especially Daniel Beland, "Ideas and Institutional Change in Social Security: Conversion, Layering, and Policy Drift," *Social Science Quarterly* 88 (1) (2007); Gerald Berk and Dennis Galvan, "How People Experience and Change Institutions: A Field Guide to Creative Syncretism," *Theory and Society* 38 (6) (2009): 543–580; and Jacobs, "Democracy and Capitalism," 250–51.

62. For a discussion of this approach, see Robert Lieberman, "Ideas, Institutions, and Political Order: Explaining Political Change," *American Political Science Review* 96 (2002): 697–712.

63. Robert Lieberman, *Shaping Race Policy: The United States in Comparative Perspective* (Princeton, NJ: Princeton University Press, 2006), 8. See also Daniel Beland, "Ideas, Institutions, and Public Policy," *Journal of European Public Policy* 16 (5) (2009): 703–4.

64. See Maris Vinovskis, *From a Nation at Risk to No Child Left Behind: National Education Goals and the Creation of Federal Education Policy* (New York: Teachers College Press, 2009); John Jennings, *Why National Standards and Tests? Politics and the Quest for Better Schools* (Washington, DC: Sage, 1998); Elizabeth DeBray-Pelot, *Politics, Ideology, and Education: Federal Policy during the Clinton and Bush Administrations* (New York: Teachers College Press, 2006).

65. R. Kent Weaver, *Ending Welfare as We Know It* (Washington, DC: Brookings Institution Press, 2000).

66. Patrick McGuinn, *No Child Left Behind and the Transformation of Federal Education Policy, 1965–2005* (Lawrence: University Press of Kansas, 2006).

67. Paul Manna, *School's In: Federalism and the National Education Agenda* (Washington, DC: Georgetown University Press, 2006).

68. For a discussion of policy intensification as a recurrent strategy in the context of America's "War on Drugs" see Eva Bertram, Morris Blachman, Kenneth Sharpe, and Peter Andreas, *Drug War Politics: The Price of Denial* (Berkeley: University of California Press, 1996).

69. Patrick McGuinn, *No Child Left Behind and the Transformation of Federal Education Policy, 1965–2005* (Lawrence: University Press of Kansas, 2006); Elizabeth DeBray, *Politics, Ideology, and Education: Federal Policy during the Clinton and Bush Administrations* (New York: Teachers College Press, 2006); Maris Vinovskis, *From a Nation at Risk to No Child Left Behind: National Education Goals and the Creation of Federal Education Policy* (New York: Teachers College Press, 2009); Kevin Kosar, *Failing Grades: The Federal Politics of Education Standards* (New York: Lynne Rienner, 2005).

70. Admittedly, in summarizing, the table makes generalizations that may not apply to each and every member of each grouping. It should also be noted that the table, and the discussion below, is meant to indicate the "long-term" preferences of each of the groups

discussed—or, rather, the preferences each appears to hold today. Initially, when the idea of improving schools by raising standards emerged on the scene, there was considerable overlap in the beliefs and preferences of the groups described below. However, as we shall see in the following chapters, the ideational differences between groups have become starker as the federal role has increased and the consequences for educational governance have become more significant.

71. On the material interests of teachers see Terry M. Moe, *Special Interest: Teachers Unions and America's Public Schools* (Washington, DC: Brookings Institution Press, 2011).

1. THE STRUCTURE OF AMERICAN EDUCATION POLICY BEFORE 1980

1. See Thomas Corcoran and Margaret Goertz, "The Governance of Public Education," in *The Public Schools*, ed. Susan Fuhrman and Marvin Lazerson (Oxford: Oxford University Press, 2005), 25–55.

2. David Cohen and James Spillane, "Policy and Practice: The Relations between Governance and Instruction," *Review of Research in Education* 18 (1992): 6. Emphasis added.

3. Geoffrey Borman and Jerome V. D'Agostino, "Title I and Student Achievement: A Meta-Analysis of Federal Evaluation Results," *Educational Evaluation and Policy Analysis* 18 (4) (1996): 309–26; Edward McDill and Gary Natriello, "The Effectiveness of the Title I Compensatory Education Program: 1965–1997," *Journal of Education for Students Placed at Risk* 3 (1998): 317–35; Maris Vinovskis, "Do Federal Compensatory Education Programs Really Work? A Brief Historical Analysis of Title I and Head Start," *American Journal of Education* 107 (3) (1999): 187–209.

4. Lee Anderson, *Congress and the Classroom: From the Cold War to "No Child Left Behind"* (University Park: Pennsylvania State University Press, 2007), 10; Patrick McGuinn, *No Child Left Behind and the Transformation of Federal Education Policy, 1965–2005* (Lawrence: University Press of Kansas, 2006), 26.

5. Hugh Davis Graham, *The Uncertain Triumph: Federal Education Policy in the Kennedy and Johnson Years* (Chapel Hill: University of North Carolina Press, 1984), xvii.

6. Advisory Panel on Intergovernmental Relations, *The Federal Role in the Federal System: The Dynamics of Growth—Intergovernmentalizing the Classroom: Federal Involvement in Elementary and Secondary Education* (Advisory Commission on Intergovernmental Relations, 1981), chap. 2.

7. McGuinn, *No Child Left Behind*, 26.

8. Harry Kursh, *The United States Office of Education: A Century of Service* (Philadelphia and New York: Chilton Books, 1965), 28–29.

9. See, for example, Joel Spring, *The American School, 1642–1996*, 4th ed. (New York: McGraw-Hill, 1997), chap. 15.

10. Gareth Davies, *See Government Grow: Education Politics from Johnson to Reagan* (Lawrence: University Press of Kansas, 2007), 9–11, chap. 1; also Gilbert Smith, *The Limits of Reform: Politics and Federal Aid to Education, 1937–1950* (New York: Garland Publishing, 1982).

11. Advisory Panel on Intergovernmental Relations, *The Federal Role in the Federal System: The Dynamics of Growth*, 21.

12. Ibid., 24.

13. James T. Patterson, *Brown v. Board of Education: A Civil Rights Milestone and Its Troubled Legacy* (Oxford: Oxford University Press, 2001), 69.

14. Michael Klarman, "How *Brown* Changed Race Relations: The Backlash Thesis," *Journal of American History* 81(1) (1994): 84.

15. Quoted in Harvey Kantor, "Education, Social Reform, and the State: ESEA and Federal Education Policy in the 1960s," *American Journal of Education* 100 (1) (1991): 53.

16. For an extended discussion see Harold Silver and Pamela Silver, *An Educational War on Poverty: American and British Policy-making, 1960–1980* (Cambridge: Cambridge University Press, 1991).

17. Davies, *See Government Grow*, 35.

18. See Graham, *Uncertain Triumph*, 73. "Title I," the initiative for compensatory education programs, authorized five-sixths of all the funding under the ESEA.

19. Maris Vinovskis, *The Birth of Head Start: Preschool Education Policies in the Kennedy and Johnson Administrations* (Chicago: University of Chicago Press, 2005), 80.

20. Kantor, "Education, Social Reform, and the State," 48.

21. Data is from the Policy Agendas Project, www.policyagendas.org. As Patrick McGuinn notes, reauthorizations of the ESEA were enacted in 1974 and 1978 by wide bipartisan margins. See McGuinn, *No Child Left Behind*, 38.

22. Harvey Kantor and Robert Lowe, "From New Deal to No Deal: No Child Left Behind and the Devolution of Responsibility for Equal Opportunity," *Harvard Educational Review* 76 (Winter 2006): 480.

23. Davies, *See Government Grow*, 282.

24. Carl Kaestle and Marshall Smith, "The Federal Role in Elementary and Secondary Education, 1940–1980," *Harvard Education Review* (Winter 1982): 405.

25. David Kirp, "The Fourth R: Reading, Writing, 'Rithmetic—and Rules," in *School Days, Rule Days: The Legalization and Regulation of Education*, ed. David L. Kirp and Donald N. Jensen (Philadelphia: Falmer Press, 1986). See also John Chubb, "Excessive Regulation: The Case of Federal Aid to Education," *Political Science Quarterly* 100 (2) (1985): 287–311.

26. Paul Manna, "Federal Aid to Elementary and Secondary Education: Premises, Effects, and Major Lessons Learned," paper commissioned by the Center on Education Policy, Washington, DC, November 2008, 5.

27. See, for example, Vinovskis, "Do Federal Compensatory Education Programs Really Work?" 187–209.

28. Kantor and Lowe, "From New Deal to No Deal," 479.

29. Thomas Timar, "Federal Education Policy and Practice: Building Organizational Capacity through Chapter 1," *Educational Evaluation and Policy Analysis* 16 (1) (1994): 51–66.

30. Manna, "Federal Aid to Elementary and Secondary Education," 7.

31. Brenda Turnbull, Marshall Smith, and Alan Ginsburg, "Issues for a New Administration: The Federal Role in Education," *American Journal of Education* 89 (4) (1981): 399.

32. For a review see, e.g. Vinovskis, "Do Federal Compensatory Education Programs Really Work?"

33. For one review of the state role in education in the nineteenth century see David Tyack and Thomas James, "State Government and American Public Education: Exploring the 'Primeval Forest,'" *History of Education Quarterly* 26 (1) (1986): 39–69. An overview of the legal and political status of the school district is provided in Richard Briffault, "The Local School District in American Law," in *Besieged: School Boards and the Future of Education Politics*, ed. William Howell (Washington, DC: Brookings Institution Press, 2005), 24–55.

34. William Howell, introduction to *Besieged: School Boards and the Future of Education Politics*, ed. William Howell (Washington, DC: Brookings Institution Press, 2005), 2.

35. Thomas Timar, "The Institutional Role of State Education Departments: A Historical Perspective," *American Journal of Education* 105 (3) (1997): 231–60.

36. Thomas James, "State Authority and the Politics of Educational Change," *Review of Research in Education* 17 (1991): 185.

37. Leonard Cantor, "The Growing Role of the States in American Education," *Comparative Education* 16 (1) (March 1980): 25–31.

38. Howell, introduction to *Besieged*, 3–4.

39. David Kirp, "Changing Conceptions of Educational Equity," in *Learning from the Past: What History Teaches Us about School Reform*, ed. Diane Ravitch and Maris Vinovskis (Baltimore: Johns Hopkins University Press, 1995).

40. Paul T. Hill, "Recovering from an Accident: Repairing Governance with Comparative Advantage," in *Who's in Charge Here? The Tangled Web of School Governance and Policy*, ed. Noel Epstein (Washington, DC: Brookings Institution, 2004); Michael Kirst, "Turning Points: A History of American School Governance," in Epstein, *Who's in Charge Here?*

41. Paul Manna, *School's In: Federalism and the National Education Agenda* (Washington, DC: Georgetown University Press, 2006), 90–91.

42. Roald Campbell, Luvern Cunningham, Raphael Nystrand, and Michael Usdan, *The Organization and Control of American Schools*, 4th ed. (Columbus, OH: Charles E. Merrill Publishing Co., 1980), 86.

43. John Dayton and Anne Proffitt Dupree, "The Spirit of *Serrano* Past, Present, and Future," *Journal of Education Finance* 32 (1) (2006): 22–35.

44. Frederick Wirt and Michael Kirst, *Schools in Conflict: The Politics of Education* (Berkeley, CA: McCutchan Publishing, 1982), chap. 9.

45. Campbell, Cunningham, Nystrand, and Usdan, *Organization and Control of American Schools*, 61.

46. Kirst, "Turning Points," 29.

47. Russell Vlaanderen, "Teacher Competency Testing: Status Report," *Educational Measurement: Issues and Practice* 1 (2) (1982): 17.

48. Timar, "Institutional Role of State Education Departments," 253.

49. George H. Gallup, *The Eleventh Annual Gallup Poll of the Public's Attitudes toward the Public Schools*, September 1979. Available at the Roper Center Public Opinion Archives, University of Connecticut, Storrs, Connecticut.

50. For an overview and critique of this literature see Andrew Karch, *Democratic Laboratories: Policy Diffusion among the American States* (Ann Arbor: University of Michigan Press, 2007).

51. National Center for Education Statistics, *Digest of Education Statistics 1995* (Washington, DC: Department of Education, 1995), Table 164. Dollar amounts are in constant 1992–93 dollars.

52. Timar, "Institutional Role of State Education Departments."

53. For a recent analysis of this variation and its consequences for education policy and student achievement see Paul Manna, "How Governance of K–12 Education Influences Policy Outputs and Student Outcomes in the United States," paper presented at the Annual Meeting of the American Political Science Association, September 3, 2006.

54. See Terry Moe, *Special Interest: Teachers Unions and America's Public Schools* (Washington, DC: Brookings Institution Press, 2011).

55. George H. Gallup, *The 12th Annual Gallup Poll of the Public's Attitudes toward the Public Schools*, September 1980, 36. Available at the Roper Center Public Opinion Archives.

2. A NEW DIRECTION IN AMERICAN EDUCATION POLICY, 1980–1988

1. A recent review of the "Great Stagflation" can be found in Alan Blinder and Jeremy Rudd, "The Supply-Shock Explanation of the Great Stagflation Revisited," paper prepared for the National Bureau of Economic Research conference on "The Great Inflation," Woodstock, Vermont, September 2008.

2. See, for example, W. Elliott Brownlee, ed., *Funding the American State, 1941–1995: The Rise and Fall of the Era of Easy Finance* (New York: Cambridge University Press, 1995).

3. The best contemporary study is Congressional Budget Office, *Educational Achievement: Explanations and Implications of Recent Trends* (Washington, DC: Congressional Budget Office, 1987).

4. Numerous scholars create the impression that *A Nation at Risk* originated the movement for excellence in education. Keith Nitta, for example, argues baldly that "the *A Nation at Risk* report launched the structural education reform movement in the United States." Similarly, Sandra Hunt and Ann Staton assert that "the publication of *A Nation at Risk*...by the National Commission on Excellence in Education (NCEE) in April of 1983 catapulted the issue of educational reform into the public sphere." In their classic *Tinkering toward Utopia*, David Tyack and Larry Cuban write that "in the mid-1980s, responding to the 'crisis' announced by *A Nation at Risk*, the states promulgated more educational laws and regulations than they had generated in the previous twenty years." See Keith Nitta, *The Structural Politics of Education Reform* (New York: Routledge, 2008), 28; Sandra L. Hunt and Ann Q. Staton, "The Communication of Educational Reform: *A Nation at Risk*," *Communication Education* 45 (4) (1996): 271; David Tyack and Larry Cuban, *Tinkering toward Utopia: A Century of Public School Reform* (Cambridge, MA: Harvard University Press, 1995), 78.

5. Education Commission of the States, *A Summary of Major Reports on Education* (Denver: Education Commission of the States, 1983).

6. On the checkered history of "blue ribbon" commissions in shaping public policy (especially education) see, for example, Hugh Davis Graham, "The Ambiguous Legacy of American Presidential Commissions," *Public Historian* 7 (2) (1985): 5–25; Daniel A. Smith, Kevin M. Leyden, and Stephen A. Borrelli, "Predicting the Outcomes of Presidential Commissions: Evidence from the Johnson and Nixon Years," *Presidential Studies Quarterly* 28 (2) (1998): 269–85; Amy B. Zegart, "Blue Ribbons, Black Boxes: Toward a Better Understanding of Presidential Commissions," *Presidential Studies Quarterly* 34 (2) (2004): 366–93; Rick Ginsberg and Robert K. Wimpelberg, "Educational Change by Commission: Attempting 'Trickle-Down' Reform," *Educational Evaluation and Policy Analysis* 9 (4) (1987): 344.

7. Quoted in Tracie Rozhon, "Conference Ponders Students' Poor Math," *New York Times*, June 8, 1980.

8. See Margaret Price, "Education Is Failing Industry," *Industry Week*, July 13, 1981, 42; Otto Sturzenegger, "We'd Better Do Something about Education," *Industry Week*, July 26, 1982, 13; Milliard Foist, "Business Must Shore Up Education," *Industry Week*, May 3, 1982, 13.

9. See David Vogel, "The Power of Business in America: A Re-appraisal," *British Journal of Political Science* 13 (1) (1983): 19–43.

10. Thomas Edsall and Mary Edsall, *Chain Reaction: The Impact of Race, Rights, and Taxes on American Politics* (New York: W. W. Norton, 1992), 167.

11. Mark Blyth, *Great Transformations: Economic Ideas and Political Change in the Twentieth Century* (Cambridge: Cambridge University Press, 2002), 156–61.

12. Quoted in Joseph Glorioso, "Can CEO's Improve Education?" *Industry Week*, September 19, 1983.

13. Thomas Toch, "New Activism Marks Corporate Role in Schools," *Education Week*, November 10, 1982.

14. Donald Clark, "Less Rhetoric and More Structure for Industry-School Ties," *Education Week*, December 22, 1982.

15. Tim Mazzoni and Richard Clugston, "Business as a Policy Innovator in State School Reform: A Minnesota Case Study," *Educational Evaluation and Policy Analysis* 9 (4) (1987): 312–24.

16. Quoted in Robert Lindsey, "Coast Executives Seek Better Schools," *New York Times*, April 23, 1983.

17. Diane Massell and Michael W. Kirst, "State Policymaking for Educational Excellence: School Reform in California," in *The Fiscal, Legal, and Political Aspects of State Reform of Elementary and Secondary Education,* ed. Van Mueller and Mary P. McKeown (Cambridge, MA: Ballinger Publishing Co., 1985); Mazzoni and Clugston, "Big Business as a Policy Innovator."

18. Frank Lutz, "Education Politics in Texas," *Peabody Journal of Education* 63 (1986): 70–89; Paul Taylor, "Perot Electrifies State of Education; Millionaire Texan Fights to Put Class in the Classrooms," *Washington Post,* May 31, 1984.

19. Michael Timpane and Laurie Miller McNeil, *Business Impact on Education and Child Development Reform: A Study Prepared for the Committee for Economic Development* (New York: Committee for Economic Development, 1991), 21. Emphasis added.

20. Thomas Toch, *In the Name of Excellence: The Struggle to Reform the Nation's Schools, Why It's Failing, and What Should Be Done* (Oxford: Oxford University Press, 1991), 21.

21. Ernest Boyer, quoted in Leonard Lund and Cathleen Wild, *Ten Years after "A Nation at Risk"* (New York: Conference Board, 1993), 20.

22. Education Commission of the States, *Action for Excellence* (Denver: Education Commission of the States, 1983), 23; "Education Commission of the States to Study Role of Schools in Economy," *Education Week,* December 15, 1982.

23. Charlie Euchner, "E.C.S. Group to Spend $725,000 to Spur Action on Its Proposals," *Education Week,* December 7, 1983.

24. Quoted in Sheppard Ranbom, "Business, Education Group Asks President to Guide Industry," *Education Week,* May 25, 1983.

25. Laurie S. Miller McNeil and Sandra K. Hamburg, "Committee for Economic Development: Shaping Policies and Partnerships for America's Children," in *Commissions, Reports, Reforms, and Educational Policy,* ed. David N. Plank (New York: Greenwood Publishing, 1995).

26. See, for example, Deborah Gold, "Rare Joint Session Held on Report," *Education Week,* September 16, 1987; "C.E.D. Seeks $11.5 Billion for Reforms," *Education Week,* May 25, 1988.

27. Reagan Walker, "The Education of Business," *Teacher Magazine,* January 1, 1990.

28. Personal interview with Cynthia Brown, March 12, 2008; also personal interview with Hayes Mizell, March 24, 2008.

29. Thomas Toch, "For School Reform's Top Salesmen, It's Been Some Year," *Education Week,* June 6, 1984.

30. Ronald Edmonds, "Effective Schools for the Urban Poor," *Educational Leadership* (October 1979): 23.

31. Ronald Edmonds, "Programs of School Improvement: An Overview," *Educational Leadership* (December 1982): 4–11.

32. See Stewart Purkey and Marshall Smith, "Effective Schools: A Review," *Elementary School Journal* 83 (4) (1983): 426–52.

33. See James P. Comer, *School Power: Implications of an Intervention Project* (New York: Free Press, 1980).

34. James P. Comer and Christine Emmons, "The Research Program of the Yale Child Study Center School Development Program," *Journal of Negro Education* 75 (3) (2006): 353–72.

35. Comer and Emmons, "Research Program of the Yale Child Study Center," 358.

36. Edward Fiske, "New Look at Effective Schools," *New York Times,* April 15, 1984.

37. Twentieth Century Fund, *Making the Grade: The Report of the Twentieth Century Fund Task Force on Federal Elementary and Secondary Education Policy* (New York: Twentieth Century Fund, 1983).

38. Ernest Boyer, *High School: A Report on Secondary Education in America* (New York: Harper & Row, 1983).

39. Kati Haycock and Patricia R. Brown, *Excellence for Whom? A Report from the Planning Committee of the Achievement Council* (Oakland, CA: Achievement Council, 1984).

40. National Commission on Secondary Education for Hispanics, *Make Something Happen: Hispanics and Urban School Reform* (New York: Hispanic Policy Development Project, 1984), 34. Jaramillo's autobiography is *Madame Ambassador: The Shoemaker's Daughter* (Tempe, AZ: Bilingual Press, 2002).

41. Arthur Powell, Eleanor Farrar, and David Cohen, *The Shopping Mall High School: Winners and Losers in the Educational Marketplace* (Boston: Houghton Mifflin, 1985).

42. Larry Cuban, "American High Schools: The Blackboard Jumble," *Washington Post,* October 6, 1985.

43. See *School Success for Students at Risk: Analysis and Recommendations of the Council of Chief State School Officers* (Orlando, FL: Harcourt Brace Jovanovich, 1988).

44. Lynn Olson, "Chiefs Urge That States 'Guarantee' School Quality for Those 'at Risk,'" *Education Week,* November 18, 1987.

45. William Taylor, *The Passion of My Times: An Advocate's Fifty-Year Journey in the Civil Rights Movement* (New York: Da Capo Press, 2004), 195.

46. See especially Joseph Adelson, *Inventing Adolescence: The Political Psychology of Everyday Schooling* (New Brunswick, NJ: Transaction Books, 1986); Diane Ravitch, *The Troubled Crusade: American Education, 1945–1980* (New York: Basic Books, 1983); Chester E. Finn Jr., "A Call for Quality Education," *American Education* 18 (1982): 31–36; William J. Bennett, *Our Children and Our Country: Improving America's Schools and Affirming the Common Culture* (New York: Simon & Schuster, 1988).

47. Fred L. Pincus, "From Equity to Excellence: The Rebirth of Educational Conservatism," in *The Great School Debate: Which Way for American Education?*, ed. Beatrice Gross and Ronald Gross (New York: Touchstone Books, 1985), 333.

48. See especially Chester E. Finn Jr., "The Future of Education's Liberal Consensus," *Change* 12 (1980): 25–30, and Finn, "Toward a New Consensus," *Change* 13 (1981): 17–21, 60–63; as well as Ravitch, *Troubled Crusade.*

49. Personal interview with Chester E. Finn Jr., November 1, 2007.

50. Chester E. Finn Jr., *Troublemaker: A Personal History of School Reform Since Sputnik* (Princeton, NJ: Princeton University Press, 2008), 118.

51. "Research and Reports," *Education Week,* April 24, 1985.

52. Finn, *Troublemaker,* 119. Examples of EEN publications include Chester E. Finn Jr., Diane Ravitch, and Robert T. Fancher, *Against Mediocrity: The Humanities in America's High Schools* (New York: Holmes & Meier, 1984); Diane Ravitch and Chester E. Finn Jr., *What Do Our 17-Year-Olds Know? A Report on the First National Assessment of History and Literature* (New York: Harper & Row, 1987).

53. See, for example, Andrew Porter, "The Role of Testing in Effective Schools," *American Educator* (January–February 1983), 25–28; Max Rafferty, "The Petard of Pragmatism," *American Educator* (July 1982), 6–11; Phil Kiesling, "The Class War We Can't Afford to Lose," *American Educator* (August–September 1982), 4–11; Dennis Gray, "The Challenge of Basic Education," *American Educator* (July 1982), 4–5; Donald Frey, "The Economy, Productivity, and Training—a CEO's View," *American Educator* (December 1982), 15–18.

54. Terrel Bell, *The Thirteenth Man: A Reagan Cabinet Memoir* (New York: Free Press, 1988), 114–43.

55. See, for example, Glen MacNowand and Cassandra Spratling, "Secretary Bell Calls on States to Carry Out Education Reforms," *Education Week,* May 25, 1983; Thomas Toch, "Forum Said Successful in Rallying Support for Change," *Education Week,* December 14, 1983.

56. David Hoffman, "Reagan Emphasizes Education," *Washington Post*, May 31, 1983. See also David L. Clark and Terry A. Astuto, "The Significance and Permanence of Changes in Federal Education Policy," *Educational Researcher* 15 (8) (1986): 4–13.

57. Gareth Davies, *See Government Grow: Education Politics from Johnson to Reagan* (Lawrence: University Press of Kansas, 2007), 274.

58. For a collection of speeches on these topics from the early 1980s see Bennett, *Our Children and Our Country*.

59. Southern Regional Education Board, *The Need for Quality: A Report to the Southern Regional Education Board by Its Task Force on Higher Education and the Schools* (Atlanta: Southern Regional Education Board, 1981), i.

60. Quoted in Nigel Hamilton, *Bill Clinton: An American Journey—Great Expectations* (New York: Random House, 2003), 408.

61. Charles Allen and Jonathan Portis, *The Comeback Kid: The Life and Career of Bill Clinton* (New York: Birch Lane Press, 1992), 82–102.

62. Bill Clinton, *My Life* (New York: Alfred A. Knopf, 2004), 312.

63. "News Update," *Education Week*, April 6, 1983; Peggy Caldwell, "Tenn. Governor Urges Merit Pay for Teachers," *Education Week*, February 9, 1983; Thomas Toch, "Tennessee Governor Presses Merit-Teacher Proposal," *Education Week*, March 16, 1983; Hope Aldrich, "Tenn. Governor, Wooing Teacher Union, Broadens Merit-Pay Plan," *Education Week*, March 30, 1983.

64. See, for example, Jennie Vanetta Carter, *How Three Governors Involved the Public in Passing Their Education Reform Programs*, unpublished dissertation, Peabody College for Teachers, Vanderbilt University, 1992, 53–69.

65. "Will Blacks Rally to Riley's Education Reforms?" *Journal of Blacks in Higher Education* 1 (1993), 83; see also Nancy Jennings and James Spillane, "Policy Review: South Carolina," *Journal of Education Policy* 11 (5) (1996): 625–31.

66. Reginald Stuart, "South Pressing for Wide Changes to Upgrade Education Standards," *New York Times*, March 20, 1983.

67. Southern Regional Education Board, *Meeting the Need for Quality: Action in the South* (Atlanta: Southern Regional Education Board, 1983), 1.

68. Fred Hechinger, "About Education," *New York Times*, March 22, 1983.

69. Robert L. Savage, "When a Policy's Time Has Come: Cases of Rapid Policy Diffusion, 1983–1984," *Publius* 15 (3) (1985): 111–25.

70. Peggy Caldwell, "Governors Call School Improvement a Top Priority," *Education Week*, January 25, 1984.

71. Of course, not all "education governors," as they were often called in the press, were southern. For example, Thomas Kean of New Jersey was a prominent proponent of excellence in education and a co-chair of the NGA's "Time for Results" panel. See Alvin Felzenberg, *Governor Tom Kean: From the New Jersey Statehouse to the 9-11 Commission* (New Brunswick, NJ: Rivergate Books, 2006), 232–57.

72. Lorraine McDonnell and Susan Fuhrman, "The Political Context of Reform," in *The Fiscal, Legal, and Political Aspects of State Reform of Elementary and Secondary Education*, ed. Van Mueller and Mary P. McKeown (Cambridge, MA: Ballinger Publishing Co., 1985), 57.

73. Of course, the various proponents of excellence in education did not agree on every point. For the purposes of exposition, however, it is worthwhile to analyze the agenda in general terms. Contemporary summaries of multiple excellence-in-education reform reports noted striking similarities (as well as some differences) among the reports. See, for example, K. Forbis Jordan, *Comparison of Recommendations from Selected Education Reform Reports* (Washington, DC: Library of Congress, Congressional Research Service, 1983); Education Commission of the States, *A Summary of Major Reports on Education* (Denver: Education Commission of the States, 1983).

74. An excellent overview of the themes of the excellence movement is Andrew Hacker, "The Schools Flunk Out," *New York Review of Books* 31 (1984).

75. See, for example, Finn, "Toward a New Consensus," 60; Education Commission of the States, *Action for Excellence;* Paul B. Salmon, "Strengthening America through Stronger Education," *American Education* 19 (1983): 27–29; National Commission on Excellence in Education, *A Nation at Risk: The Imperative of Education Reform* (Washington, DC: U.S. Department of Education, 1983).

76. National Commission on Excellence in Education, *A Nation at Risk*, 5.

77. Quoted in Toch, *In the Name of Excellence*, 16.

78. Andrew Oldenquist, "The Decline of American Education in the '60s and '70s," *American Education* 19 (1983): 18.

79. Joseph Adelson, *Inventing Adolescence: The Political Psychology of Everyday Schooling* (New Brunswick, NJ: Transaction Books, 1986).

80. For a collection of speeches on these topics from the early 1980s see Bennett, *Our Children and Our Country*.

81. Boyer, *High School;* Powell, Farrar, and Cohen, *Shopping Mall High School*.

82. Twentieth Century Fund, *Making the Grade;* Education Commission of the States, *Action for Excellence;* National Commission for Excellence in Education, *A Nation at Risk;* Mortimer Adler, *The Paideia Proposal: An Educational Manifesto* (New York: Macmillan, 1982).

83. Quoted in "Business Awakes to the Crisis in Education," *Business Week*, July 4, 1983, 32.

84. Ravitch, *Troubled Crusade*, chap. 7.

85. Diane Ravitch, "The Debate about Standards: Where Do We Go from Here?" *American Educator* (January 1982).

86. For a sharp critique of teachers and the teaching profession see Keisling, "Class War," 4–11.

87. Finn, "Toward a New Consensus," 62.

88. Task Force on Education for Economic Growth, *Action for Excellence*.

89. Finn, "Toward a New Consensus," 17.

90. Some prominent educational liberal critiques of excellence in education, along with rejoinders from business entrepreneurs, civil rights entrepreneurs, educational conservatives, and state leaders, are anthologized in Beatrice Gross and Ronald Gross, eds., *The Great School Debate: Which Way for American Education?* (New York: Simon and Schuster, 1985).

91. Quoted in Anne Bridgman, "Coalition Assails Reform Movement for Ignoring Equity Issues," *Education Week*, October 10, 1984.

92. John Goodlad, *A Place Called School* (New York: McGraw-Hill, 1984), 140.

93. See especially Jeannie Oakes, *Keeping Track: How Schools Structure Inequality* (New Haven: Yale University Press, 1985). Oakes's famous 1985 book was preceded by earlier important articles that helped jump-start the excellence movement. See, for example, Oakes, "Classroom Social Relationships: Exploring the Bowles and Gintis Hypothesis," *Sociology of Education* 55 (4) (1982): 197–212; Oakes, "Tracking and Ability Grouping in American Schools: Some Constitutional Questions," *Teachers College Record* 84 (4) (1983): 801–19.

94. Powell, Farrar, and Cohen, *Shopping Mall High School*, 294.

95. Oakes, *Keeping Track*, 206–7.

96. Quoted in Linda Chion-Kenney, "Educators Warned That Reform May Peril Minority-Student Gains," *Education Week*, November 7, 1984.

97. Susan H. Fuhrman and Richard F. Elmore, "Understanding Local Control in the Wake of State Education Reform," *Educational Evaluation and Policy Analysis* 12 (1) (1990): 82–96.

98. David L. Clark and Terry A. Astuto "The Significance and Permanence of Changes in Federal Education Policy," *Educational Researcher* 15 (8) (1986): 6.

99. Quoted in Thomas Toch, "'The Wax Is Warm' Says National Endowment Chairman," *Education Week*, October 24, 1984.

100. See Finn, "Future of Education's Liberal Consensus"; and Finn, "Toward a New Consensus."

101. Fred Hechinger, "Raising the Question of Federal 'Interference,'" *New York Times*, May 24, 1983.

102. Robert Pear, "Caution Signals Flash at the Federal Level," *New York Times*, November 13, 1983; Cindy Currence, "Education Lobbies Shift Focus to States," *Education Week*, October 2, 1985.

103. Richard F. Elmore and Milbrey Wallin McLaughlin, *Steady Work: Policy, Practice, and Reform of American Education* (Washington, DC: RAND Corp., 1988), 53–59; Catherine Cornbleth, "Ritual and Rationality in Teacher Education Reform," *Educational Researcher* 15 (4) (1986): 5–14.

104. Lawrence C. Stedman and Marshall S. Smith, "Weak Arguments, Poor Data, Simplistic Recommendations," in Gross and Gross, *The Great School Debate*, 102.

105. Paul E. Peterson, "Did the Education Commissions Say Anything?" *Brookings Review* 2 (1983), 62. Emphasis added. See also Rick Ginsberg and Robert K. Wimpelberg, "Educational Change by Commission: Attempting 'Trickle-Down' Reform," *Educational Evaluation and Policy Analysis* 9 (4) (1987): 344–60.

106. On 1970s-era precursors of excellence in education, see William Firestone, "Continuity and Incrementalism after All: State Responses to the Excellence Movement," in *The Educational Reform Movement of the 1980s: Perspectives and Cases*, ed. Joseph Murphy (Berkeley, CA: McCutchan Publishing, 1990), 146–47.

107. Quoted in Currence, "Education Lobbies Shift Focus to States."

108. U.S. Department of Education, *The Nation Responds* (Washington, DC: U.S. Department of Education, 1984); Margaret E. Goertz, *State Educational Standards: A Fifty-State Survey* (Princeton, NJ: Educational Testing Service, 1986); Goertz, *State Educational Standards in the 50 States: An Update* (Princeton, NJ: Educational Testing Service, 1988); Laurie Miller McNeill, *The State Education Reform Movement and the Reform of the State Politics of Education*, unpublished dissertation, Teachers' College, Columbia University, 1989.

109. Thomas B. Timar and David L. Kirp, "Education Reform in the 1980s: Lessons from the States," *Phi Delta Kappan* 70 (7) (1989): 506.

110. Susan Fuhrman and Richard Elmore, "Understanding Local Control in the Wake of State Education Reform," *Educational Evaluation and Policy Analysis* 12 (1) (1990): 82.

111. National Education Association, "Legislative Program for the 98th Congress," *NEA Handbook 1982–83* (Washington, DC: National Education Association, 1982), 240–41.

112. William H. McGuire, "Speeches to the Representative Assembly: Report of the President," *Proceedings of the Sixty-Second Representative Assembly*, Philadelphia, July 2–5, 1983 (Washington, DC: National Education Association, 1983), 10.

113. See also "New N.E.A. Head Discusses Union's Views on Pay Plans," *Education Week*, June 8, 1983.

114. Richard D. Kahlenberg, *Tough Liberal: Albert Shanker and the Battles over Schools, Unions, Race, and Democracy* (New York: Columbia University Press, 2007), 275–80.

115. Albert Shanker, *Albert Shanker's Address to the 1983 AFT Convention* (Washington, DC: American Federation of Teachers, 1983), 11.

116. Gene Maeroff, "National Education Association: Meeting Over, Work Starts on New Image," *New York Times*, July 4, 1985; Keith Richberg, "Chiefs Redirect Teachers' Unions: Historic Shift Called Enlightened Self-Interest," *Washington Post*, May 27, 1985.

117. National Education Association, *Teachers' Views on Excellence in Education: Six NEA Booklets* (Washington, DC: National Education Association, 1983).

118. National Education Association, *An Open Letter to America on Schools, Students, and Tomorrow* (Washington, DC: National Education Association, 1984), 8.

119. Tom Mirga, "Bell Raps Union's Report on Education Funding," *Education Week*, September 7, 1983.

120. Lisa Jennings, "Survey Finds Teachers 'Dispirited,' Uninvolved in Reform," *Education Week*, May 25, 1988.

121. See AFT Task Force on the Future of Education, *The Revolution That Is Overdue: Looking toward the Future of Teaching and Learning* (Washington, DC: American Federation of Teachers, 1986).

122. Two prominent radical critics of the excellence in education paradigm were Michael Apple and Ira Shor, both career academics. See, for example, Apple, "National Reports and the Construction of Inequality," *British Journal of Sociology of Education* 7 (2) (1986): 171–90; Shor, *Culture Wars: School and Society in the Conservative Restoration* (Chicago: University of Chicago Press, 1992).

3. FEDERAL SCHOOL REFORM BUILDS MOMENTUM, 1989–1992

1. When I use the term "standards-based reforms," I refer to reforms that seek to align many of the major components of the education system—especially student assessments, school accountability, teacher training, and (perhaps) school finance—around explicit, state-determined standards of what children should know and be able to do. The various groups promoting standards-based reforms did not agree on each and every principle of this strategy, but there was sufficient overlap among these groups to warrant discussing the agenda as a shared one. While I use the term "standards-based reform" to refer to this agenda, some of its proponents also used the terms "systemic reform" or "restructuring" to refer to the same ideas and concepts. Contemporary analysts saw coherence in the various versions of standards-based reform; as the National Governors Association reported in 1991, "There are numerous lists of critical components, strategies, and conceptual frameworks designed to help guide state restructuring efforts. Contributors to this enterprise include the National Governors Association, The Business Roundtable, the Center for Policy Research in Education, the Education Commission of the States, and the National Center on Education and the Economy. Although details and strategies may vary, these different conceptions of restructuring, and each state's own version, share a core of basic operating assumptions, including: The goal of restructuring the education system is to ensure that all children reach high performance standards. Restructuring refers to systemic change in which many pieces and levels of the education system and supporting systems, including preschool and basic health services, must be transformed and linked for the system to become effective. Restructuring education aims to create a performance-based system in which school faculties have the knowledge, authority, and resources to make instructionally relevant decisions in exchange for real accountability for results. In a restructured system, challenging goals for the performance of all students are reflected in a demanding curriculum and corresponding meaningful assessments of performance. Restructuring the system requires that professional preparation and ongoing learning be fundamentally redesigned to prepare current and future administrators and teachers for the new curriculum and their new roles." National Governors Association, *From Rhetoric to Action: State Progress in Restructuring the Education System* (Washington, DC: National Governors Association, 1991), 1.

2. Thomas Timar and David Kirp, "State School Reform Efforts in the 1980s: Lessons from the States," *Phi Delta Kappan* 70 (1989): 506.

3. Paul Manna, *School's In: Federalism and the National Education Agenda* (Washington, DC: Georgetown University Press, 2006), 99–106.

4. Robert E. Feir, "Political and Social Roots of Education Reform: A Look at the States in the Mid-1980s," paper presented at the 1995 meeting of the American Educational Research Association, San Francisco, April 18–22.

5. Office of Educational Research and Improvement State Accountability Study Group, *Creating Responsible and Responsive Accountability Systems* (Washington, DC: U.S. Department of Education, 1988), 11.

6. For broad discussion of these trends see William A. Firestone, Susan Fuhrman, and Michael W. Kirst, *The Progress of Reform: An Appraisal of State Education Initiatives* (New Brunswick, NJ: CPRE, 1989); William A. Firestone, Sheila Rosenblum, Beth D. Bader, and Diane Massell, *Education Reform from 1983 to 1990: State Action and District Response* (New Brunswick, NJ: CPRE, 1990); Susan H. Fuhrman, William Clune, and Richard Elmore, "Research on Education Reform: Lessons on the Implementation of Policy," *Teachers College Record* 90 (2) (1988): 237–57.

7. Firestone, Fuhrman, and Kirst, *Progress of Reform*, 12, emphasis added. See also Firestone, Fuhrman, and Kirst, "An Overview of Education Reform since 1983," in *The Educational Reform Movement of the 1980s: Perspectives and Cases*, ed. Joseph Murphy (Berkeley, CA: McCutchan Publishing, 1990); Diane Massell and Susan Fuhrman, *Issues and Strategies in Systemic Reform* (New Brunswick, NJ: CPRE, 1992), 6.

8. William H. Clune with Paula White and Janice Patterson, *The Implementation and Effects of High School Graduation Requirements: First Steps toward Curricular Reform* (New Brunswick, NJ: CPRE, 1989), 39.

9. David K. Cohen and James P. Spillane, "Policy and Practice: The Relations between Governance and Instruction," *Review of Research in Education* 18 (1994), 51–54; Rolf K. Blank and Diane Schilder, "State Policies and State Role in Curriculum," *The Politics of Curriculum and Testing: The 1990 Yearbook of the Politics of Education Association* (London: Falmer Press, 1991), 59–60. See also Office of Educational Research and Improvement, *Creating Responsible and Responsive Accountability Systems* (Washington, DC: U.S. Department of Education, 1988), ix.

10. William A. Firestone, Sheila Rosenblum, and Beth D. Bader, "Recent Trends in State Educational Reform: Assessment and Prospects," *Teachers College Record* 94 (2) (1992): 254–77.

11. See National Center for Education Statistics, *NAEP 2008 Trends in Academic Progress: Reading 1971–2008* (Washington, DC: U.S. Department of Education, 2010); National Center for Education Statistics, *NAEP 2008 Trends in Academic Progress, Mathematics 1973–2008* (Washington, DC: U.S. Department of Education, 2010).

12. General Accounting Office, *Education Reform: Initial Effects in Four School Districts; Report to Congressional Requesters* (Washington, DC: General Accounting Office, 1989).

13. Jennifer O'Day and Marshall Smith, "Systemic Reform and Educational Opportunity," in *Designing Coherent Education Policy: Improving the System*, ed. Susan H. Fuhrman (San Francisco: Jossey-Bass, 1993), 262.

14. Roger B. Porter, "Memorandum for Governor Sununu: Education Policy Advisory Committee," June 1, 1989, Open P2–P5 Documents, box 1, documents 1–300, folder 200–250, Papers of President George H. W. Bush, George H. W. Bush Presidential Library, College Station, Texas (hereafter *GHWB*).

15. Ken Yale, "Draft—The Education President: Defining the Education Agenda," *GHWB*, Open P2–P5 Documents, box 1, documents 1–300, folder 200–250, document 206.

16. A useful discussion of Congress's response to Bush's initial educational offering can be found in Maris Vinovskis, *From a Nation at Risk to No Child Left Behind: National*

Education Goals and the Creation of Federal Education Policy (New York: Teachers College Press, 2009), 39–42.

17. An informal survey of the views of education policymakers by *Education Week* found that many leaders were frustrated by Bush's lackluster policy leadership. See Lynn Olson and Julie A. Miller, "The 'Education President' at Midterm: Mismatch between Rhetoric, Results?" *Education Week*, January 9, 1991. For additional discussion of Bush's inactivity on education issues in 1990 see, for example, Holly G. McIntush, "Political Truancy: George Bush's Claim to the Mantle of 'Education President,'" in *The Rhetorical Presidency of George H. W. Bush*, ed. Martin J. Medhurst (College Station: Texas A&M Press, 2006).

18. See Vinovskis, *From a Nation at Risk to No Child Left Behind*, chap. 2.

19. My argument sheds new light on the emergence of the standards-based reform paradigm, which provided the ideological rationale for major federal education reforms such as Bill Clinton's Improving America's Schools Act of 1994, George W. Bush's No Child Left Behind Act of 2002, and Barack Obama's Race to the Top and Elementary and Secondary Education Act reauthorization. A few previous studies—especially works by Keith Nitta and Jal Mehta—have underscored the importance of the standards-based reform paradigm in the development of education policy, but they have underestimated the extent to which these ideas developed as a reaction to the slow progress of excellence in education and thus have difficulty accounting for the emergence of the paradigm. Unlike previous accounts, my analysis also grounds the diffusion of standards-based reform in the entrepreneurial activities of various education entrepreneurs, providing a more robust accounting of the enduring influence of this paradigm. See Keith Nitta, *The Politics of Structural Education Reform* (New York: Routledge, 2008); Jal Mehta, "The Transformation of American Educational Policy, 1980–2001: Ideas and the Rise of Accountability Politics," unpublished dissertation, Higher Degrees in Social Policy, Harvard University, 2006.

20. National Governors Association, *From Rhetoric to Action: State Progress in Restructuring the Education System* (Washington, DC: National Governors Association, 1991), 1.

21. William Miller, "Employers Wrestle with 'Dumb' Kids," *Industry Week*, July 4, 1988.

22. Business Roundtable, "The Education Decade: A Business Commitment to America's Children," 1989, *GHWB*, WHORM: Education File, box 6, documents 073666–075562.

23. National Alliance of Business, *Corporate Action Agenda: The Business of Improving Public Education* (Washington, DC: National Alliance of Business, 1989).

24. Business Roundtable, *Essential Components of a Successful Education System: The Business Roundtable Education Public Policy Agenda* (New York: Business Roundtable, 1989), 5.

25. Business Roundtable, *The Essential Components of a Successful Education System: Putting Policy into Practice* (New York: Business Roundtable, 1992), 2.

26. Ibid., 1.

27. Business Roundtable, *Transforming Education Policy: Assessing 10 Years of Progress in the States* (New York: Business Roundtable, 1999).

28. Edward Rust, "No Turning Back: A Progress Report on the Business Roundtable Education Initiative," New York: Business Roundtable, 1999.

29. "Plan to Pair Business with Government for Reform is Stymied in Many States," *Education Week*, February 13, 1991.

30. National Alliance of Business, *Business Strategies That Work: A Planning Guide for Education Restructuring, Corporate Action Package* (Washington, DC: National Alliance of Business, 1990).

31. "Centers to Expand Linkages between Businesses, Schools," *Education Week*, April 18, 1990.

32. "Minutes: National Alliance of Business, Center for Excellence in Education, Board of Directors, National Alliance of Business Headquarters, Washington, D.C.," December 6, 1990, Papers of Albert Shanker, President of the American Federation of Teachers, Walter P. Reuther Library, Wayne State University, Detroit, Michigan (hereafter *AS*), box 81, folder 19, National Alliance of Business, 1986–91; "National Alliance of Business, Center for Excellence in Education, Board of Directors," November 21, 1990, *AS*, box 81, folder 19, National Alliance of Business, 1986–91.

33. Letter from William Kolberg to Albert Shanker, January 11, 1991, *AS*, box 81, folder 19, National Alliance of Business 1986–91.

34. National Center on Education and the Economy, Commission on the Skills of the American Workforce, *America's Choice: High Skills or Low Wages!* (Rochester: National Center on Education and the Economy, 1990).

35. Letter from Marc Tucker to Hillary Clinton, November 11, 1992, *AS*, box 85, folder 26, National Center on Education and the Economy, 1989–92.

36. Marshall S. Smith and Jennifer O'Day, "Systemic School Reform," in *The Politics of Curriculum and Testing: The 1990 Yearbook of the Politics of Education Association*, ed. Susan H. Fuhrman and Betty Malen (London: Falmer, 1990/91), 238.

37. Ibid., 246.

38. See, e.g. O'Day and Smith, "Systemic Reform and Educational Opportunity."

39. Maris Vinovskis, "An Analysis of the Concept and Uses of Systemic Educational Reform," *American Educational Research Journal* 33 (1) (1996): 59.

40. Personal interview with Marshall S. Smith, November 11, 2007.

41. Pew Forum on Education Reform, "Progress Report: June 15, 1994," *AS*, box 90, folder 23, Pew Forum on Education Reform Correspondence.

42. Vinovskis, "Analysis of the Concept and Uses of Systemic Educational Reform."

43. Susan Fuhrman and Diane Massell, *Issues and Strategies in Systemic Reform* (New Brunswick, NJ: Consortium for Policy Research in Education, 1992), 3. Emphasis added.

44. See, for example, "Putting the Pieces Together: Systemic School Reform," *CPRE Policy Briefs* (New Brunswick, NJ: Consortium for Policy Research in Education, 1991); "Equality in Education: Progress, Problems, and Possibilities," *CPRE Policy Briefs* (New Brunswick, NJ: Consortium for Policy Research in Education, 1991); Susan Fuhrman, ed., *Designing Coherent Education Policy: Improving the System* (New York: Jossey-Bass, 1993).

45. Lynn Olson, "Fed Up with Tinkering, Reformers Tout Systemic Approach," *Education Week*, September 9, 1992.

46. Quoted in "A Look Ahead: Education and the New Decade," *Education Week*, January 10, 1990.

47. "Blueprint for State's New School System Advances in Kentucky," *Education Week*, March 7, 1990.

48. Fuhrman and Massell, *Issues and Strategies in Systemic Reform*. Indeed, KERA was almost immediately the subject of a major scholarly symposium, which was subsequently turned into an academic volume. See Thomas R. Guskey, ed., *High Stakes Performance Assessment: Perspectives on Kentucky's Educational Reform* (New York: Corwin Press, 1994).

49. Chester E. Finn Jr., "A Nation Still at Risk," *Commentary* 87 (May 1989): 20.

50. Chester E. Finn Jr., *We Must Take Charge: Our Schools and Our Future* (New York: Basic Books, 1991), 135.

51. Educational Excellence Network, "Network Accomplishments (Fall 1988 to Winter 1991)," *AS*, box 75, folder 22, Educational Excellence Network, 1988–92.

52. For a discussion of these activities see Educational Excellence Network, "Request for Support of Core Activities: September 1991–August 1994," in *AS*, box 75, folder 22, EEN 1988–92; Letter from Chester E. Finn Jr. and Jean M. Barthurst to Albert Shanker, August 30, 1991, *AS*, box 75, folder 22, Education Excellence Network 1988–92.

53. Personal interview with Gordon Ambach, December 11, 2007.

54. Personal interview with Richard Riley, October 31, 2007; Southern Regional Education Board, *A Progress Report and Recommendations on Educational Improvements in the SREB States: A Report to the Southern Regional Education Board by Its Commission for Educational Quality* (Atlanta: Southern Regional Education Board, 1987).

55. Southern Regional Education Board, *Challenge 2000: Goals for Education* (Atlanta: Southern Regional Education Board, 1988).

56. Education Commission of the States, *Introduction to Systemic Education Reform: Restructuring the Education System* (Denver: Education Commission of the States, 1992), 2.

57. National Governors Association, *Results in Education 1988: The Governors' 1991 Report on Education* (Washington, DC: National Governors Association, 1988), 11.

58. See, for example, National Governors Association, *From Rhetoric to Action.*

59. Education Commission of the States, *Introduction to Systemic Education Reform: Restructuring the Education System* (Denver: Education Commission of the States, 1992); Education Commission of the States, *Bringing Coherence to State Policy: Restructuring the Education System* (Denver: Education Commission of the States, 1992); Education Commission of the States, *Creating Visions and Standards to Support Them: Restructuring the Education System* (Denver: Education Commission of the States, 1992).

60. Conference Board, *Beyond Business/Education Partnerships: The Business Experience* (New York: Conference Board, 1988), 17. Emphasis added.

61. Quoted in Deborah Cohen, "National School Goals: Old Idea Surfaces with Newfound Intensity," *Education Week,* September 27, 1989; see also Chester E. Finn Jr., "National Standards: A Plan for Consensus," *Teachers College Record* 91 (1988), 32; personal interview with Bruno Manno, November 5, 2007.

62. National Governors Association, *Results in Education 1988,* 2.

63. See Reagan Walker, "Education Summit's 'When' and 'Where' Are Set, but the 'Why' Remains Unsettled," *Education Week,* September 6, 1989.

64. The governors, of course, were already familiar with the idea of goal setting as a central facet of educational improvement, due to the work of the Southern Regional Education Board.

65. Personal interview with Michael Cohen, November 2, 2007; personal interview with Raymond Scheppach, January 15, 2008.

66. Roger B. Porter, "Memorandum for Governor Sununu: Education Summit Conference Objectives," September 20, 1989, *GHWB,* Files Proposed for Opening—Released, box 181, MC001910–040212, scanned through MC003, 128572–148146 unscanned, folder MC 083346–084715. Emphasis added.

67. An insider's account of the wrangling over the content of the National Education Goals is provided by Christopher Cross, who was serving in Bush's Department of Education at the time. See Cross, *Political Education: National Policy Comes of Age* (New York: Teachers College Press, 2004), chap. 6.

68. Vinovskis, *From a Nation at Risk to No Child Left Behind,* 38.

69. Letter from Lauren Resnick to the Members of the National Council on Education Standards and Testing, "Standard Setting," July 14, 1991, Papers of Chester E. Finn Jr., Hoover Institution on War, Revolution, and Peace, Stanford University, Palo Alto, California (hereafter *CEF*), box 131, folder NCEST: Standards Task Force.

70. Robert Rothman, "Panel Unveils Proposed Assessments to Measure Progress toward Goals," *Education Week,* April 3, 1991.

71. For a discussion of the overlapping groups considering national standards see Lynn Olson, "'Confusing' Array of Players Chart Course toward National Standards," *Education Week,* October 23, 1991.

72. The formulation of America 2000 is discussed in greater detail later in this chapter. In response to America 2000's recommendation to "create new American Achievement Tests," Roger Porter wrote Alexander that "in principle, I agree with this recommendation,

but I believe it needs to be the product of the consensus process currently underway with the National Education Goals Panel." Similarly, Porter responded to America 2000's proposal to "develop an interim system of individual testing for reading, writing, and mathematics" with the rejoinder that "an interim system is currently contemplated by the National Education Goals Panel." See Roger B. Porter, "Memorandum for Secretary Lamar Alexander—America 2000: An Education Strategy," March 20, 1991, *GHWB*, Open P2–P5 Documents, box 51, folder 14201–14475.

73. Business Roundtable, *American Excellence in a World Economy: A Report of the Business Roundtable on International Competitiveness* (New York: Business Roundtable, 1987), 27; Business Roundtable, *The Role of Business in Education Reform: A Blueprint for Action* (New York: Business Roundtable, 1988), 19–20.

74. Corporate frustration was such that executives including Stewart Orton of the Federated Stores Foundation, David Kearns of Xerox, Owen Butler of Procter & Gamble, and John Scully of Apple Computers publicly berated federal officials during the 1988 election campaign for failing to take action. Orton complained that "we have people running for office who keep saying that education is the most important issue, but they are not coming up with a program....There seems to be no national agenda." See Stewart Orton in Conference Board, *Beyond Business/Education Partnerships: The Business Experience* (New York: Conference Board, 1988), 17; David T. Kearns, "An Education Recovery Plan for America," *Phi Delta Kappan* 69 (1988): 566; Steven Pearlstein, "Neither Candidate Satisfies CEOs on Issue of Education: Executives Say Dukakis, Bush Ducking Key Choices," *Washington Post*, October 9, 1988; "Education: What Business Can Do," *Washington Post*, October 13, 1988.

75. "Roundtable Asks CEO's Commitment," *Industry Week*, October 16, 1989; personal interview with Christopher Cross, November 7, 2007.

76. John Akers, letter to President George H. W. Bush, September 18, 1989, *GHWB*, Bush Presidential Records, White House Office of Records Management, Education (ED): box 6, folder 073666–075562. The report, *The Education Decade: A Business Commitment to America's Children*, proclaimed that "America desperately needs a national vision for education. Together, our challenge is to develop this vision, which should include widely accepted goals for restructuring as well as the adoption of national standards for higher levels of achievement—for students and for teachers."

77. Robert Rothman, "What to Teach: Reform Turns Finally to the Essential Question," *Education Week*, May 17, 1989.

78. Quoted in Edward Fiske, "Concerns Raised on School Quality," *New York Times*, June 6, 1989.

79. In a letter to O'Neill, Chester Finn, a member of PEPAC, congratulated O'Neill for "your thoughtful (and deft) persistence in getting a credible 'national testing' plan through our group." Letter from Chester E. Finn Jr. to Paul O'Neill, January 23, 1991, *CEF*, box 156, folder PEPAC (typed).

80. Letter from Paul O'Neill to Roger Porter, February 26, 1991, *CEF*, box 156, folder "PEPAC" (written). Emphasis added.

81. "See Business Core Group, April 18, 1991," *CEF*, box 95, blue folder; Jonathan Weisman, "Educators Watch with a Wary Eye as Business Gains Policy Muscle," *Education Week*, July 31, 1991.

82. A top Bush education adviser, Charles Kolb, passed this quote from Kolberg along to Bush's domestic policy adviser, Roger Porter, in December 1990. See Kolb, "Memorandum for Roger B. Porter: Education Speeches," December 27, 1990, *GHWB*, WHORM: Education File, box 18, 202078–205949.

83. Quoted in William Raspberry, "Better Education, Better Business," *Washington Post*, November 21, 1990.

84. "The New Player," *Teacher Magazine,* October 1, 1991.

85. Weisman, "Educators Watch with a Wary Eye."

86. Jonathan Weisman, "Businesses Sign On to Bush Plan, but Many Are Raising Concerns," *Education Week,* May 8, 1991.

87. Reagan Walker, "Business Leaders Challenge Bush's School Priorities," *Education Week,* November 8, 1989; Susan Chira, "A Sea of Doubt Swells around Bush's Education Plan," *New York Times,* July 22, 1991. Indeed, during the strident congressional debate over America 2000, which centered on the plan's voucher provisions, William Kolberg of the NAB emphasized that "[while] there are those who believe that choice is the only thing we need to do, an ideological panacea, we do not believe that. Our attitude at this stage is that choice needs to have a lot more experimentation done" (quoted in Chira, "Sea of Doubt").

88. Julie A. Miller, "Bush's School Plan Is 'Lamar's Baby,'" *Education Week,* June 5, 1991.

89. Robert Rothman, "Bennett Offers High School's 'Ideal' Content," *Education Week,* January 13, 1988.

90. Chester E. Finn Jr., "National Standards: A Plan for Consensus," *Teachers College Record* 91 (Fall 1989): 7.

91. See Letter from Chester Finn to William Bennett, undated, *CEF,* box 156, Charlottesville Education Summit.

92. Educational Excellence Network, "Request for Support of Core Activities: September 1991–August 1994," *AS,* box 75, folder 22, Educational Excellence Network 1988–92.

93. Charles Kolb, who served in an education policymaking role in the Bush White House, argues that Cavazos was retained more for his electoral value (he was the first Hispanic-American to hold a Cabinet-level position) than for his energy or programmatic agenda. See Kolb, *White House Daze: The Unmaking of Domestic Policy in the Bush Years* (New York: Free Press, 1994), 127–28.

94. Personal interview with Bruno Manno, November 5, 2007; personal interview with Chester E. Finn Jr., November 1, 2007.

95. Personal interview with Chester E. Finn Jr., November 1, 2007.

96. Lamar Alexander to the President, "A Proposed Education Plan," Draft 2/3/91, *GHWB,* Office of Policy Development: Randolph Beales Papers, America 2000 Development and Lamar Alexander Transition Team Materials, OA/ID 07959.

97. See Finn's handwritten notes from meetings with top administration officials on America 2000, *CEF,* box 95, brown folder no. 2.

98. Kati Haycock and Susana Navarro, *Unfinished Business: Fulfilling Our Children's Promise* (Oakland, CA: Achievement Council, 1988); Phyllis McClure, *Mississippi's Future—Will the Schools Meet the Challenge? A Report to the Mississippi State Board of Education and the Citizens of Mississippi* (Washington, DC: NAACP Legal Defense Fund, 1988).

99. See, for example, "'Small Changes' Won't Do, Says California Panel," *Education Week,* June 8, 1988; "Trained for 'Ideal' Students, New Teachers Encounter 'At Risk,'" *Education Week,* June 22, 1988; "In the Urban Crucible," *Education Week,* June 22, 1988; Lynn Olson, "Despite Years of Rhetoric, Most Still See Little Understanding," *Education Week,* September 21, 1988.

100. David W. Hornbeck, "New Paradigms for Action," in *Human Capital and America's Future: An Economic Strategy for the '90s,* ed. David W. Hornbeck and Lester M. Salamon (Baltimore: Johns Hopkins University Press, 1991), 361.

101. Marshall S. Smith, "The Pew Forum on K–12 Education Reform in the United States: A Proposal to the Pew Charitable Trusts," January 1991, Papers of Gordon M. Ambach, Education Policy Papers, B1829, New York State Archives, Cultural Education Center, Albany, New York (hereafter *GMA*), box 168, folder 5, "Pew Forum Publications and Proposals." Emphasis added.

102. Marshall Smith, "Selecting Students and Services for Chapter 1," in *Policy Options for the Future of Compensatory Education: Conference Papers*, ed. Denis P. Doyle, Joan S. Michie, and Barbara I. Williams (Chapel Hill, NC: Research and Evaluation Associates, 1986), 110–34.

103. Robert Rothman, "Educators, Analysts Hail Strategy as Bold Departure," *Education Week*, April 24, 1991.

104. White House Office of the Press Secretary, "America 2000 Excellence in Education Fact Sheet," *GHWB*, Domestic Policy Council: Domestic Policy Council Files, Education: America 2000 OA/ID 04793 [1 of 3].

105. Julie Miller and Mark Pitsch, "Bush and Kennedy Bills Set Stage for Federal Debate," *Education Week*, May 29, 1991.

106. Quoted in "The Administration's Education Reform Proposal," Hearing Examining the Administration's Proposal to Reform the National Education System before the Committee on Labor and Human Resources, United States Senate, 102nd Congress, 1st Sess., 1991, 2.

107. Vinovskis, *From a Nation at Risk to No Child Left Behind*, 39–42.

108. National Education Association, "General Financial Aid to Education," March 1992, *GMA*, box 234, folder 6, "R H/S C Comments from Members."

109. See "Memorandum: Possible Meeting with the Majority Leader," August 2, 1991, Papers of Senator Claiborne Pell of Rhode Island, University Library Special Collections and Archives Unit, University of Rhode Island, Kingston, Rhode Island (hereafter *CP*), Subject Files, box 30, folder 565.

110. See John F. Jennings, *Why National Standards and Tests?* (New York: Russell Sage, 1998); Patrick McGuinn, *No Child Left Behind and the Transformation of Federal Education Policy, 1965–2005* (Lawrence: University Press of Kansas, 2006); Vinovskis, *From a Nation at Risk to No Child Left Behind*.

111. America 21, a coalition of some of the major education groups, created its own "Framework for Legislation" that pressed for comprehensive social services, the expansion of Head Start and other federal education programs, and a system of research and development and demonstration programs to promote excellence in education. See America 21, "Achieving the National Education Goals: A Framework for Action," June 27, 1991, *GMA*, box 93, folder 7, "NAB Center for Excellence in Education Board Meeting, July 1991."

112. Jill Zuckman, "Bush Primed to Push 'Choice' in School Reform Bill," *CQ Weekly*, January 18, 1992.

113. "Statement of Administration Policy: S.2.—The Neighborhood Schools Improvement Act," January 21, 1992, *CP*, Education Subject Files, box 63, folder 562.

114. Zuckman, "Bush Primed."

115. The administration was deeply disturbed by the new "school delivery" standards. In a letter to the office of Democratic senator Claiborne Pell, Diane Ravitch, at that time assistant secretary of education, wrote that "as presently written, this bill will allow a group in Washington to write school delivery standards—which describe HOW education is to be delivered, which practices and which policies are most appropriate for the classroom—that will in the final analysis be mandated throughout the nation. This represents a dramatic change in the federal role in education and creates the power to prescribe the actions of every teacher and the policies of every state and local school board in the nation. Such a change should not occur without careful public discussion." Letter from Diane Ravitch to David Evans, September 24, 1992, *CP*, Education Subject File, box 64, folder 567.

116. Jill Zuckman, "Panel Gives Listless Approval to Scorned Reform Bill," *CQ Weekly*, May 23, 1992; Julie A. Miller, "House's Bill Would Authorize Standards, but Not Assessment," *Education Week*, May 27, 1992.

117. Vinovskis, *From a Nation at Risk to No Child Left Behind*, 49.

4. A NEW FEDERAL ROLE IS BORN, 1993–1994

1. Quotes are from Keith Nitta, *The Politics of Structural Education Reform* (New York: Routledge, 2008), 47; Patrick McGuinn, *No Child Left Behind and the Transformation of Federal Education Policy, 1965–2005* (Lawrence: University Press of Kansas, 2006), 75; and Lorraine McDonnell, "No Child Left Behind and the Federal Role in Education: Evolution or Revolution?" *Peabody Journal of Education* 80 (2): 30.

2. McDonnell, "No Child Left Behind"; McGuinn, *No Child Left Behind;* John F. Jennings, *Why National Standards and Tests?* (New York: Russell Sage, 1998).

3. Policy Studies Associates, *Status of New State Curriculum Frameworks, Standards, Assessments, and Monitoring Systems* (Washington, DC, 1993).

4. Robin Chait et al., *High Standards for All Students: A Report from the National Assessment of Title I on Progress and Challenges since the 1994 Reauthorization* (Washington, DC: U.S. Department of Education, 2001). See also U.S. General Accounting Office, *Title I Program: Stronger Accountability Needed for Performance of Disadvantaged Students* (Washington, DC, 2000); Margaret Goertz and Mark Duffy, *Assessment and Accountability Systems in the 50 States: 1999–2000* (Philadelphia: Consortium for Policy Research in Education, 2001); Planning and Evaluation Services, *Federal Education Legislation Enacted in 1994: An Analysis of Implementation and Impact* (Washington, DC: U.S. Department of Education, 1999).

5. National Center for Education Statistics, *NAEP 2008 Trends in Academic Progress: Reading 1971–2008, Mathematics 1973–2008* (Washington, DC: U.S. Department of Education, 2010), 2. To be fair, there was a notable uptick in mathematics scores among nine-year-olds between 1986 and 1990, and more-modest improvement among thirteen-year-olds in the same period.

6. See, for example, Michael S. Knapp et al., *What Is Taught and How to the Children of Poverty: Interim Report of a Two-Year Investigation* (Washington, DC: Policy Studies Associates / SRI International, 1991); Abt Associates and Policy Studies Associates, *The Chapter 1 Implementation Study Final Report* (Cambridge, MA, and Washington, DC: Abt Associates / Policy Studies Associates, 1991); Joyce L. Epstein and Douglas J. MacIver, *Opportunities to Learn: Effects on Eighth Graders of Curriculum Offerings and Instructional Approaches* (Baltimore: Center for Research on Effective Schooling for Disadvantaged Students, 1992); Jomillis H. Braddock and Robert E. Slavin, *Life in the Slow Lane: A Longitudinal Study of Effects of Ability Grouping on Student Achievement, Attitudes, and Perceptions* (Baltimore: Center for Research on Effective Schooling for Disadvantaged Students, 1992).

7. Indeed, the civil rights entrepreneur–led Commission on Chapter 1, which would provide the framework for the Improving America's Schools Act, complained that "though the 1988 amendments sharpened and expanded the goal and objectives of Chapter 1, the legislated changes have been implemented slowly. Many schools have not yet implemented the requirements to identify their desired outcomes in terms of advanced skills expected for all children and to then shape their programs to achieve those outcomes." Commission on Chapter 1, "The Commission on Chapter 1: October 1990," *GMA*, box 256, folder 9, "Chapter 1 Commission Meeting [2 of 2]."

8. Maris Vinovskis, "Do Federal Compensatory Education Programs Really Work? A Brief Historical Analysis of Title I and Head Start," *American Journal of Education* 107 (3) (1999): 187–209.

9. "Transcript of 2nd TV Debate between Bush, Clinton, and Perot," *New York Times*, October 16, 1992.

10. Quoted in Julie Miller, "On Familiar Political Turf, Alexander Hits the Campaign Trail," *Education Week*, September 30, 1992.

11. Julie Miller, "Bush Stand on School Choice Is Seen Bolder," *Education Week*, September 9, 1992.

12. "The Clinton Education Reform Plan: A New Covenant for Learning," Office of the Undersecretary of Education: Papers of Marshall S. Smith, National Archives of the United States, College Park, Maryland (hereafter *OUSE: MS*), 1996 (UD-O7W Entry 4), box 1, Brief Materials 1996 (first folder).

13. Quoted in Julie Miller, "With a Track Record on Education, Campaigner Clinton Speaks with Authority," *Education Week*, February 5, 1992.

14. On Clinton's long involvement in the standards-based reform movement and his knowledge of education issues see Julie Miller, "Clinton's Search for Education Advice: 'Coals to Newcastle,'" *Education Week*, October 14, 1992.

15. See, for example, "New American Choice Resolutions," Resolutions adopted at the DLC Convention, Cleveland, Ohio, May 1, 1991, 10–12, 20–21; Ted Kolderie, "Beyond Choice to New Public Schools: Withdrawing the Exclusive Franchise in Public Education," *PPI Policy Report* (Washington, DC: Progressive Policy Institute, 1990); John T. Woolley and Gerhard Peters, "Democratic Party Platform of 1992, July 13, 1992," the American Presidency Project, University of California at Santa Barbara, www.presidency.ucsb.edu, 4, 6; Ted Kolderie, Robert Lerman, and Charles Moskos, "Educating America: A New Compact for Opportunity and Citizenship," in *Mandate for Change*, ed. Will Marshall and Martin Schram (New York: Berkley Books, 1993), 129–52.

16. Memo from Marshall Smith to Michael Cohen, March 23, 1992, *OUSE: MS*, 1996 (UD-O7W Entry 4), box 1, Brief Materials 1996 (first folder).

17. See, for example, "Revised Education Transition Guide, November 4, 1992," *AS*, box 70, folder 13, Council of Chief State School Officers, 1992–94; "K–12 Transition Team Executive Summary," Papers of President William J. Clinton, William J. Clinton Presidential Library, Little Rock, Arkansas (hereafter *WJC*), Clinton Administration History Project, History of the Department of Education, box 17, folder 10, "Education—Volume 1[2] (OA23863)."

18. Personal interview with Tom Lindsley, January 24, 2008.

19. Jonathan Weisman, "Plan to Pair Business with Government for Reform Is Stymied in Many States," *Education Week*, February 13, 1991; Jonathan Weisman, "Business Roundtable Assessing State Progress on Reforms," *Education Week*, November 20, 1991.

20. Quoted in Mark Walsh, "Slow Pace of School Reform Worries Business Leaders," *Education Week*, October 13, 1993.

21. "Made in America" advertisement, in *GMA*, box 15, folder 6, "Investment 21 Meeting, 3/12/1991 (1 of 2)."

22. Business Roundtable, *Transforming Education Policy: Assessing 10 Years of Progress in the States* (New York: Business Roundtable, 1999), 1.

23. See, for example, Business Roundtable, *The Essential Components of a Successful Education System: Putting Policy into Practice* (New York: Business Roundtable, 1992).

24. Quoted in Mark Walsh, "Business Leaders Say Commitment to Education Still Strong," *Education Week*, June 2, 1993.

25. Walsh, "Business Leaders Say."

26. "RE: December 1 Minutes," to BCER Elementary and Secondary Education Act Roundtable Meeting Attendees and Invitees, December 23, 1992, *AS*, box 81, folder 20, National Alliance of Business 1992–94.

27. Quoted in Walsh, "Business Leaders Say."

28. Quoted in Cathie Jo Martin, *Stuck in Neutral: Business and the Politics of Human Capital Investment Policy* (Princeton, NJ: Princeton University Press, 2000), 202.

29. Richard Riley, "Education Reform through Standards and Partnerships, 1993–2000," *Phi Delta Kappan* 83 (9) (2002): 700–707.

30. Gordon M. Ambach to Bill Halter, "Revised Education Transition Guide, November 4, 1992," *AS*, box 70, folder 13, Council of Chief State School Officers, 1992–94.

31. Michael Cohen, "Goals 2000: Educate America Act. Draft: Document in Progress," February 19, 1993, *WJC*, Carol Rasco Subject Files, box 12, folder 13, "Fast Track Education Reform Legislation."

32. See documents in *GMA*, box 93, folder 6, "NAB Center for Excellence in Education Board Meeting, July 1990."

33. William Miller, "That Other Clinton Initiative: His Education/Training/Jobs Package Is Overshadowed by Health-Care Reform. But Its Impact Could Be Just as Big," *Industry Week*, April 4, 1994.

34. "Hill Outreach on Goals 2000," Office of the Assistant Secretary of Education: Records of Kay Casstevens, National Archives and Records Administration, College Park, Maryland (hereafter *OASE: KC*), box 2, "Goals 2000 Statements and Clips"; Letter from Gordon Ambach to Richard Riley, March 26, 1993, *OASE: KC*, box 2, "Goals 2000 Statements and Clips."

35. Memorandum from Richard Riley to President Clinton, "Goals 2000 Legislation," *WJC*, Clinton Administration History Project, History of the Department of Education, box 17, folder 12, "Education—Volume I [2]," (OA23863).

36. Memorandum from Jennifer Davis to Mike Cohen, Ray Cortines, Mike Smith, Kay Casstevens, and Terry Peterson, March 31, 1993, *OASE: KC*, box 2, "Goals 2000 Statements and Clips."

37. Kati Haycock and Susanna Navarro, *Unfinished Business: Fulfilling Our Children's Promise* (Oakland: Achievement Council, 1988), 3–4.

38. Pew Forum on Education Reform, "Progress Report: June 15, 1994," *GMA*, box 166, folder 3, "Pew Forum on Education Reform."

39. Susan Fuhrman, ed., *Designing Coherent Education Policy: Improving the System* (San Francisco: Jossey-Bass, 1993).

40. Consortium for Policy Research in Education, "Developing Content Standards: Creating a Process for Change," October 1993; Consortium for Policy Research in Education, "On the Design and Purposes of State Curriculum Guides: A Comparison of Mathematics and Social Studies Guides from Four States," April 1994; Consortium for Policy Research in Education, "Challenges of Systemic Education Reform," January 1994.

41. Letter from Gordon Ambach to Robert Schwartz, March 2, 1992, *GMA*, box 164, folder 1, "Pew Forum on Education Reform."

42. Personal interview with Hayes Mizell, March 24, 2008; Personal interview with Cynthia Brown, March 12, 2008; Kati Haycock and David Hornbeck, "Making Schools Work for Children in Poverty," in *National Issues in Education: Elementary and Secondary Education Act*, ed. John F. Jennings (Bloomington, IN: Phi Delta Kappa International, 1995), 78.

43. Commission on Chapter 1, "The Commission on Chapter 1: October 1990," *GMA*, box 256, folder 9, "Chapter 1 Commission Meeting [2 of 2]."

44. "Draft for Discussion: Commission on Chapter 1—Principles to Guide Its Work," February 1991, *GMA*, box 256, folder 8, "Chapter 1 Commission Meeting [1 of 2]."

45. "Meeting Dates: Commission on Chapter 1," *GMA*, box 256, folder 9, "Chapter 1 Commission Meeting [2 of 2]"; Letter from William L. Taylor and Dianne Piché to the Chapter 1 Commission, "Recommended Changes in 7/24/92 Draft," September 10, 1992, *GMA*, box 257, folder 6, "Revision Drafts of Chapter 1 Statutory Framework."

46. Commission on Chapter 1, "Report of First Meeting," December 11–12, 1991, Papers of Bella Rosenberg, American Federation of Teachers, Walter P. Reuther Library, Wayne State University, Detroit, Michigan (hereafter *BR*), box 11(1/6), folder Bella Rosenberg, National Commission on Chapter 1, 1990–94.

47. Commission on Chapter 1, *Making Schools Work for Children in Poverty: A New Framework* (Washington, DC: Commission on Chapter 1, 1992), v–vi, 6–7.

48. Memorandum from Kati Haycock to the Members of the Commission on Chapter 1, February 23, 1993, *BR*, box 11(1/6), folder Bella Rosenberg, National Commission on Chapter 1, 1990–94.

49. Julie A. Miller, "Chapter 1 Panel Calls for Radical Set of Revisions," *Education Week*, December 16, 1992.

50. Personal interview with William Taylor, January 14, 2008.

51. Kati Haycock, Letter to Members of the Commission on Chapter 1, February 23, 1993, *BR*, box 11 (1/6), folder Bella Rosenberg, National Commission on Chapter 1, 1990–94; see also "Commission Update, June 1993" and "Commission Update, August/ September 1993," both in the *BR*, box 11(1/6), folder Bella Rosenberg, National Commission on Chapter 1, 1990–94.

52. Marshall S. Smith, Letter to Members of the Pew Forum on K–12 Education Reform, October 8, 1992, *GMA*, box 164, folder 4, "Pew Forum, Disadvantaged Children."

53. Reauthorization of Hawkins/Stafford Consortium, "Recommendations to the House Education and Labor Committee on the Reauthorization of the Hawkins/Stafford Amendments of 1988," December 2, 1992, *GMA*, box 234, folder 9, "R H/C C Final Report Original."

54. Commission on Chapter 1, "Commission Update: August/September 1993," *BR*, box 11(1/6), folder Bella Rosenberg, National Commission on Chapter 1, 1990–94.

55. Thomas Payzant, "Administration's Response to the Steering Committee of the Commission on Chapter 1's Analysis of the Administration's Title I Proposal," *BR*, box 11(1/6), folder Bella Rosenberg, National Commission on Chapter 1, 1990-94.

56. Commission on Chapter 1 members were not enthused by these aspects of the administration's proposals but likely realized that further progress on these measures was not politically possible at the time. See Letter from Kati Haycock to Members, Commission on Chapter 1, October 27, 1993, *BR*, box 11(1/6), folder Bella Rosenberg, National Commission on Chapter 1, 1990–94.

57. Julie Miller, "E.S.E.A. Plan Would Retool Chapter 1, Eliminate Block Grant," *Education Week*, August 4, 1993.

58. Memorandum from MD & MS to DE, "RE: Major ESEA reauthorization issues and proposals," September 8, 1994, *CP*, Elementary and Secondary Education Act Subject Files, box 15, folder 129.

59. Personal interview with John F. Jennings, February 13, 2008.

60. Personal interview with Michael Cohen, November 7, 2007.

61. "Minutes: National Alliance of Business Council on Excellence in Education, ANA Westin Hotel, Washington, D.C.," June 16, 1992, *AS*, box 81, folder 20, National Alliance of Business, 1992–94.

62. Mark Pitsch, "Timing of Clinton Budget, Outlook for Education Uncertain," *Education Week*, December 9, 1992; Mark Pitsch, "Deficit Reduction Tagged Key Budget Goal," *Education Week*, January 20, 1993.

63. Julie A. Miller, "Lobbyists See Minuses for Education in Clinton Budget Plan," *Education Week*, March 3, 1993.

64. Quoted in Miller, "Lobbyists See Minuses."

65. The quote from Hornbeck can be found in "The Roundtable: Raising Public Awareness," *Education Week*, April 21, 1993; Austin's quote is from Mark Walsh, "Signing Up the Public," *Education Week*, April 7, 1993.

66. *The 25th Annual Phi Delta Kappa / Gallup Poll of the Public's Attitudes toward the Public Schools*, Fall 1993, 138–39. Available at the Roper Center for Public Opinion Research, University of Connecticut, Storrs, Connecticut.

67. See Elisabeth Clemens, "Lineages of the Rube Goldberg State: Building and Blurring Public Programs, 1900–1940," in *Rethinking Political Institutions: The Art of the State*, ed. Ian Shapiro, Stephen Skowronek, and Daniel Galvin (New York: NYU Press, 2006).

68. Memorandum from Secretary Richard Riley to President Bill Clinton, "Goals 2000 Legislation," *WJC*, Clinton Administration History Project, History of the Department of Education, box 17, folder 12, "Education—Volume I [4]," OA23863.

69. Quoted in Jill Zuckman, "Clinton's School Reform Plan Has High Hopes, Low Funds," *CQ Weekly*, April 24, 1993.

70. Quoted in Mark Pitsch, "Pitched Battle over Clinton Plan to Shift Chapter 1 Aid Seen," *Education Week*, September 22, 1993.

71. Reauthorization of Hawkins/Stafford Consortium, "Concepts for Reauthorization of the Hawkins/Stafford Amendments of 1988: Achieving National Education Goals and the Hawkins/Stafford Reauthorization," *GMA*, box 234, folder 9, "R H/S C Final Report Original."

72. National Coalition of Educational Equity Advocates, *Educate America: A Call for Equity in School Reform* (Chevy Chase, MD: National Coalition of Educational Equity Advocates, 1993), vii.

73. Letter from Republican Representatives Bill Goodling, Marge Roukema, Steve Gunderson, Duke Cunningham, Buck McKeon, and Dan Miller to Secretary Richard Riley, April 21, 1993, *OASE: KC*, box 2, "Goals 2000 Statements and Clips."

74. Representatives Dick Armey, Cass Ballenger, John Boehner, and Pete Hoekstra, "Parent and Student Empowerment Act: Time for a Change," October 12, 1993, Papers of Texas Representative Richard Armey, Carl Albert Center, University of Oklahoma, Norman, Oklahoma (hereafter *RA*), box 51, folder 6.

75. Quoted in Laurel Shaper Walters, "Goals 2000 Act Broadens Federal Role," *Christian Science Monitor*, April 11, 1994.

76. "House Republicans Condemn Education Bill as Federal Takeover of Schools," February 24, 1994, *RA*, box 51, folder 7.

77. Roy Romer, "Memorandum to All Governors Serving on the NGA Task Force on Education: RE: Conference Call Thursday, April 15, 4:30 pm EDT to Discuss the Clinton Administration's education reform bill, "Goals 2000: Educate America Act," April 14, 1993. Accessed, with permission, from the National Governors Association Historical Files, National Governors Association, Washington, DC (hereafter *NGA*); National Governors Association, "Education Task Force Agenda: Strategic Investment: Achieving the National Education Goals," Draft Talking Points. January 31, 1993. Accessed from *NGA*.

78. Personal interview with Raymond Scheppach, January 15, 2008.

79. Personal interview with Gordon Ambach, December 11, 2007.

80. National Governors Association, "Statement of the NGA Task Force on Education," August 16, 1993, *The Debate on Opportunity to Learn Standards* (Washington, DC: National Governors Association, 1993).

81. Quoted in Julie Miller, "E.D. and House Democrats Negotiate on 'Goals 2000' Bill," *Education Week*, August 4, 1993.

82. To be sure, because it worked as a series of amendments to the underlying Elementary and Secondary Education Act—which was due for reauthorization—there was some pressure to pass the act in order to continue funding for ESEA programs. But this pressure did not determine the legislative outcome; Congress could simply have chosen to authorize funding for the act as it was currently structured, as it later did between 2000 and 2002, and again between 2007 and 2012.

83. Letter from President Bill Clinton to William Ford, June 3, 1993, *WJC*, Carol Rasco Subject Files, box 34, folder 1, "Goals 2000: Educate America Act," (OA7454) [1].

84. When faced with a similar amendment in the Senate offered by liberal Democratic senators Paul Simon of Illinois and Paul Wellstone of Minnesota, Democrat Claiborne Pell of Rhode Island reminded Democrats that removing the language was necessary to protect the bill: "[I] am very concerned that inclusion of this language will risk bipartisan

support, which is essential to passing this bill and strengthening the federal education reform effort." The amendment was defeated. "School Finance Amendment," *CP*, Elementary and Secondary Education Subject File, box 21, folder 193.

85. Julie Miller, "'Goals 2000' Clears First Hurdle, but Obstacles Remain," *Education Week*, May 12, 1993.

86. Senator Claiborne Pell, handwritten notes from luncheon with Mike Smith, June 10, 1993. *CP*, Elementary and Secondary Education Act Subject Files, box 1, folder 1.

87. Thomas Sawyer, quoted in *Congressional Record*, 103rd Congress, 1st Sess., 1993, 139, 7741–42.

88. Kevin Kosar, *Failing Grades: The Federal Politics of Education Standards* (New York: Lynne Rienner, 2005), 132–36.

89. McGuinn, *No Child Left Behind*, 90; See also Robert Schwartz and Marian Robinson, "Goals 2000 and the Standards Movement," *Brookings Papers on Education Policy* (Washington, DC: Brookings Institution Press, 2000), 173–206. For a sense of moderate Republicans' concerns about, and support for, Goals 2000, see Rep. Bill Goodling et al., Letter to Honorable Richard Riley, Secretary of Education, April 21, 1993, *OASE: KC*, 1994–97, box 2, folder Goals 2000 Statements and Clips.

90. Letter from the Pew Forum on K–12 Education Reform to its members, July 13, 1994, *AS*, box 90, folder "Pew Forum on Education Reform, Summer 1994(21)."

91. Testimony of Richard Riley, Hearing before the Committee on Labor and Human Resources, "Goals 2000: Educate America Act," May 4, 1993, United States Senate, 103rd Congress, 1st Sess., 6.

92. Martin, *Stuck in Neutral*, 203–4.

93. Personal interview with Susan Traiman, February 11, 2008.

94. "A G.O.P. Divided: O.B.E. Drives Wedge in Party," *Education Week*, June 15, 1994.

95. For vote tallies see McGuinn, *No Child Left Behind*, 90; Kosar, *Failing Grades*, 130.

96. Kosar, *Failing Grades*, 164.

97. Jennings, *Why National Standards and Tests?* 135.

98. William Taylor, *The Passion of My Times: An Advocate's Fifty-Year Journey in the Civil Rights Movement* (New York: Da Capo Press, 2004), 199.

99. Personal interview with John F. Jennings, February 13, 2008.

100. Campbell quoted in *Congressional Record*, 103rd Congress, 2nd Sess., 1994, 140, 1120.

101. Quoted in Joseph Garcia, "Federal Aid for Schools Called Poor; Chapter 1 Program Ineffective, Panel Says," *Dallas Morning News*, December 11, 1992.

102. Personal interview with Tom Lindsley, January 24, 2008.

103. Quoted in Jennings, *Why National Standards and Tests?* 140.

104. Jennings, *Why National Standards and Tests?* 149.

105. Maris Vinovskis, *From a Nation at Risk to No Child Left Behind: National Education Goals and the Creation of Federal Education Policy* (New York: Teachers College Press, 2009), 83–84.

106. Quoted in Elizabeth DeBray, *Politics, Ideology and Education: Federal Policy during the Clinton and Bush Administrations* (New York: Teachers College Press, 2006), 31.

107. Benjamin Superfine, "The Politics of Accountability: The Rise and Fall of Goals 2000," *American Journal of Education* 112 (2005): 10–43.

108. *Federal Education Legislation Enacted in 1994: An Evaluation of Implementation and Impact* (Washington, DC: U.S. Department of Education, 1999), 6.

5. THE ROAD TO NO CHILD LEFT BEHIND, 1995–2002

1. Gail Sunderman and James Kim, "The Expansion of Federal Power and the Politics of Implementing the No Child Left Behind Act," *Teachers College Record* 109(5) (2007): 1057–58.

2. Scott Abernathy, *No Child Left Behind and the Public Schools* (Ann Arbor: University of Michigan Press, 2007), 2–3.

3. See especially Patrick McGuinn, "Swing Issues and Policy Regimes: Federal Education Policy and the Politics of Policy Change," *Journal of Policy History* 18(2) (2006): 205–40.

4. Quoted in Steven Gillon, *The Pact: Bill Clinton, Newt Gingrich, and the Rivalry That Defined a Generation* (Oxford: Oxford University Press, 2008), 126.

5. House Education Task Force, "104th Congress: Privatize, Localize, Consolidate, Eliminate. Back to Basics Education Reform Act," *OASE: KC,* box 1, "Department."

6. Robert Johnston, "Clinton Spares Education from Cuts in Balanced-Budget Plan," *Education Week,* June 21, 1995.

7. President William J. Clinton, State of the Union Address, January 23, 1996.

8. Patrick McGuinn, *No Child Left Behind and the Transformation of Federal Education Policy, 1965–2005* (Lawrence: University Press of Kansas, 2006), 117–19.

9. Survey by CNN and *USA Today,* April 9–10, 1996, archived at the Roper Center for Public Opinion Research, University of Connecticut, Storrs, Connecticut.

10. Quoted in Mark Pitsch, "Polls Confirm Key Role of Education in Political Arena," *Education Week,* June 19, 1996.

11. McGuinn, *No Child Left Behind,* 118.

12. "Possible Department of Education Goals for Calendar Year 1996," November 12, 1995, Office of the Undersecretary: Records of Marshall Smith, 1996, box 1, "Brief Materials (6)," National Archives of the United States, College Park, Maryland. Emphasis added.

13. See McGuinn, *No Child Left Behind,* 109.

14. Quoted in Mark Pitsch, "To Placate Conservatives, Measure Alters Goals 2000," *Education Week,* May 1, 1996.

15. "Dear Senator" letter from Richard Riley to U.S. senators, July 14, 1995, Office of the Undersecretary: Records of Marshall Smith, 1996, box 1, "Brief Materials (6)," National Archives of the United States, College Park, Maryland.

16. Kenneth Wong and Gail Sunderman, "Education Policy as a Presidential Priority: No Child Left Behind and the Bush Presidency," *Publius: The Journal of Federalism* 37 (3) (2007), 5; see also Erik W. Robelen, "States Sluggish on Execution of 1994 ESEA," *Education Week,* November 28, 2001.

17. Clinton's postelection education policies are handled expertly in McGuinn, *No Child Left Behind,* chap. 7.

18. President William J. Clinton, State of the Union address, February 4, 1997.

19. See McGuinn, *No Child Left Behind,* 134.

20. Citizens' Commission on Civil Rights, *Closing the Deal: A Preliminary Report on State Compliance with Final Assessment and Accountability Requirements under the Improving America's Schools Act of 1994* (Washington, DC: Citizens' Commission on Civil Rights, 2001).

21. U.S. General Accounting Office, *Title I Program: Stronger Accountability Needed for Performance of Disadvantaged Students* (Washington, DC: U.S. General Accounting Office, 2000), 32–38.

22. Independent Review Panel, *Improving the Odds: A Report on Title I from the Independent Review Panel* (Washington, DC: U.S. Department of Education, 2001), 13.

23. Citizens' Commission on Civil Rights, *Closing the Deal;* see also SRI International / Policy Studies Associates, *Evaluation of Title I Accountability Systems and School Improvement Efforts (TASSIE): First-Year Findings* (Washington, DC: U.S. Department of Education, 2004), ix; Margaret E. Goertz, Marc C. Duffy, and Kerstin C. LeFloch, *Assessment and Accountability Systems in the 50 States: 1999–2000* (New Brunswick, NJ: CPRE, 2001), 34.

24. Quoted in Mark Walsh, "Businesses' Enthusiasm for Reform Seen Flagging," *Education Week,* June 14, 1995.

25. Peter Applebaum, "Business Leaders and Governors Gather to Map Route to Elusive New Era of Education," *New York Times*, March 26, 1996.

26. "Summit," *AS*, box 86, folder National Education Summit Correspondence.

27. Robert B. Schwartz, "The Emerging State Leadership Role in Education Reform: Notes of a Participant-Observer," in *A Nation Reformed? American Education 20 Years after "A Nation at Risk,"* ed. David T. Gordon (Cambridge, MA: Harvard University Press, 2003), 143.

28. Louis Gerstner, Remarks at Opening Plenary Session, 1996 Education Summit, *GMA*, box 147, folder 4, "1996 National Education Summit, Speeches."

29. Ruth Wattenberg, Memorandum to Al Shanker, Gene Kemble, Matt Gandal, John Mitchell, Joan Snowden, Bella Rosenberg, and Liz Smith, June 7, 1996, "RE: Follow-up work on the 'Entity,'" *AS*, box 66, folder 57, Achieve 1996–97.

30. "Year Later, Progress since Summit Questioned," *Education Week*, April 2, 1997.

31. Norman Augustine, Ed Lupberger, and James Orr, from a written statement, "A Common Agenda for Improving American Education," The Business Roundtable Education Task Force, the U.S. Chamber of Commerce, and the National Alliance of Business, September 26, 1996.

32. Personal interview with Susan Traiman, February 11, 2008.

33. Personal interview with Sandy Boyd, January 29, 2008.

34. In testimony before Congress, Edward Rust, chairman and CEO of State Farm Insurance, chairman of the National Alliance of Business, and chair of the Education Task Force for the Business Roundtable, reported that the Business Coalition for Education Reform (of which he was also a key player) was "linked to over 500 local business-led education coalitions across the country working directly" on standards, testing, accountability, and teacher quality issues. Testimony of Edward Rust, "Education Success=Business Success," May 25, 1999, Hearing before the Committee on Small Business, U.S. Senate, 106th Cong., 1st sess., 80.

35. Personal interview with Milton Goldberg, January 21, 2008.

36. Business Coalition for Education Reform, Letter to Representative William Goodling of Pennsylvania, June 28, 1999. Document provided to the author by Tom Lindsley of the National Center for Educational Achievement.

37. Business Coalition for Education Reform, "Principles for Reauthorizing the Elementary and Secondary Education Act," 1999. Available from Internet Archive, http://web.archive.org/web/20001007105701/www.nab.com/content/aboutus/resources/presea.htm.

38. Statement of Edward B. Rust Jr., chairman and CEO, State Farm Insurance Companies, before the Committee on Education and the Workforce, U.S. House of Representatives, on "Business Issues in Elementary and Secondary Education," July 1, 1999.

39. "The Republican vs. Democratic Education Agendas: Although Their Rhetoric Has Changed, GOP *Still* Doesn't Support Policies to Improve Public Education," Papers of Patsy Mink, Representative of Hawaii, Manuscript Division, Library of Congress, Washington, DC (hereafter *PM*), box 1548, folder 5, "Democratic Caucus Education Task Force," 1999.

40. "Democratic Education Agenda: Democrats Must Act Now!" *PM*, box 2024, folder 1, "Democratic Caucus: Education Task Force Memoranda/Agenda," 1995–99, n.d.

41. U.S. House Democratic Policy Committee, "GOP Congress Rejects Democratic Class-Size Reduction Initiative," March 12, 1999, *PM*, box 1563, folder 4, "Teaching/Class Size Reduction, 1999–2000." Emphasis added.

42. *Education at a Crossroads: What Works and What's Wasted in Education Today.* Subcommittee on Oversight and Investigations, Committee on Education and the Workforce, U.S. House of Representatives, July 17, 1998, xiii.

43. Andrew Rudalevige, "Forging a Congressional Compromise," in *No Child Left Behind? The Politics and Practice of School Accountability*, ed. Paul Peterson and Martin West (Washington, DC: Brookings Institution Press, 2003), 32.

44. See Elizabeth DeBray, *Politics, Ideology, and Education: Federal Policy during the Clinton and Bush Administrations* (New York: Teachers College Press, 2006), 45–47, for an overview of congressional Republicans' approach to school reform in 1998–99.

45. This term is used by John Kingdon in his classic work, *Agendas, Alternatives, and Public Policies* (New York: Little, Brown, 1984), 137.

46. Texas Business and Education Coalition, "History," Texas Business and Education Coalition website: http://tbec.org/about/history.

47. Tyce Palmaffy, "The Gold Star State," *Policy Review* 88 (March/April 1998); see also William DeSoto, "A New Force in School Politics: The Texas Business and Education Coalition," *Education* 115 (Spring 1995).

48. Emily Pyle, "Te$t Market: Sandy Kress Has Ridden High-Stakes Accountability to Fame and Fortune. What about the Kids?" *Texas Observer*, May 13, 2005, provides useful information, albeit in an unsympathetic portrait of Kress.

49. See Keith Nitta, *The Politics of Structural Education Reform* (New York: Routledge, 2008), 86–87. A historically informative, but largely unsympathetic, portrait of Kress is presented in Mark Donald, "The Resurrection of Sandy Kress: Or, How a Democrat and Reviled Former DISD Board President Found a Happy Home Pushing 'Educational Accountability' for the GOP," *Dallas Observer*, October 19, 2000.

50. John Stevens, "Education Improved under Bush," *Dallas Morning News*, June 13, 1999.

51. Peter Beinart, "The Big Debate: George W. Bush Battles the Republican Right," *New Republic*, March 16, 1998.

52. Paul Burka, "The Disloyal Opposition," *Texas Monthly*, December 1998.

53. Paul Teske, "President Bush and the U.S. Department of Education: The Texas Mafia, Scientific Education Policy, and No State Left Behind," in *President George W. Bush's Influence over Bureaucracy and Policy: Extraordinary Times, Extraordinary Powers*, ed. Colin Provost and Paul Teske (New York: Palgrave Macmillan, 2009), 105.

54. Patrick McGuinn provides evidence that education was a primary concern in voters' minds during the 2000 election campaign. See McGuinn, *No Child Left Behind*, chap. 8. Bush's major statement on "compassionate conservatism" can be found in his speech, "The Duty of Hope," Indianapolis, Indiana, July 22, 1999, http://www.cpjustice.org/stories/storyreader$383.

55. Quoted in Nicholas Lemann, "Testing Limits: Can the President's Education Crusade Survive Beltway Politics?" *New Yorker*, July 2, 2001.

56. Quoted in Lemann, "Testing Limits."

57. Personal interview with Sandy Kress, January 3, 2008.

58. See Robert Maranto and Laura Coppeto, "The Politics behind Bush's No Child Left Behind Initiative: Ideas, Elections, and Top-Down Education Reform," in *George W. Bush: Evaluating the President at Midterm*, ed. Bryan Hilliard, Tom Lansford, and Robert Watson (New York: SUNY Press, 2004), 105–19.

59. 2000 Republican Party Platform, July 31, 2000, available at the American Presidency Project Online: www.presidency.ucsb.edu/ws/index.php?pid = 25849.

60. "Interview with Margaret Spellings," *Texas Monthly*, May 1, 2008, http://www.texasmonthly.com/preview/2008-05-01/talks.

61. Gore had proposed to require states to adopt annual school report cards and shut down failing schools; increase federal funding for charter schools; establish a system of voluntary national standards and tests; and institute a system of grants to encourage states to adopt high school exit exams. He also called for an additional $115 billion for teacher

recruitment and salary increases, class-size reduction, and universal preschool. See Joetta Sack, "Candidates' K–12 Policies Share Themes," *Education Week*, September 6, 2000.

62. Personal interview with Susan Traiman, February 11, 2008.

63. President George W. Bush, *No Child Left Behind* (Washington, DC: U.S. Department of Education, 2001).

64. Personal interview with Tom Lindsley, January 28, 2008.

65. Quoted in Joetta Sack, "Group Seeks Help for Minority Achievement," *Education Week*, December 15, 1999.

66. Sack, "Group Seeks Help."

67. Personal interview with Krista Kafer, January 25, 2008.

68. Dianne Piché, with the assistance of Phyllis McClure and Stephanie Schmelz, *Title I at Midstream: The Fight to Improve Schools for Poor Kids* (Washington, DC: Citizens' Commission on Civil Rights, 1998), 2.

69. Margot Rogers and Christine Stoneman, *Triggering Educational Accountability* (Washington, DC: Center for Law and Education, 1999).

70. *Dispelling the Myth: High Poverty Schools Exceeding Expectations* (Washington, DC: Education Trust, 1999).

71. Leadership Conference on Civil Rights, "Accountability," April 2000. Available from Internet Archive, http://web.archive.org/web/20010423202837/www.civilrights.org/policy_and_legislation/pl_issues/education/accountability.html. See also Leadership Conference on Civil Rights, "Title I's Impact on Student Achievement: Myths and Realities," April 2000, in which the LCCR calls for reaffirming and strengthening the IASA. Available from Internet Archive, http://web.archive.org/web/20010423202242/www.civilrights.org/policy_and_legislation/pl_issues/education/myth.html

72. Personal interview with Charles Barone, January 16, 2008.

73. Personal interview with Kati Haycock, February 1, 2008.

74. Personal interview with Gordon Ambach, December 11–12, 2007; personal interview with Kati Haycock, February 1, 2008.

75. Personal interview with Kati Haycock, February 1, 2008.

76. "Title I Fact Sheet #1: Accountability—All Must Mean All and Progress Must Mean Progress," Education Trust, September 13, 1999.Emphasis added.

77. Rudalevige, "Forging a Congressional Compromise," 32; DeBray, *Politics, Ideology, and Education*, 48.

78. DeBray, *Politics, Ideology, and Education*, 72.

79. In fact, Sandy Kress, a Democrat and DLC member, claimed to have borrowed ideas from the Three R's bill while fleshing out the No Child Left Behind proposal. Rudalevige, "Forging a Congressional Compromise," 34.

80. Andrew Rotherham, "Modernizing Title I for the 21st Century," *Title I Monitor*, January 1, 2001.

81. See Andrew Rotherham, "Toward Performance-Based Federal Education Funding: Reauthorization of the Elementary and Secondary Education Act," Progressive Policy Institute, April 1999. The primary discussion of ESEA Title I is on pp.5–7, with corresponding citations on pp. 20–21.

82. See Rudalevige, "Forging a Congressional Compromise."

83. Personal interview with Sandy Kress, January 3, 2008; see also Frederick Hess and Michael Petrilli, "Wrong Turn on School Reform," *Policy Review* 153 (2009): 55–68.

84. See Sandy Kress, "Confessions of an NCLB Supporter," *Education Next* 7 (2) (Spring 2007). Emphasis added. Available at http://educationnext.org/confessions-of-a-no-child-left-behind-supporter/.

85. "Comparison of Education Proposals: President Bush, Lieberman/Roemer/Dooley, Miller/Kildee," February 15, 2001, *PM*, box 1681, folder 7, Elementary and Secondary Education Act, No Child Left Behind (HR 1), binder B (1 of 3).

86. Personal interview with Raymond Scheppach, January 15, 2008.

87. Wilkins quoted in Jim Yardley, "The Education Issue: Critics Say a Focus on Test Scores Is Overshadowing Education in Texas," *New York Times*, October 30, 2000; Lewis quoted in Gail Russell Chaddock, "All Eyes on Reform," *Christian Science Monitor*, January 18, 2000.

88. Citizens' Commission on Civil Rights, *Analysis of President George W. Bush's Education Plan* (Washington, DC: Citizens' Commission on Civil Rights, 2001), 4.

89. Quoted in Erik Robelen, "Civil Rights Group Decries Implementation of Title I," *Education Week*, September 22, 1999.

90. For civil rights entrepreneurs' perceptions of resistance of federally led standards-based reforms, see prepared statement of William Taylor, "Examining Legislation Authorizing Funds for the Elementary and Secondary Education Act, Focusing on Title I, Education Programs for the Disadvantaged," Hearing of the Committee on Health, Education, Labor, and Pensions, United States Senate, 106th Congress, 1st sess., March 16, 1999, 30.

91. Personal interview with Sandy Kress, January 3, 2008.

92. Dianne Piché with Phyllis McClure and Stephanie Schmelz, *Title I in Midstream: The Fight to Improve Schools for Poor Kids* (Washington, DC: Citizens' Commission on Civil Rights, 1999), 24–25 (using ERIC numbers).

93. Kress, "Confessions of a 'No Child Left Behind' Supporter."

94. See George Miller, "Major Public School Improvement Bill Would Provide Significant New Resources in Exchange for Tough Accountability: Real Resources for Real Reform," press release, January 31, 2001, *PM*, box 2025, folder 1, Elementary and Secondary Education Act, No Child Left Behind Committee binder, 2001; George Miller, "The Excellence and Accountability in Education Act," January 31, 2001, *PM*, box 2025, folder 1, Elementary and Secondary Education Act, No Child Left Behind Committee binder, 2001; George Miller, "Statement by Rep. George Miller Regarding President Bush's Education Proposal: Yes on Accountability and Teacher Quality, No on Vouchers, President Must Submit Strong Education Budget Request," press release, January 23, 2001, *PM*, box 1681, folder 7, Elementary and Secondary Education Act, No Child Left Behind, HR 1, binder B (1 of 3); Andrew Rotherham, "The New Three R's of Education," *Blueprint Magazine*, February 7, 2001.

95. See, for example, "Comparison of Education Proposals: President Bush, Lieberman/Roemer/Dooley, Miller/Kildee," *PM*, box 1681, folder 7, Elementary and Secondary Education Act, No Child Left Behind, HR 1, binder B (1 of 3).

96. Personal interview with Kati Haycock, February 2, 2008.

97. Survey by Cable News Network, *USA Today*, Gallup, January 13–16, 2000. Data provided by the Roper Center for Public Opinion Research, University of Connecticut, Storrs, Connecticut.

98. *Phi Delta Kappa / Gallup Poll of the Public's Attitudes toward the Public Schools*, June 5–29, 2000, conducted by the Gallup Organization. Data provided by the Roper Center for Public Opinion Research.

99. Chester E. Finn Jr., Bruno Manno, and Diane Ravitch, *Education 2001: Getting the Job Done; A Memorandum to the President-Elect and the 107th Congress*, December 2000.

100. Personal interview with Joel Packer, February 9, 2010.

101. Remark by Margaret Spellings in White House Domestic Policymaking Symposium, Session 1: From Campaigning to Governing, June 12, 2009, Oral History Program, Miller Center of Public Affairs, University of Virginia, Charlottesville, Virginia. Audio and video of the session are available at http://millercenter.org/scripps/archive/conference/detail/5471.

102. DeBray, *Politics, Ideology, and Education*, 66–71.

103. Testimony of Ralph M. Tanner, Kansas state representative, National Conference of State Legislatures, before the Committee on Education and the Workforce of the

United States House of Representatives, regarding the Academic Achievement for All (Straight A's) Act, May 20, 1999.

104. Siobhan Gorman, "Education: Behind Bipartisanship," *National Journal*, July 14, 2001, 2228–33; Robert Schlesinger, "Compromise Drove Education Bill—Bipartisanship Won Day for Bush," *Boston Globe*, June 16, 2001.

105. Bush used a personal touch to woo Kennedy. As Margaret Spellings recalls, "A couple of the first things that Bush did when he came to office, literally in the first week, was to have George Miller and Ted Kennedy and John Boehner and the whole fam damily over to watch the movie—I can't remember the name of it—about the Cuban Missile Crisis [the movie is Thirteen Days]. It was a surreal moment for me to watch Senator Kennedy and President Bush sit in the front row of the White House movie theater watching this movie about Senator Kennedy's brother, literally feet away from the oval office, and the entirety of the movie virtually takes place in the Oval Office." Remark by Margaret Spellings in White House Domestic Policymaking Symposium, Session 3: Selling Domestic Policy from the White House, June 13, 2009, Oral History Program, Miller Center of Public Affairs, University of Virginia, Charlottesville, Virginia. Audio and video of the session are available at http://millercenter.org/scripps/archive/conference/detail/5471.

106. David Nather and Mary Agnes Carey, "Health, Education: Assertive Dealmaker," *CQ Weekly*, May 26, 2001; see also David Broder, "Long Road to Reform: Negotiators Forge Education Legislation," *Washington Post*, December 17, 2001.

107. David Nather, "Compromises on ESEA Bills May Imperil Republican Strategy," *CQ Weekly*, May 5, 2001.

108. David Nather, "Democrats Leaving Their Stamp on Bush's Education Bill," *CQ Weekly*, May 12, 2001; Lisa Fine, "ESEA, Minus Vouchers, Easily Passes House," *Education Week*, May 30.

109. Nather and Carey, "Health, Education: Assertive Dealmaker."

110. Kathy Kiely, "Bush Explains Compromises on Education Bill," *USA Today*, May 21, 2001; David Nather, "Education Bill Nears Final Hurdle with 'Deal-Breakers' Swept Aside," *CQ Weekly*, June 16, 2001.

111. Nather, "Democrats Leaving Their Stamp."

112. Personal interview with Andrew Rotherham, March 4, 2008.

113. In April 2000, the Leadership Conference on Civil Rights declared that "The 1994 reforms [that is, the IASA] should be given a chance to work." In the same document, the LCCR also called for increased federal funding, an end to teaching of poor children by "uncertified, out-of-field, and less experienced teachers," public reporting of achievement data and teachers' qualifications, a right of students to transfer from "failing schools," and tests to "measure the progress of schools." See Leadership Conference on Civil Rights, "Title I Reauthorization: What's at Stake for Students and Parents," April 2000. Available from Internet Archive, http://web.archive.org/web/20010423202536/http://www.civilrights.org/policy_and_legislation/pl_issues/education/at_stake.html.

114. Craig Jerald, *Real Results, Remaining Challenges: The Story of Texas Education Reform* (Washington, DC: Education Trust, 2001).

115. Personal interview with David Shreve, January 23, 2008.

116. David Nather, "As Education Bill Heads for Floor Votes, Big Ideological Tests Loom in House," *CQ Weekly*, May 19, 2001.

117. DeBray, *Politics, Ideology, and Education*, 101.

118. Nather, "Compromises on ESEA Bills."

119. Quoted in Susan Crabtree and John Bresnahan, "Boehner Facing Plenty of Heat from Conservatives," *Roll Call*, May 3, 2001.

120. Quoted in David Nather, "Compromises on ESEA Bills."

121. Dana Milbank, "House Education Bill Got It Wrong for Some Critics on the Right, But Conservatives Generally Award Bush High Marks," *Washington Post*, May 7, 2001.

122. Personal interview with Michael Petrilli, February 8, 2010.

123. Business Coalition for Excellence in Education, "Fact Sheet," provided to the author by Tom Lindsley, National Center for Educational Achievement; Business Coalition for Excellence in Education, "Summary of Activities and Products," provided to the author by Tom Lindsley, National Center for Educational Achievement.

124. "Business Roundtable Brings Employers to Capitol Hill to Make the Case for Education Reform," Business Roundtable press release, March 20, 2001. Available from Internet Archive, http://web.archive.org/web/20011225092617/http://www.brtable.org/press.cfm/518.

125. Personal interview with Tom Lindsley, January 28, 2008.

126. Business Coalition for Excellence in Education, "Principles for K–12 Education Legislation," handout provided to the author by Tom Lindsley, National Center for Educational Achievement.

127. Remarks by Spellings during a "Newsmaker Luncheon with Education Secretary Margaret Spellings," National Press Club, September 26, 2006.

128. For further discussion see DeBray, *Ideology, Politics, and Education*, 122–24.

129. Personal interview with David Shreve, January 23, 2008.

130. Julie Blair, "Unions' Positions Unheeded on ESEA," *Education Week*, November 6, 2002.

131. Quoted in Erik Robelen, "ESEA Passage Awaits a Deal on Spending," *Education Week*, December 12, 2001.

132. Personal interview with Raymond Scheppach, January 15, 2008.

133. Personal interview with Patricia Sullivan, January 22, 2008.

134. However, supporters of expanded federal spending failed in their effort to "fully fund" the federal government's commitment to the Individuals with Disabilities Education Act, the law serving disabled students. Erik Robelen, "ESEA to Boost Federal Role in Education," *Education Week*, January 9, 2002.

135. See Rebecca Skinner and Erin Caffrey, *Educational Testing: Implementation of ESEA Title I-A Requirements under the No Child Left Behind Act* (Washington, DC: Congressional Research Service, 2010).

136. Rudalevige, "Forging a Congressional Compromise," 41.

137. Robelen, "ESEA Passage Awaits a Deal on Spending."

138. Siobhan Gorman, "Bipartisan Schoolmates," *Education Next* 2 (2) (Summer 2002), http://educationnext.org/files/ednext20022_36.pdf.

139. Center on Education Policymaking, *A Call to Restructure Restructuring: Lessons from the No Child Left Behind Act in Five States* (Washington, DC, 2008).

140. According to Joel Packer, then a top lobbyist with the National Education Association, the teachers unions played a critical role in negotiating the "teacher quality" measures contained in NCLB. Personal interview with Joel Packer, February 9, 2010.

141. For a discussion of these and other aspects of NCLB's "teacher quality" reforms, see U.S. Department of Education, *State and Local Implementation of the No Child Left Behind Act—Volume 8—Teacher Quality under NCLB: Final Report* (Washington, DC: U.S. Department of Education, 2010).

6. "YES WE CAN" IMPROVE AMERICA'S SCHOOLS?

1. Barack Obama, "Change that Works for You," Raleigh, North Carolina, June 9, 2008.

2. Dan Froomkin, "Obama as the Anti-Bush," *Washington Post*, August 29, 2008.

3. Adam Nagourney, "Obama: Racial Barrier Falls in Decisive Victory," *New York Times*, November 5, 2008.

4. "Full Text of Obama's Education Speech," *Denver Post*, May 28, 2008.

5. David Hoff, "Obama Sounds as If He Wants to Get NCLB Right," *Education Week*, July 15, 2008.

6. Arne Duncan, "Reauthorization of ESEA: Why We Can't Wait," U.S. Department of Education Press Release, September 24, 2009.

7. Nick Anderson, "Unions Criticize Obama's School Proposals as 'Bush III,'" *Washington Post*, September 25, 2009.

8. Quoted in Paul Manna, "Control, Persuasion, and Educational Accountability: Implementing the No Child Left Behind Act," *Educational Policy* 20 (3) (2006): 480–81.

9. See also William Erpenbach, Ellen Forte-Fast, and Abigail Potts, *Statewide Educational Accountability under NCLB* (Washington, DC: Council of Chief State School Officers, 2003); Ellen Fast and William Erpenbach, *Revisiting Statewide Educational Accountability under NCLB* (Washington, DC: Council of Chief State School Officers, 2004).

10. Erik Robelen, "Department Levies $783,000 Title I Penalty on Georgia," *Education Week*, May 28, 2003.

11. Quoted in Alyson Klein, "Spellings' Worldview: There's No Going Back on K-12 Accountability," *Education Week*, December 10, 2008.

12. Fast and Erpenbach, *Revisiting Statewide Educational Accountability under NCLB*, 26. See also Lynn Olson, "Approval of States' ESEA Plans Suggests Flexibility," *Education Week*, January 22, 2003.

13. On the early debate over the costs of implementing NCLB's provisions see David Hoff, "Debate Grows on True Costs of School Law," *Education Week*, February 4, 2004; Joetta Sack, "'No Child' Law Vies for Scarce State Resources," *Education Week*, January 8, 2003.

14. Furthermore, while only 13 percent of Title I districts (i.e., those receiving ESEA funds) were identified for improvement in 2006–7, these districts enrolled 40 percent of the nation's students (or about 18 million students). For discussion of implementation of accountability policies under NCLB, see U.S. Department of Education, *State and Local Implementation of the No Child Left Behind Act; Volume 9—Accountability under NCLB: Final Report* (Washington, DC: 2010), chap. 4.

15. Personal interview with Joan Wodiska, February 11, 2010.

16. Alan Richard and Erik Robelen, "Federal Law Is Questioned by Governors," *Education Week*, March 3, 2004.

17. "The States of NCLB," *Teacher Magazine*, October 1, 2004; Bryan Shelly, "Rebels and Their Causes: State Resistance to No Child Left Behind," *Publius: The Journal of Federalism* 38 (3) (2008): 444–45.

18. Personal interview with Joel Packer, formerly of the National Education Association, February 9, 2010.

19. Personal interview with Bruce Hunter, February 17, 2010.

20. On the limited impact of the NEA and other teacher organizations on the debate leading to enactment of NCLB see Julie Blair, "Unions' Positions Unheeded on ESEA," *Teacher Magazine*, November 6, 2002.

21. Weaver and Chanin were quoted in Bess Keller, "NEA Seeks Allies to Bring Lawsuit on ESEA Funding," *Education Week*, August 6, 2003.

22. Bess Keller, "NEA Takes Stand against Bush Education Law," *Education Week*, July 7, 2003.

23. Paul Manna, "Teachers Unions and No Child Left Behind," in *Collective Bargaining in Education: Negotiating Change in Today's Schools*, ed. Jane Hannaway and Andrew Rotherham (Cambridge, MA: Harvard Education Press, 2006), 159–79.

24. Quoted in Karla Scoon Reid, "Paige Blasts NAACP Leaders' 'Hateful' Rhetoric on Bush," *Education Week*, September 20, 2004.

25. Quoted in Andrea Stone, "Conservatives to Challenge Bush," *USA Today*, December 20, 2004.

26. Quoted in Michelle Davis, "Congress' Shift to Right May Be Felt in Schools," *Education Week*, November 9, 2004.

27. Education Testing Service, *Equity and Adequacy: Americans Speak on Public School Funding* (Education Testing Service, 2004).

28. *The 36th Annual Phi Delta Kappa / Gallup Poll of the Public's Attitudes toward the Public Schools* (2004), available from the Roper Center Public Opinion Archives, University of Connecticut, Storrs, Connecticut.

29. Results for America, "No Child Left Behind Survey," January 22–February 4, 2004, available from the Roper Center Public Opinion Archives.

30. Erik Robelen, "'No Child' Law Faulted in Democratic Race," *Education Week*, January 14, 2004.

31. Quoted in Erik Robelen, "Kerry Softens Rhetoric on 'No Child Left Behind,'" *Education Week*, September 20, 2004.

32. Erik Robelen, "Bill Would Make 'No Child' Flexibility Retroactive," *Education Week*, June 23, 2004; Erik Robelen, "Kennedy Hints at Amending 'No Child' Law," *Education Week*, February 25, 2004; Erik Robelen, "Kennedy Bill Would Give States, Districts Leeway," *Education Week*, September 23, 2004.

33. Quoted in Sean Cavanagh, "Bush Takes On Critics of No Child Left Behind," *Education Week*, May 19, 2004.

34. Gail Sunderman, "The Unraveling of No Child Left Behind: How Negotiated Changes Transform the Law," Civil Rights Project, Harvard University, February 2006, 9.

35. Indeed, some proponents of strong accountability claimed that these administrative changes allowed states to "game the system" by allowing poor and minority students to be exempt from NCLB's accountability system. As Charles Barone, a former aide to George Miller, contended in 2007, "Miller accuses the Bush Administration of opening regulatory loopholes in NCLB, such as by allowing large numbers of poor and minority students to be exempt from NCLB's accountability system under the guise of statistical 'reliability.' Miller is spot on. States have used specious technical arguments to game the system. And [Margaret] Spellings (following the path of her predecessor Rod Paige) has, for whatever reason, let them get away with it." Charles Barone, "Loopholes, Stalemates, and Common Ground," Democrats for Education Reform, September 14, 2007.

36. U.S. Department of Education, "Secretary Spellings Announces More Workable, 'Common Sense' Approach to Implement No Child Left Behind Law," press release, April 7, 2005; David Hoff, "Education Department Announces More Flexible Approach to NCLB Law," *Education Week*, April 7, 2005.

37. William Erpenbach, *Statewide Educational Accountability under the NCLB Act—A Report on 2008 Amendments to State Plans* (Washington, DC: Council of Chief State School Officers, 2008), 17–18.

38. Joe Williams, "Job One for Rupert Murdoch at WSJ," Democrats for Education Reform, September 28, 2007.

39. This section builds on contributions by other scholars. See, for example, Maris Vinovskis, *From a Nation at Risk to No Child Left Behind: National Education Goals and the Creation of Federal Education Policy* (New York: Teachers College Press, 2009); Paul Manna, "NCLB in the States: Fragmented Governance, Uneven Implementation," in *No Remedy Left Behind: Lessons from a Half-Decade of NCLB*, ed. Frederick Hess and Chester E. Finn Jr. (Washington, DC: AEI Press, 2007); Lance Fusarelli, "Restricted Choice, Limited

Options: Implementing Choice and Supplemental Educational Services in No Child Left Behind," *Educational Policy* 21 (1) (2007): 132–54; Gail Sunderman and Gary Orfield, "Domesticating a Revolution: No Child Left Behind Reforms and State Administrative Response," *Harvard Educational Review* 76 (4) (2006): 526–55.

40. U.S. Department of Education, *State and Local Implementation of the No Child Left Behind Act: Volume 9—Accountability under NCLB: Final Report* (Washington, DC: 2010), xx.

41. U.S. Department of Education, *State and Local Implementation of the No Child Left Behind Act: Volume 8—Teacher Quality under NCLB: Final Report* (Washington, DC: 2010), xix.

42. *The 39th Annual Phi Delta Kappa / Gallup Poll of the Public's Attitudes toward the Public Schools* (2007), available from the Roper Center Public Opinion Archives.

43. George Miller, "Chairman Miller Remarks on the Future of the No Child Left Behind Education Law," prepared remarks for speech at the National Press Club, Washington, DC, July 30, 2007.

44. Susan Traiman, director of public policy, Business Roundtable, testimony to the Commission on No Child Left Behind, Aspen Institute, Hearing on Assessing the Quality and Consistency of State Standards, August 31, 2006. See also NCLB Works!, *Top Ten Myths about No Child Left Behind*, www.nclbworks.org; NCLB Works!, *Success Stories: How the No Child Left Behind Act Is Helping to Transform Schools across the Country*, www .nclbworks.org.

45. Margaret Spellings, remarks delivered on the No Child Left Behind Act to the National Press Club, Washington, DC, January 10, 2008.

46. See Thomas Donohue, "Education Reform: A Moral Imperative," address in Washington, DC, December 5, 2007; Arthur Rothkopf, senior vice president and counselor to the president of the U.S. Chamber of Commerce, statement before the Senate Committee on Health, Education, Labor, and Pensions and the House Committee on Education and Labor, March 13, 2007; Business Coalition for Student Achievement, "Framework for Reauthorizing the No Child Left Behind (NCLB) Act: Recommendations to Improve and Strengthen the Law," Business Coalition for Student Achievement, www.biz4achievement.org; Kati Haycock, director of the Education Trust, written testimony before the Commission on No Child Left Behind, Aspen Institute, September 25, 2006; NCLB Works!, *NCLB Works! A Campaign to Reauthorize and Strengthen No Child Left Behind*, www.nclbworks.org.

47. See, for example, Business Coalition for Student Achievement, "Framework for Reauthorizing the No Child Left Behind (NCLB) Act: Recommendations to Improve and Strengthen the Law," Business Coalition for Student Achievement, www.biz4achievement. org; United States Chamber of Commerce and the Center for American Progress, *A Joint Platform for Education Reform* (Washington, DC: U.S Chamber of Commerce and Center for American Progress, 2007), 2–3; William Taylor, chairman of the Citizens' Commission on Civil Rights, testimony before the Commission on No Child Left Behind, Aspen Institute, May 9, 2006; Amy Wilkins, vice president for government affairs and communication, Education Trust, written testimony for the Senate Committee on Health, Education, Labor, and Pensions, March 6, 2007.

48. Kati Haycock, director of the Education Trust, written testimony before the Commission on No Child Left Behind, Aspen Institute, September 25, 2006.

49. Business Coalition for Student Achievement, "Framework for Reauthorizing the No Child Left Behind (NCLB) Act: Recommendations to Improve and Strengthen the Law," www.biz4achievement.org.

50. Amy Wilkins, written testimony, Senate Committee on Health, Education, Labor, and Pensions, March 6, 2007.

51. Letter from Monty Neill of FairTest, on behalf of the Forum on Educational Accountability, to the presidential candidates, December 19, 2007, http://www.edaccountability.org/FEALetterPresCandDec07.pdf.

52. Forum on Educational Accountability, "Empowering Schools and Improving Learning: A Joint Organizational Statement on the Federal Role in Public Schooling," http://www.edaccountability.org/Empowering_Schools_Statement.html.

53. See, for example, Forum on Educational Accountability, "Joint Organizational Statement on No Child Left Behind (NCLB) Act," October 21, 2004; Forum on Educational Accountability, "Key Recommendations for ESEA/NCLB Reauthorization"; Forum on Educational Accountability, "Dear Member of Congress" letter on George Miller's NCLB Reauthorization "Discussion Draft," October 3, 2007. All are available at www.edaccountability.org.

54. Neal McCluskey and Andrew Coulson, "End It, Don't Mend It: What to Do with No Child Left Behind," *Cato Institute Policy Analysis No. 599*, September 5, 2007.

55. Dan Lips, "Reforming No Child Left Behind by Allowing States to Opt Out: An A-PLUS for Federalism," *Heritage Foundation Backgrounder No. 2044*, June 19, 2007.

56. John Chubb, *Learning from No Child Left Behind* (Palo Alto, CA: Stanford University Press / Hoover Institution Press, 2008), "Lessons and Recommendations."

57. David Hoff, "NCLB Law Needs Work, Legislators Assert," *Education Week*, February 24, 2005.

58. Letter from Donna Stone, president of the National Conference of State Legislatures, to George Miller and Howard McKeon of the House Committee on Education and Labor, "RE: Staff Discussion Draft of Title I of ESEA," September 5, 2007.

59. National Governors Association, Council of Chief State School Officers, and National Association of State Boards of Education, "Joint Statement on Reauthorization of the No Child Left Behind Act (NCLB)," June 7, 2007.

60. Jay Matthews, "Congressman Offers Revisions to 'No Child'; Proposal Would Lessen Some Penalties," *Washington Post*, August 29, 2007; Mark Walsh and Alyson Klein, "Miller's NCLB Priorities Spark Fresh Debate," *Education Week*, August 15, 2007.

61. See, for example, George Miller, "Chairman Miller Remarks on the Future of the No Child Left Behind Education Law," remarks for speech at the National Press Club, Washington, DC, July 30, 2007; Walsh and Klein, "Miller's NCLB Priorities Spark Fresh Debate"; Michael Sandler, "'No Child' Author Starts Questioning the Test," *CQ Weekly*, October 8, 2007.

62. Quoted in Peter Baker, "An Unlikely Partnership Left Behind," *Washington Post*, November 5, 2007.

63. Letter from Craig Barrett, chairman of Intel, Arthur Ryan, chairman and CEO of Prudential Financial, and Edward Rust, chairman and CEO of State Farm, to Representatives George Miller, Howard McKeon, Dale Kildee, and Michael Castle of the House Education and Labor Committee, September 5, 2007.

64. Quoted in "Education Trust Statement on House No Child Left Behind Reauthorization Draft," Education Trust, August 29, 2007.

65. Letter from Monty Neill of FairTest, on behalf of the Forum on Educational Accountability, to members of Congress, October 3, 2007, http://www.edaccountability.org/pblclttrtoCngrssOCT07.pdf

66. Joan Wodiska, director of NGA Education, Early Childhood, and Workforce Committee, testimony before the House Education and Labor Committee on Reauthorization of the No Child Left Behind Act, September 10, 2007.

67. Dan Lips, "Education Notebook: Making No Child Left Behind Worse," Heritage Foundation, September 7, 2007.

68. David Hoff, "Conservative Plan Would Shift Accountability to the States," *Education Week*, March 13, 2007.

69. David Hoff, "Republican Starts Attempt to Suspend NCLB Accountability," *Education Week*, NCLB: Act II blog, June 13, 2008, http://blogs.edweek.org/edweek/NCLB-ActII/2008/06/republican_starts_attempt_to_s.html; William Taylor and Crystal Rosario, "National Teachers' Unions and the Struggle over School Reform," Citizens' Commission on Civil Rights, July 2009, 31; Kati Haycock, "Ed Trust Opposes NCLB Recess until Reauthorization Act," letter to U.S. House of Representatives, June 20, 2008; Leadership Conference on Civil Rights, "Oppose the No Child Left Behind Recess until Reauthorization Act," letter to U.S. House of Representatives, June 18, 2008; Craig Barrett and Edward Rust, "This Recess Is Really from Accountability," *Wall Street Journal*, July 31, 2008; National Education Association, letter to Sam Graves supporting the NCLB Recess until Reauthorization Act, June 18, 2008.

70. Leadership Conference on Civil Rights, "Oppose the No Child Left Behind Recess until Reauthorization Act," letter to U.S. House of Representatives, June 18, 2008, http://www.civilrights.org/advocacy/letters/2008/nclb-recess.html. Emphasis added.

71. Alyson Klein, "Would Education Be a Priority in an Obama Administration?" *Education Week*, Politics K–12 blog, October 29, 2008, http://blogs.edweek.org/edweek/campaign-k-12/2008/10/will_education_be_a_priority_i.html.

72. See Carlo Rotella, "Class Warrior: Arne Duncan's Bid to Shake Up Schools," *New Yorker*, February 1, 2010; Amanda Paulson, "Education Secretary Arne Duncan: Headmaster of US School Reform," *Christian Science Monitor*, August 30, 2010.

73. Dakarai Aarons, "Chicago Record Shows Duncan as Collaborator," *Education Week*, January 7, 2009. On Rogers and his relationship with Obama see, for example, Roger Crockett, "Obama's Business Backers Look Ahead," *Business Week*, November 6, 2008; Lauren Young, "Mr. Rogers' Neighborhood," *Smart Money*, February 21, 2002; Ellen McGirt, "The Brand Called Obama," *Fast Company*, March 19, 2008.

74. These latter figures viewed him as a union buster and shill for corporate interests. However, it should be noted that Duncan actually enjoyed a collegial relationship with the major Chicago teachers unions, even if the two sides did not always agree. For a taste of the most critical views see, for example, Henry Giroux and Kenneth Saltman, "Obama's Betrayal of Public Education? Arne Duncan and the Corporate Model of Schooling," *Critical Studies, Critical Methodologies* 9 (6) (2009): 772–79; Pauline Lipman and David Hursh, "Renaissance 2010: The Reassertion of Ruling-Class Power through Neoliberal Policies in Chicago," *Policy Futures in Education* 5 (2) (2007): 160–78; William Ayers and Michael Klonsky, "Chicago's Renaissance 2010: The Small Schools Movement Meets the Ownership Society," *Phi Delta Kappan* 87 (6) (2006): 453–57.

75. Greg Burns, "Education Secretary Arne Duncan Counting on Business Leaders to Help Push Through School Reforms," *Chicago Tribune*, July 6, 2009.

76. Letter from Wade Henderson, president and CEO, and Nancy Zirkin, executive vice president, Leadership Conference on Civil Rights, to Senators Edward Kennedy and Michael Enzi, "Support Arne Duncan for Secretary of Education," January 13, 2009, http://www.civilrights.org/advocacy/letters/2009/duncan.html.

77. Duncan quoted in "President-elect Obama Announces Arne Duncan as Secretary of Education," Change.gov: The Office of the President-Elect, December 16, 2008: http://change.gov/newsroom/entry/president_elect_obama_announces_arne_duncan_as_secretary_of_education/.

78. Arne Duncan, "Reauthorization of ESEA: Why We Can't Wait," U.S. Department of Education, September 24, 2009.

79. Nick Anderson, "Unions Criticize Obama's School Proposals as 'Bush III,'" *Washington Post*, September 25, 2009.

80. U.S. Department of Education, "Race to the Top Program: Executive Summary," November 2009.

81. Jason Song, "U.S. Schools Chief to Push Disclosure of Education Data," *Los Angeles Times*, August 25, 2010. See also U.S. Department of Education, *Race to the Top: Application for Initial Funding*, CFDA no. 84.395A (Washington, DC: 2009). According to *Education Week*, "During the 30-day public review period for the proposed regulations [prior to their final codification], 1800 comments were submitted, many of them critical of what was described as highly prescriptive reforms from the federal government. Critics said the models might now work in communities where teacher and principal shortages exist, where teachers' union contracts pose barriers, or where closing an entire school isn't feasible. But, for the most part, the Department refused to budge." See "Final Rules Set for School Turnaround Grants," *Education Week*, December 9, 2009.

82. Michael Shear and Nick Anderson, "A \$4 Billion Push for Better Schools," *Washington Post*, July 24, 2009.

83. See, for example, "Obama Team's Advocacy Boosts Charter Momentum," *Education Week*, June 16, 2009; Sam Dillon, "Administration Takes Aim at State Laws on Teachers," *New York Times*, July 24, 2009; Sam Dillon, "Dangling \$4.3 Billion, Obama Pushes States to Shift on Education," *New York Times*, August 17, 2009; Associated Press, "Duncan Weighs In on Lifting NY Charter Cap," May 18, 2010.

84. See, for example, Michele McNeil, "Racing for an Early Edge: States Jockey for Position as the U.S. Education Department Readies Billions of Dollars in 'Race to the Top' Awards—the Stimulus Program's Grand Prize," *Education Week*, July 15, 2009; Erik Robelen, "'Race to Top' Driving Policy Actions across States," *Education Week*, December 23, 2009; Erik Robelen, "States Change Policies with Eye to Winning Federal Grants," *Education Week*, January 9, 2010.

85. Education Week, *Schools and the Stimulus: A Midterm Report on an Unprecedented Federal Commitment* (Washington, DC: Education Week, 2010), 6; Robelen, "'Race to Top' Driving Policy Actions."

86. Michele McNeil, "Delaware and Tennessee Win Race to Top," *Education Week*, March 29, 2010.

87. Sam Dillon, "Winners of Aid for Education Are Mostly in the East," *New York Times*, August 25, 2010.

88. Sean Cavanagh, "Race to Top Now Faces Acid Test," *Education Week*, August 31, 2010.

89. Paul Manna correctly advises that we should suspend judgment of RTT's educational effects until appropriate data is available. See Manna, *Competitive Grant-Making and Education Reform: Assessing Race to the Top's Current Impact and Future Prospects*, American Enterprise Institute Working Paper, October 2010.

90. Craig Barrett, William Green, and Edward Rust, "Co-Chairs of the Business Coalition for Student Achievement on Race to the Top," Business Coalition for Student Achievement, press release, April 22, 2010.

91. Education Trust, "Statement on President Obama's Speech at the National Urban League Centennial Conference," July 29, 2010.

92. Alyson Klein, "Jobs Bill Collides with Obama Agenda," *Education Week*, July 2, 2010.

93. Stephen Sawchuk, "NEA's Delegates Vote 'No Confidence' in Race to the Top," *Education Week*, July 4, 2010.

94. Michele McNeil, "Civil Rights Groups Call for New Federal Education Agenda," *Education Week*, July 26, 2010. However, the groups later appeared to backtrack, with former Urban League president Hugh Price calling the Obama-Duncan education agenda "the most muscular federal education policy I've ever seen" and adding that "we've got your back." See Michele McNeil, "Duncan Deflects Civil Rights Groups' Criticism: You're 'Wrong,'" *Education Week*, July 28, 2010.

95. President Barack Obama, "Remarks by the President on Education Reform at the National Urban League Centennial Conference," Washington Convention Center, Washington, DC, July 29, 2010.

96. Alyson Klein, "Obama Defends Race to Top," *Education Week*, July 29, 2010.

97. Cavanagh, "Race to Top Now Faces Acid Test."

98. Michele McNeil, "Losing States in Race to Top Scramble to Meet Promises," *Education Week*, February 22, 2011.

99. Michele McNeil, "Race to Top Winners Work to Balance Promises, Capacity," *Education Week*, March 29, 2011.

100. Chad Aldeman, "How Race to the Top Could Inform ESEA Reauthorization," *Education Week*, June 29, 2010.

101. Alyson Klein, "Congress Wraps Up 2011 Budget," *Education Week*, April 19, 2011. Michelle McNeil, "Education a Priority of New Federal Grant," *Education Week*, May 9, 2011. Congress also required that early childhood education be a major priority in "round three" of Race to the Top.

102. Arne Duncan, "The Obama Administration's Elementary and Secondary Education Act Reauthorization Blueprint," testimony before the House Committee on Education and Labor, March 17, 2010.

103. U.S. Department of Education, "A Blueprint for Reform: The Reauthorization of the Elementary and Secondary Education Act," March 2010.

104. Alyson Klein, "Push to Renew ESEA Faces Steep Policy, Political Hurdles," *Education Week*, May 17, 2010.

105. Quoted in "Duncan Upbeat Despite Election Blow," Associated Press, November 5, 2010.

106. Quoted in "GOP Gains Could Prompt Funding, Policy Shifts," *Education Week*, November 4, 2010.

107. As in the past, the major Republican ESEA proposals taking shape in Congress seem to privilege flexibility for states and localities in implementing regulations and using federal funds. Alyson Klein, "Outlines of ESEA's Future Emerging on Capitol Hill," *Education Week*, May 17, 2011.

108. Michelle McNeil, "Duncan Issues Far More NCLB Waivers Than Predecessors," *Education Week*, April 22, 2011; Michelle McNeil, "Obama Gives Go-Ahead for NCLB Waivers to States," August 8, 2011, Education Week Politics K–12 blog, http://blogs.edweek.org/edweek/campaign-k-12/2011/08/obama_gives_go-ahead_for_waivers.html?qs=No+Child+Left+Behind.

109. "Ed Secretary: States to Get School Test Waivers," *Education Week*, August 8, 2011.

110. The letter, "Education Reform Coalition Urges State and Local Accountability for Closing Achievement Gaps as Key Elements of ESEA/NCLB Reauthorization," was sent March 29, 2011, http://www.uschamber.com/sites/default/files/issues/education/files/2011_03_28_Coalition%20Statement%20of%20Principles%20ESEA%20Accountability.pdf.

111. Letter, "Education Reform Coalition," 1. Emphasis in original.

112. Quoted in Alyson Klein, "Advocates Worry ESEA Rewrite May Weaken Law," *Education Week*, April 1, 2001.

CONCLUSION

1. Scott Abernathy, *No Child Left Behind and the Public Schools* (Ann Arbor: University of Michigan Press, 2007), 2–3.

2. Helen Ladd and Douglas Lauen, "Status versus Growth: The Distributional Effects of School Accountability Policies," *Journal of Policy Analysis and Management* 29 (3) (2010): 426–50.

3. Thomas Dee and Brian Jacob, "The Impact of No Child Left Behind on Students, Teachers, and Schools," *Brookings Papers on Economic Activity*, Fall 2010, 149–94; other findings on positive achievement effects, using state level data, are found in Hanley Chiang, "How Accountability Pressure on Failing Schools Affects Student Achievement," *Journal of Public Economics* 93 (9/10) (2009): 1045–57; and David Figlio and Cecelia Elena Rouse, "Do Accountability and Voucher Threats Improve Low-Performing Schools?" *Journal of Public Economics* 90 (2006), 239–55.

4. See, for example, Martin Carnoy and Susanna Loeb, "Does External Accountability Affect Student Outcomes? A Cross-State Analysis," *Educational Evaluation and Policy Analysis* 24(4) (Winter 2002): 305–31; Eric Hanushek and Margaret Raymond, "Does School Accountability Lead to Improved Student Performance?" *Journal of Policy Analysis and Management* 24(2) (2005): 297–327; Randall Reback, "Teaching to the Rating: School Accountability and the Distribution of Student Achievement," *Journal of Public Economics* 92 (5/6) (2008), 1394–1415; Derek Neal and Diane Withmore Schanzenbach, "Left Behind by Design: Proficiency Counts and Test-Based Accountability," *Review of Economics and Statistics* 92(2) (2010): 263–83.

5. Brian Jacob and Steven Levitt, "Rotten Apples: An Investigation of the Prevalence and Predictors of Teacher Cheating," *Quarterly Journal of Economics* 118(3) (2003): 843–77; David Figlio and Joshua Winicki, "Food for Thought: The Effects of School Accountability Plans on School Nutrition," *Journal of Public Economics* 89 (2) (2005), 381–94; John Kreig, "Are Students Left Behind? The Distributional Effects of the No Child Left Behind Act," *Education Finance and Policy* 3 (2) (2008): 250–81.

6. National Center for Education Statistics, *NAEP 2008 Trends in Academic Progress: Reading 1971–2008, Mathematics 1973–2008* (Washington, DC: U.S. Department of Education, 2010), 14–17.

7. Terry Moe, *Special Interest: Teachers Unions and America's Public Schools* (Washington, DC: Brookings Institution Press, 2011), 13–14.

8. Michael Apple, *Educating the "Right" Way: Markets, Standards, God, and Inequality*, 2nd ed. (New York: Routledge, 2006), 55. Emphasis added.

9. See Daniel Carpenter, *The Forging of Bureaucratic Autonomy: Reputations, Networks, and Policy Innovation in Executive Agencies, 1862–1928* (Princeton, NJ: Princeton University Press, 2001).

10. Patrick McGuinn, *No Child Left Behind and the Transformation of Federal Education Policy, 1965–2005* (Lawrence: University Press of Kansas, 2006).

11. As Margaret Weir notes in an important essay, "In democratic political systems . . . elite political strategies require acceptance—or at least acquiescence—from below if they are to be successful." Weir, "When Does Politics Create Policy? The Organizational Politics of Change," in *Rethinking Political Institutions: The Art of the State*, ed. Ian Shapiro, Stephen Skowronek, and Daniel Galvin (New York: NYU Press, 2007), 171–72.

12. Stephen Skowronek, *The Politics Presidents Make: Leadership from John Adams to Bill Clinton*, 2nd ed. (Cambridge, MA: Harvard University Press, 1997).

13. Christopher Howard, *The Welfare State Nobody Knows: Debunking Myths about U.S. Social Policy* (Princeton, NJ: Princeton University Press, 2007).

Index

Numbers in *italics* refer to figures and tables.